The Spirit of the Old Testament

SIDNEY B. SPERRY

Second Edition, Revised and Enlarged

Deseret Book Company
Salt Lake City, Utah
1980

Other Volumes in the Classics
in Mormon Literature Series

An Approach to the Book of Mormon, by Hugh Nibley
The Gospel: God, Man and Truth, by David H. Yarn, Jr.
Key to the Science of Theology and A Voice of Warning, by Parley P. Pratt
Outlines in Ecclesiastical History, by B. H. Roberts
Why the King James Version, by J. Reuben Clark
Essentials in Church History, by Joseph Fielding Smith

PREFACE
to the
CLASSICS IN MORMON LITERATURE
EDITION

In recent years The Church of Jesus Christ of Latter-day Saints has placed great emphasis on the importance of studying the scriptures. Beginning in the fall of 1972, Church members studied each of the four standard works over an eight-year period in Gospel Doctrine classes, with correlated lessons in Relief Society, priesthood, and other manuals. With publication of the Latter-day Saints edition of the King James Version of the Bible in 1979, even greater interest in study of the Bible has been shown.

To help Church members gain greater understanding of the Old Testament, Deseret Book is reissuing *The Spirit of the Old Testament* by Dr. Sidney B. Sperry, in this Classics in Mormon Literature edition. Dr. Sperry first prepared and published this work in the 1940s; it was later revised and published by Deseret Book in 1970.

The characters of many of the Old Testament prophets come to life vividly as Dr. Sperry introduces them in this informative work, and their teachings take on new dimensions for present-day students of the scriptures. Dr. Sperry taught Old Testament history, literature, and languages at Brigham Young University for many years. He received his M.A. and Ph.D. degrees from the University of Chicago, specializing in Old Testament languages and literature. He also studied in Palestine and Europe, and became well acquainted with biblical archaeology and the excavations of Bible lands.

Deseret Book is pleased that this work is now available in this attractive library edition, to help a new generation of Latter-day Saints gain greater appreciation for and understanding of the Old Testament.

LITHOGRAPHED BY

IN THE UNITED STATES OF AMERICA

PREFACE

to the

SECOND EDITION

The first edition of this little book appeared nearly thirty years ago and has been long out of print. It was written in order to provide Latter-day Saint students attending our own educational institutions with materials for a short course in Old Testament appreciation. The book was not written for experts; nevertheless, a number of non-Mormon scholars wrote me appreciative letters.

Many of my friends and colleagues have urged me to issue another edition of the book and I now respond with this revised and enlarged edition. There is a dearth of Latter-day Saint publications on the Old Testament and I trust that my efforts will find a welcome among Church scholars and members generally. My aim has been to focus attention on the religious and devotional aspects of selected Old Testament books rather than on the critical aspects of them. Where questions of biblical criticism have been dealt with, conservative views in harmony with the gospel have been adopted.

The text of the Old Testament used in this work has been the dignified translation of The Jewish Publication Society of America (1917), though I have not hesitated in a few instances to use other translations if I thought they gave added clearness. On rare occasions I have made my own translation.

I wish to acknowledge the encouragement and clerical help provided by Dean Daniel Ludlow of the College of Religion of Brigham Young University in producing this edition of my book. Thanks are also extended to my good colleague and former student, Assistant Professor Keith Meservy, for counseling with me on a few matters pertaining to Old Testament chronology and the bibliography.

The views expressed in this book, unless otherwise indicated, are my own; nevertheless, I trust they are generally in harmony with the scriptures accepted by our Church.

Sidney B. Sperry

Brigham Young University
December 1, 1969.

CONTENTS

Chapter I

WHAT THE OLD TESTAMENT IS

A Record of How God Worked with a Covenant People. We may define the Old Testament as that body of literature or collection of Hebrew scriptures which records in the form of history, law, prophecy, psalms, and wisdom the relations of God with covenant peoples, more particularly the descendants of Abraham. Stated in another way it is "primarily the written record of the origin, terms, and history of the solemn agreement which existed between the Israelitish nation and Jehovah."[1] The Old Testament is, indeed, a vital and inseparable part of that *one* Book which we call the Bible. It provides an indispensable foundation for the New Testament and furnishes much preparatory material needful for that record's proper understanding. In fact, apart from the Old Testament the New Testament loses much of its meaning. As we study the Old Testament we shall be impressed with it as a book of religious faith in which inspired scribes and prophets have recorded the manner in which God attempted to bring spiritual enlightenment and salvation to men through His covenant people, Israel.

Back of the Old Testament is a vast variety of vital experiences, national and individual, political and spiritual, social and ethical, pleasurable and painful. Back of all these deeply significant experiences is God Himself, through them making known his character and laws and purpose to man.[2]

The Old Testament has delighted, captivated, and enthralled mankind through the centuries and will continue to do so because it has recorded in beautiful form the truths of life and is satisfying to the yearnings of the human spirit.

---

[1]C. F. Kent, *The Origin and Permanent Value of the Old Testament*, p. 22.
[2]*Ibid.*, p. 26.

Why the Name Old Testament. The title *Testament* is derived from the Latin Vulgate's[3] *Testamentum*. The latter in turn is a translation of the Greek word *diatheke* which was often used to translate *berith*, the Hebrew word for covenant. The Latin *testamentum* would be acceptable if it were the correct translation of the Greek *diatheke*. The latter has a number of meanings of which we may notice the following: (1) a *covenant* between two parties. (2) a *last will, testament.* The Latin *testamentum* has only the last of these meanings and is the proper rendering of diatheke, *will* or *testament*, not diatheke, *covenant*. We believe that it would be far better, therefore, to speak of the Hebrew scriptures as the Old Covenant than as the Old Testament. It should be remembered that the idea of a covenant between God and a chosen group of people is one of the outstanding characteristics of the Hebrew scriptures. (See Gen. 9:8-17; 17:1-21; 26:1-4; Exo. 19:5; Jer. 31:31-34.)

The Order of the Books of the Old Testament. If we examine our English version we shall find that it contains thirty-nine books in the order of that assigned to them in the Greek translation (Septuagint) of the Hebrew Bible which was made sometime between B. C. 250 and B. C. 150. But in the Greek translation the various books are grouped according to their content. First come the historical books (Genesis—Esther), then the poetic books (Job —Song of Solomon), with the prophetic books (Isaiah— Malachi) in last place. While this order is convenient for some purposes, we ask ourselves whether it is the one used anciently by the Jews in Palestine.

Let us turn to the New Testament and see if there is any evidence bearing on the order of the books of the Old Testament as used by Christ and, in general, by the Jews of His day. In Luke 24:44 we find the risen Lord saying to His disciples, "These are the words which I spake unto you, while I was yet with you, that all things must be fulfilled,

---

[3]The Vulgate was a Latin translation of the Bible made by St. Jerome about A. D. 400.

which were written in the law of Moses, and in the prophets, and in the psalms, concerning me." It is to be noted that our Lord divides the Old Testament into three divisions, the Law, the Prophets, and the Psalms. If we examine a modern Hebrew Bible and compare the order of its books we shall find that they also fall into three divisions—*The Law, The Prophets, The Writings.* We further observe that the Book of Psalms forms the first and leading book of the last division. It is possible that our Lord singled it out as an especially good witness of Himself in that division of the canon.[4] Now let us list the books in order under each major division.

The Threefold Division of the Hebrew Bible
The Law
    1. Genesis
    2. Exodus
    3. Leviticus
    4. Numbers
    5. Deuteronomy

The Prophets
    Former ---- 6. Joshua
                  7. Judges
                  8. Samuel
                  9. Kings
    Latter -----10. Isaiah
                  11. Jeremiah
                  12. Ezekiel
                  13. The Twelve (Hosea—Malachi)

The Writings
    14. Psalms
    15. Proverbs
    16. Job

---

[4]See W. H. Green, *General Introduction to the Old Testament,* (The Canon), p. 142. For a definition of canon see near the end of this chapter.

17. Song of Songs
18. Ruth
19. Lamentations   The Five Rolls (Megilloth)
20. Ecclesiastes
21. Esther
22. Daniel
23. Ezra—Nehemiah
24. Chronicles

Inspection reveals that the Hebrew Bible has but twenty-four books in contrast with thirty-nine in our more familiar English version, the above list showing that I and II Samuel, I and II Kings, I and II Chronicles, Ezra and Nehemiah, and the Twelve Minor Prophets are each reckoned as one book. The facts would seem to indicate that Christ was familiar with a Bible having the same general order as that in our present Hebrew Bible. The late John E. McFadyen, eminent Old Testament scholar, emphasized the importance of the Hebrew order of the books as follows: "It would somewhat simplify the scientific study even of the English Bible, if the Hebrew order could be restored, for it is in many ways instructive and important."[5]

New Testament References to the Hebrew Scriptures. The New Testament indicates that the Old Testament was the Bible used by Christ and His followers. They revered it and loved it, and made constant reference to it in their preaching and writing. A good example of this is to be found in the use of the Old Testament in the Gospel of Matthew. It will be instructive to note some references the New Testament makes to the Hebrew writings. Thus the Lord speaks of "The Scriptures," (Matt. 21:42) and Paul of "the Holy Scriptures," (Romans 1:2) "the oracles of God," (Romans 3:2) of "the sacred writings," (2 Timothy 3:15)[6] etc. In a number of cases—Matt. 5:17; Luke 16:16, 29, 31; John

---

[5]*Introduction to the Old Testament* (New Edition), pp. 13f. The Hebrew order is preserved in a modern English translation entitled, *The Holy Scriptures*, Jewish Publication Society of America, Philadelphia, 1917. More recent translations in the Hebrew order are also available.

[6]A. V. renders "the Holy Scriptures."

1:45; Acts 24:14; Romans 3:21 are good examples—the Hebrew scriptures are designated as "the law and the prophets" by which title or appellation is apparently meant the whole of scripture. Sometimes the lone term "prophets" is used in a broad sense to include all the inspired writers. (See Hebrews 1:1)[7]

The Old Testament a Survival of Early Hebrew Literature. The Old Testament is practically all that survives of Hebrew literature prior to B. C. 350.[8] Latter-day Saints know from our modern scriptures that the Lord has preserved much of Hebrew sacred literature, but the time has not as yet arrived to reveal it to His people. (See I Nephi 5:10, 18, 19; 2 Nephi 27:7-9.) The Hebrew sacred writings have been spoken of as a national literature, and, while that is true, it represents to the writer the actual writings of but relatively few men. There can be no doubt that the Hebrew people had a rich and varied literature, but our Old Testament represents, unfortunately, only a small part of it.

The catastrophes that befell the Hebrew people through the centuries were probably responsible for the destruction of a large number of records of all kinds. Those which were saved may have been the ones that were regarded as particularly precious and necessary to the religious welfare of Israel.

A Record Compiled Over a Period of One Thousand Years. If it be admitted that the Pentateuch[9] was composed in the days of Moses—a fact denied by many—we could say that the Old Testament represents the writings of men over a period of about one thousand years. These writings in turn deal with events that took place during

---

[7]Note the references to the Hebrew scriptures in I Nephi 3:3; 7:11; 19:23.

[8]Some scholars think that Daniel, Ezekiel, and certain other writings of the Old Testament appeared at a later date. The writer does not agree entirely with the views presented by them.

[9]From the Greek *pente* (five) and *teuchos* (tool or implement). The term was applied finally to a sheath or case in which five scrolls or books were kept. The use of the term *Pentateuch* as a name for the five books of Moses can be traced to early Christian times.

thousands of years of time—indeed, from the Creation to about B. C. 350.

The Old Testament Has a Remarkable Unity. Despite the fact that the Old Testament was written or compiled over a long period of time, it has a remarkable unity. The organic unity which we believe it displays is due primarily to the fact that most of the men who wrote it were prophets or historians who understood God's purposes with Israel. Latter-day Saints can understand this unity in the same manner that they understand the unity pervading the remarks of our Church Authorities published in the Conference Reports from Joseph Smith's day to the present time. The unity which prevails in the Hebrew scriptures is best appreciated by those who are most willing to study them prayerfully and intelligently.

The Old Testament Comes From an Oriental Culture. While the Old Testament is a rather complex book containing history, laws, prophecy, psalms, and wisdom it must not be forgotten that it comes out of an oriental culture. The Hebrews were a Semitic[10] people whose language, manners, and customs were much different from our own. Their thought patterns and psychology make it impossible at this day for us to completely capture the charm and spirit of the Old Testament in any English version, beautiful as the latter may be. Few of us may take the trouble to learn the Old Testament languages, but we can increase our appreciation by studying books in English dealing with the customs, habits, and psychology of the native peoples of that land and of other lands bordering the Mediterranean Sea.[11] The real student of the Old Testament will not only attempt to learn its languages, but will fulfill the other requirements as well. The dividends are large in satisfaction and in spiritual development.

The Canon of the Old Testament. Inasmuch as the word *canon* is often used in connection with the scrip-

---

[10]The word Semitic or Shemitic was derived from the name of Noah's son, Shem, who was the traditional ancestor of the Hebrews.

[11]A suitable number of such books will be found in the bibliography.

tures it is well to explain it here. It comes from the Greek word *kanon* which in turn was possibly derived from the Hebrew word *qaneh* (a reed used for measuring; cf. Ezek. 40:3, 5). Originally the word seems to have been applied to an object which was used as a measure, a rule, or a model. Finally, it seems to have acquired a derived meaning which was applied to something measured or ruled. In a metaphorical sense in Greek it is equivalent to a "rule" or "standard" of what is considered to be right and best. Its technical use with reference to books of the Bible seems to have become current among Greek and Latin authors by A. D. 350. Its use by Athanasius, Nazianzen, Rufinus, Priscillian, Jerome and others will attest that fact.

Latter-day Saints may assume that the expression "the canon of the Old Testament" has reference to that body of Hebrew scriptures which is considered by the Church to be divinely inspired, the word of God when the original words of the authors are correctly translated, and which contains an authoritative rule of faith and life for its people. The only book of the Old Testament which the Prophet Joseph Smith considered uninspired, hence uncanonical, was the *Song of Songs.*

The Language of the Old Testament. All of the books of the Old Testament were written in Hebrew, with the exception of Daniel 2:4-7:28; Ezra 4:8-6:18; 7:12-26, which are written in Aramaic, a language having many affinities with Hebrew. The Book of Jeremiah also contains a verse of Aramaic (10:11) where it appears suddenly and with no good reason in a Hebrew context denouncing idolatry. Two words of Aramaic also occur in Genesis 31:47.

Chapter II

THE SOURCES FOR
OLD TESTAMENT STUDY

Importance of Sources. Sources are of the greatest importance to the historian. It is not our purpose in this chapter to present in detail the sources for Old Testament study. We do wish, however, to point out to the Latter-day Saint reader the general sources on which the Old Testament specialist draws, not to mention the additional literary sources available to the Latter-day Saint scholar.

For convenience we may divide Old Testament sources into three general groups. (1) archaeological and epigraphical,[1] (2) literary, (3) comparative folklore and history of religions.

Archaeological and Epigraphical Sources. a) *Hebrew, Aramaic, Phoenician, Akkadian* (Babylonian and Assyrian), *Sumerian, Ugaritic, Hittite, Egyptian, Greek,* and *Latin inscriptions.* Many of these have been collected in convenient form for the use of scholars. The number and variety of inscriptions are constantly increasing as archaeologists and linguists pursue their hungry search for information respecting the history of Palestine and other Bible lands.[2] The Mesopotamian and Egyptian sources are especially numerous and instructive. Professor Adolphe Lods, of the Sorbonne, Paris, says of them, "The documents unearthed in Egypt and in Mesopotamia are an inexhaustible mine of information and facts of vital importance for the understanding of the history of Canaan, both before and after the Israelite settlement."[3]

---

[1]Epigraphy is that science which deals with the deciphering and interpreting of ancient inscriptions.

[2]See D. Winton Thomas (Ed.), *Documents from Old Testament Times* (Thos. Nelson and Sons, 1958). A very useful and valuable collection for students of the Old Testament.

[3]*Israel* (English ed. trans. by Hooke), p. 5.

b) *Monuments.* Such are relatively scarce in Palestine. The most notable are the buildings in Samaria and Jericho, the remains of irrigation systems and graves of the dead. The Arch of Titus in Rome may also be mentioned. Through the years excavators have uncovered much of interest in Megiddo, Beth-shan, Debir, Tell-en-Nasbeh (possibly the Biblical Mizpah), Shiloh, Bethel, Ai, Gibeah, Beth-zur, Jericho, and many other sites of importance. One is tremendously impressed with the exactness and care with which modern archaeologists excavate and report the results of their work. Those who would like to read an interesting book on Palestinian excavation are referred to Dr. William F. Albright's *The Archaeology of Palestine* (Baltimore. Penguin Books, Fully Revised, 1961).[4] Dr. Albright is the world's foremost Biblical archaeologist.

c) *Coins.* These comprise the Jewish, Seleuciden, and those of the independent cities of Palestine.

d) *Hebrew and other seals of state.*

e) *Pottery.* Pottery from the various levels of ancient Biblical sites has been found in great abundance. It is of great importance to the archaeologist, enabling him to date with reasonable accuracy the remains of various cultures with which it is associated. In fact, pottery may be called the archaeologist's chronometer.[5]

f) *Various articles used in daily life.* Such are oil and wine presses, handmills, baking ovens, mortars, spindles, stones used in slingshots, bone articles, metal utensils, and ornaments.

g) *Religious articles.* These comprise such articles as altars, sacrificial pillars, images, and amulets.

The Literary Sources. a. *The Old Testament.* This is, of course, our most important source of knowledge of the ancient Hebrews and their patriarchal predecessors. One of

---

[4]See also G. Ernest Wright, *Biblical Archaeology* (Westminster Press, 1957); J. B. Pritchard, *Archaeology and the Old Testament* (Princeton University Press, 1958).

[5]See G. Ernest Wright, *The Pottery of Palestine from the Earliest Times to the End of the Early Bronze Age* (New Haven, American Schools of Oriental Research, 1937).

America's greatest Semitists, Duncan B. Macdonald, in his
book, *The Hebrew Literary Genius,* said:

> The contributions of the Hebrews to the records of History are
> no longer regarded with primary suspicion. With the passing of bibli-
> olatry, the distinction between traditionalists and critics has also
> passed, and it has become plain that, through the racial tenacity of
> the Hebrews, there has been preserved for us in the Old Testament a
> unique and trustworthy key to the history of the Near East. It is
> now possible to read together Herodotus, Jeremiah, and Ezekiel and
> to profit by the comparison of these first-hand records. How exactly
> true this is any one may verify by turning to the volumes of the *Cam-
> bridge Ancient History* which touch even remotely upon the Hebrews.
> There it will be found that the old "critical" suspicious attitude towards
> the historical tradition of the Hebrews has vanished and that these
> records are given equal credence with those—often much scantier—
> of the other peoples. It is true that this is part of a general reversal of
> historical attitude from extreme scepticism to a recognition of a basal
> truth in national tradition. Homer has come back and with him the
> tale of Troy divine. We need not, then, be surprised that Sinai and
> Jerusalem have also come back, and that Moses is on his way back.[6]

b. *The Apocrypha.* This consists of a number of uncanonical books written by the Jews during the last two or
three centuries B. C. and the first century A. D.

As to the term "Apocrypha", this was used, in the first instance,
of books containing hidden teaching not to be disclosed to ordinary
people. The Greek word *apokryphos,* in its technical sense, "is derived from the practice, common among sects, religious or philosophic,
of embodying their special tenets or formulae in books withheld from
public use, and communicated to an inner circle of believers."[7]

Dr. W. O. E. Oesterley assigns the apocryphal books
to three distinct periods as follows:[8]

---

[6]P. 217. There can be no doubt that a reaction has set in against the extreme
critical views that have held sway for so long in Old Testament study. See Lods,
op. cit., p. 9; W. F. Albright, *The Biblical Period from Abraham to Ezra* (Harper Torchbook, 1963), pp. 1-23; M. F. Unger, *Introductory Guide to the Old Testament* (Zondervan
1951), pp. 42-43.

[7]W. O. E. Oesterley, *An Introduction to the Books of the Apocrypha* (Macmillan,
1935), p. 4. But see C. C. Torrey, *The Apocryphal Literature* (Yale Univ. Press, 1945), pp. 7-9.

[8]*Ibid.,* p. 25.

Pre-Maccabaean:

I Esdras, circa B. C. 300.
Tobit, circa B. C. 200.
Ecclesiasticus, B. C. 200-180
The Hymn in the *Song of the Three Holy Children* probably belongs to this period.

Maccabaean:

The Prayer in the Song of the Three Holy Children, circa B. C. 168.
Judith, circa B. C. 150.
Additions to Esther, circa B. C. 140-130.

Post-Maccabaean:

I Maccabees, circa B. C. 90-70.
II Maccabees, circa B. C. 50.
Susanna, B. C.?
Bel and the Dragon, B. C.?
Wisdom, circa 40 A. D.
Baruch, after 70 A. D.
II Esdràs, circa 100 A. D.
Prayer of Manasses?

The Apocrypha contains material of great interest for the study of the Old Testament.[9] It is particularly valuable for the study of later Hebrew history. Many things in it are true, but it also contains many things that are not true, which may be regarded as interpolations by the hands of men. (D&C 91:1-2)

c. The *Pseudepigrapha.* These are spurious works purporting to emanate from Biblical characters. They are books not in the Apocrypha in the Protestant sense, but are designated as apocrypha by the Roman Church, though also *pseudepigrapha* in the broad sense. They may be dated at about the same period as the Apocrypha. (B. C. 300- A. D. 100)

The chief characteristic of their form is that of revelation or *apocalypse.* In these books the author is supposed to say only what is directly revealed to him by visions or by

---

[9]In addition to the books already cited see L. H. Brockington, *A Critical Introduction to the Apocrypha* (Duckworth & Co., London, 1961); E. J. Goodspeed, *The Story of the Apocrypha* (Chicago, 1939); Bruce Metzger, *An Introduction to the Apocrypha* (New York, 1957); R. H. Pfeiffer, *History of New Testament Times with an Introduction to the Apocrypha* (New York, 1949).

angelic visitors. The term *pseudo* is applied to these works because the purported revelations are given not to their real authors but to their assumed ones, to ancient Israelite heroes or saints. The assumed authorship was supposed to give the writings more authority.

Their contents deal mainly with such problems as immortality, the Messiah, the day of judgment, and the new world to follow the destruction of this world, and the problem of suffering.

The pseudepigraphical books are very numerous and their number is increasing by reason of scholarly researches. The names of some of the most important ones are as follows: (1) Book of Enoch, (2) The Book of Jubilees, (3) Testaments of the Twelve Patriarchs, (4) Psalms of Solomon, (5) Apocalypse of Baruch, (6) Assumption of Moses, (7) 2 or 4 Ezra, (8) Book of Adam and Eve, (9) Slavonic Enoch, (10) Sibylline Oracles.

These works are of special value for the study of the period in which they were written, and since they refer to so many biblical matters the Old Testament specialist takes notice of them.[10]

d. *The New Testament.* The New Testament is especially valuable as a source for Old Testament study because it is a witness to the way our Lord, His apostles, and others used and regarded it. The New Testament confirms and explains many Old Testament themes. Professor William Henry Green, great American Hebraist, in discussing how Christ and the writers of the New Testament viewed the Hebrew scriptures said:

> They have not left us a list of these books, but they have clearly indicated their mind in this matter, so that we need be under no mistake as to their meaning. They give their . . . authoritative sanction to the canon as it existed among the Jews. [11]

---

[10]For discussions of the Pseudepigrapha the student is referred to R. H. Charles, *The Apocrypha and Pseudepigrapha of the Old Testament* (2 Vols. Oxford, 1913).

[11]*General Introduction to the Old Testament* (The Canon), p. 41.

Quotations are made in the New Testament of every Old Testament book with the exception of Ezra, Nehemiah, Esther, Ecclesiastes, and the Song of Solomon.

Incidentally, scholars have been divided on the question as to whether the New Testament writers ever quote from The Apocrypha.[12] It should be pointed out, however, that whatever the view taken, none of the Apocrypha are cited by name in our New Testament.

The New Testament will prove to be a very interesting and illuminating source of information to the close student of the Old Testament.

3. *The Works of Flavius Josephus.* The works of Josephus are valuable in many respects as a source. He discloses the Old Testament views of a cultured Jew of the period immediately following the time of Christ, and is an important source of later Hebrew history. Many scholars feel that Josephus is guilty of exaggeration in his attempts to magnify his people and their scriptures in the eyes of the Gentiles; consequently, that his writings must be used with caution. "His work was of a general historical character, but Josephus was essentially an apologist and not a historian."[13] There can be no doubt, however, that Josephus has been too severely criticized by some writers.[14]

f. *Philo of Alexandria.* Philo was an eminent Alexandrian Jew who flourished about the time of Christ. His writings have been classed as "gnomic" or "wisdom" literature. He was very industrious and is said to have been the most voluminous writer in all Hebrew history. Philo came of a very wealthy family and had unusual opportunities to become acquainted with Greek life and culture. In-

---

[12]See W. H. Green, *op. cit.,* pp. 145f.; A. T. Robertson, *A Grammar of the Greek New Testament in the Light of Historical Research* (Fifth Ed.), p. 126; F. W. Danker, *Multipurpose Tools for Bible Study* (St. Louis, 1960), p.94.

[13]H. E. Dana, *New Testament Criticism* (2nd Ed., Forth Worth, 1928), p. 106. For Jewish accounts of Josephus see Meyer Waxman, *A History of Jewish Literature* (3 vols. New York, 1930), I, 100-108; Norman Bentwich, *Josephus* (Phila., 1914). The student may also be referred to F. J. Foakes—Jackson, *Josephus and the Jews* (New York, 1930); H. St. J. Thackeray, *Josephus, the Man and the Historian* (New York, 1929).

[14]See J. Garrow Duncan, *The Accuracy of the Old Testament,* Introduction, X.

deed, he became a devoted admirer of Hellenistic philosophy and as a true Eclectic attempted to explain the teachings of Moses and the Israelites in terms of Greek philosophy.

The supreme passion and effort of his life was to form a synthesis of Greek philosophy and Jewish religion, but with chief emphasis on the latter. "Philo's chief aim . . . is to demonstrate the universal validity of Jewish religion as enshrined in the Old Testament, and *par excellence*, in the Pentateuch" (Kennedy; Philo's *Contribution to Religion*, p. 31). His writings exhibit great deference for the law . . . Philo devoted but little attention to the prophets, though he breathed quite freely in their spiritual atmosphere.[15]

Philo's repeated references to the books of the Old Testament, and his comments thereon, make him of some value as a source despite his faulty allegorical methods of interpretation.

g. *Rabbinic Literature.* This literature consists of the scientific treatment of the Old Testament in the form of commentaries (Midrashim and Targums) and systematic works such as the Talmud literature (Mishnah, Tosephta, the Jerusalem and Babylonian Talmud) as these were compiled in the second century A. D. The rabbinical productions contain source materials of great worth to the later periods of Jewish history and also traditions that bear upon the earlier periods.[16] Rabbinical literature is vast and difficult to handle even by erudite scholars.

h. *Greek and Roman Classics.* Such works as those by Herodotus, Tacitus, Diodorus Siculus, Strabo, Pliny, etc., contain materials that serve as background for the study of the Hebrew records. Such sources often need critical evaluation.[17]

i. *Arabic Literature.* The nomadic Arabs of Palestine and surrounding countries live in many respects under the

---

[15]See H. E. Dana, *The New Testament World* (2nd ed., rev., Forth Worth, 1928), p. 160; Waxman, *op. cit.,* gives a good account of Philo and his work. Consult the index.

[16]A good discussion of this literature will be found in Waxman, *op. cit.,* pp. 251ff.; G. F. Moore, *Judaism* (3 vols. Cambridge, 1927-30). Moore's work is very learned and critical, indeed, one of the greatest treatises on Jewish religion.

[17]Samuel A. B. Mercer's *Extra-Biblical Sources for Hebrew and Jewish History* (New York, 1913) contains a handy compilation of Greek and Latin sources.

same cultural circumstances as the ancient Hebrews did. Their literature contains much of value, therefore, for background in Old Testament study. The Arabic language, though secondary to Assyrian and Babylonian in this respect, is of great value in understanding the history of the Hebrew language. Arabic literature by no means reaches the spiritual heights of the Old Testament but Professor Duncan MacDonald made this interesting comparison between Hebrew and Arabic literary art:

> The Hebrews, it has become plain, were simply an Arab clan which, under strange and unique guidance, entered Palestine and settled there. But they remained Arab, although they denounced the name. And their literature, throughout all their history and to this day, in its methods of production and in its recorded forms, is of Arab scheme and type. Every kind of literature in the Old Testament, with partial exception of the Psalms, finds a pigeonhole for itself in the great scheme of Arabic letters. Many even of the Psalms find their parallels in the poems of the desert. And, further, while the Hebrew literature has often a spirit, a variety of picture, and an essential life lacking in that of the Arabs, it is in comparison, small in amount.[18]

j. *Works on the Modern Near East.* These comprise the modern literature that has arisen in consequence of the travels and researches of numerous scholars all over the Near East. The works of Edward Robinson, Charles Doughty, J. L. Burckhardt, E. W. Lane, and Gustaf Dalman are good examples. Such literature reveals that the whole Mediterranean basin is a modern laboratory in which much that is in the Old Testament can be studied at close range.

k. *The Dead Sea Scrolls.* The finding in 1947 of the Dead Sea Scrolls at Qumran, near the northern end of the Dead Sea, created a sensation among Biblical scholars. These scrolls, together with the important documents and numerous fragments discovered in the years since, now prove to be important sources for both Old and New Testament studies. Not only do these finds provide us with a complete text of Isaiah a thousand years older than any previous copy of a book of the Hebrew Bible known to us, but they

---

[18]*The Hebrew Literary Genius* (Princeton, 1935), pp. 1f.

also give us extensive materials of especial value to the Old Testament scholar in the fields of Old Testament interpretation and textual criticism. Linguistic studies can now be made which are bound to enrich our knowledge of the history of the Hebrew language to a considerable degree.[19]

1. *The Book of Mormon.* The Latter-day Saint Old Testament scholar will find the Book of Mormon an indispensable source for his work. To be sure, the Nephite record as a scource cannot be said to be "scientific" in the usual sense of the term. It has a spiritual origin that transcends the scope and methods of science. But science is not the only way of arriving at the truth. The experiences of the Prophet Joseph Smith teach us that through the instrumentality of His servants, God may reveal truths which could not otherwise be made known to men. The scientist' may, however, claim the right to test, as conditions make it possible, the products of revelation, and rightly so. Thus, certain linguistic and archaeological tests might be made of the Book of Mormon as time and advance of science makes it expedient to do so.

As a source, the Book of Mormon is of special interest to Old Testament scholars in the Church for the following reasons among others:

1. Most of the peoples with which it deals were of Hebrew descent, had copies of the Hebrew scriptures as recorded down to B. C. 600, and were obviously well acquainted with their contents. Even the peoples dealt with in the Book of Ether (the Jaredites) were probably of the same general race as the patriarchal predecessors of the Hebrews and had similar traditions. (Cf. Ether 1:1-5)

2. The Hebrew scriptures on the Brass Plates in pos-

---

[19]The following books on the Dead Sea Scrolls may be recommended: Millar Burrows, *The Dead Sea Scrolls* (New York, 1955); *More Light on the Dead Sea Scrolls* (New York, 1958); Frank M. Cross, Jr., *The Ancient Library of Qumran and Modern Biblical Studies* (New York, 1958); J. T. Milik, *Ten Years of Discovery in the Wilderness of Judaea* (Naperville, Ill., 1959); F. F. Bruce, *Second Thoughts on the Dead Sea Scrolls* (Grand Rapids, 1956); G. R. Driver, *The Judaean Scrolls* (New York, 1966); T. H. Gaster, *The Dead Sea Scriptures in English Translation* (Garden City N. Y., 1964).

session of the Nephites contained the five books of Moses or Pentateuch, not to mention a "record of the Jews from the beginning, even down to the commencement of the reign of Zedekiah; and also many prophecies which have been spoken by the mouth of Jeremiah." (1 Nephi 5:11-13).

3. The Book of Mormon from the first is Christ centered. It reveals that the gospel was in the world from the beginning and that our Bible should be interpreted in that light.

4. The Book of Mormon affirms that Israel was a record-keeping people from the earliest times. One of their great records, the Brass Plates, has been preserved on this continent and will in due time be revealed to the world. (1 Nephi 5:17-19).

Even a fairly well read layman can recognize from what has been said the tremendous significance and importance of the Book of Mormon to Old Testament study.[20]

m. *The Doctrine and Covenants.* Like the Book of Mormon, the Doctrine and Covenants is another unique source for the study of the Old Testament. It is not in many respects as valuable and prolific a source as the Nephite record which fact we should rather expect since it deals mainly with problems incident to the restoration of the Church of Christ in our own age. Nevertheless, it does contain materials of the greatest importance for the understanding of certain parts of the Old Testament. Nearly sixty sections of the Doctrine and Covenants would be recognized by close students of the Old Testament as having some bearing on that scripture. And of these sections the following would be acknowledged as being outstanding in importance: Sections 2, 13, 20, 27, 29, 45, 68, 76, 84, 91, 98, 107, 110, 113, 116, 124, 128, 132, 133.

---

[20]For study of the Nephite record see S. B. Sperry, *Our Book of Mormon* (Salt Lake City, 1963); *Book of Mormon Compendium* (Salt Lake City, 1968); *Answers to Book of Mormon Problems* (Salt Lake City, 1967); Hugh Nibley, *An Approach to the Book of Mormon* (Salt Lake City, 1957); *Since Cumorah* (Salt Lake City, 1967); F. W. Kirkham, *A New Witness for Christ in America* (Independence, 1951); W. E. Berrett, *Teachings of the Book of Mormon* (Salt Lake City, 1962); Eldin Ricks, *The Case of the Book of Mormon Witnesses* (Salt Lake City, 1961.)

Some of the subjects dealt with in the Doctrine and Covenants that illumine the Old Testament are these: (1) The ancient patriarchs from Adam to Moses and Aaron, (2) the Aaronic and Melchizedek priesthoods, (3) the work and mission of Elijah as referred to in Malachi 4:5-6, (4) the origin and nature of Israel's religion including the law of Moses (cf. D&C 84:6-28), (5) the nature of the fall and the atonement, (6) the gospel given to man from the beginning, (7) the nature of the relationship existing between ancient and modern Israel, (8) the reason for plural marriage among the ancient Hebrews, (9) the Urim and Thummim, (10) the lost tribes of Israel, (11) temples and their uses.[21]

n. *The Pearl of Great Price.* This collection of modern scriptures, like the Book of Mormon and the Doctrine and Covenants, is an extraordinarily rich source for the study of the Old Testament. In its modern dress, the Pearl of Great Price is divided into three parts, (1) The Book of Moses consisting of eight chapters containing the visions and writings of Moses, (2) The Book of Abraham in five chapters which consists of a translation by Joseph Smith of Abraham's writings upon papyrus when he was in Egypt, (3) the Writings of Joseph Smith, comprising his "inspired" revision of Matthew 23:39-24:51 and extracts from his own history.

Some of the reasons that the Book of Moses is such a valuable Old Testament source will be gleaned from the following:

1. Chapter One tells about a vision in which Moses speaks with God face to face some time after his experience at the burning bush (vs. 17). Here he learns about the creation of worlds but more especially about this earth and its inhabitants. Moses also has an encounter with Satan. This chapter has an extemely important bearing upon the origin of Israel's religion, one of the Old Testament's greatest problems.

---

[21]See S. B. Sperry, *Doctrine and Covenants Compendium* (Salt Lake City, 1960). See bibliography on pages 768-769. See also Roy W. Doxey, *The Latter-day Prophets and the Doctrine and Covenants*, 4 vols. (Salt Lake City; 1963).

2. Chapters Two to Eight deal with the writings of Moses as revealed to the Prophet Joseph Smith in December, 1830. These chapters deal with important matters from the Creation to the Flood. They have an important bearing on the greatest literary problem of the Old Testament—the problem of the authorship of the Pentateuch. The Book of Moses supports in an interesting way the Book of Mormon evidence that Moses did write five books dealing among other things with the Creation and also with Adam and Eve. (See I Nephi 5:11; cf. Moses 2:1-4:32) The Book of Moses also throws much light on the fall, on the Cain and Abel episode, upon the ministry and work of Enoch, and upon events prior to the Deluge, not to mention doctrinal and textual difficulties that have plagued scholars for generations in the early chapters of Genesis.

The Book of Abraham is important as a source to the Latter-day Saint student of the Old Testament for the following reasons:

1. It gives Abraham's own account of his early life in Ur of the Chaldees and of his successive removals to Haran, Canaan, Egypt, and back to Canaan.

2. It gives much information about the nature of the early religion in Chaldea, about the founding of the Egyptian government, about the Holy Priesthood, and informs us that the written records of the early patriarchs had fallen into his hands.

3. Abraham teaches important matters pertaining to astronomy, philosophy, and the doctrine of pre-existence.

4. It reveals to us that Abraham was a seer and throws much light on the use of the Urim and Thummim which the Lord had given him in Ur of the Chaldees.

5. It throws additional light on the creation of the world.

6. It corrects certain misconceptions concerning Abraham and his wife when they came to Egypt, corrects certain textual errors in Genesis, and gives us hope that

many important records in Abraham's hands are yet in existence and may someday be forthcoming.

The "Writings of Joseph Smith" contain some materials of great interest to Latter-day Saint scholars but since they are included in the next source we shall mention it is not necessary to consider them at this point.[22]

o. *The Documentary History of the Church by Joseph Smith.* This is officially published by the Church under the title *History of the Church of Jesus Christ of Latter-day Saints.* The Prophet's work in six volumes was edited by President B. H. Roberts of the First Council of Seventy who provided an introduction and notes.[23] Aside from revelations now contained in the Doctrine and Covenants the Prophet frequently makes reference to the Old Testament and gives explanations of passages of scripture of great interest. We shall give but two illustrations of what the Prophet did, since the material is scattered throughout the volumes concerned. In Volume I, pp. 12-13, the Prophet makes reference to the Urim and Thummim and what consitituted "Seers" in ancient times, not to mention explanations concerning Chapters 3 and 4 of Malachi, Chapter 11 of Isaiah, and Chapter 2:28-32 of Joel. The explanations given are very useful to the Old Testament scholar. In Volume II, pp. 436-440, the Prophet gives his views on abolition which in his day was a subject of burning interest. His discussion of slavery in the light of Genesis 9:25-26 and of slavery among the Hebrews is of great interest to us. In the course of this volume we shall often have occasion to refer to the Prophet's views on Old Testament topics as found in the Documentary History (DHC, hereafter).

---

[22]For works on the Pearl of Great Price or parts of it consult S. B. Sperry, *Ancient Records Testify* (Salt Lake City, 1938); J. R. Clark, *The Story of the Pearl of Great Price* (Salt Lake City, 1955); Milton R. Hunter, *Pearl of Great Price Commentary* (Salt Lake City, 1948). H. L. Andrus, *Doctrinal Commentary on the Pearl of Great Price* (Deseret Book, 1967). See also articles in "The Improvement Era," Volumes 71 and 72 (1968-69) by Hugh Nibley.

[23]See editions as published by the Deseret Book Co., Salt Lake City; volumes of various dates.

p. *The "Inspired" Revision of the Bible.* Between the years 1830 and 1833 the Prophet Joseph Smith revised the Bible through the spirit of revelation. Unfortunately, he never lived long enough to complete the work in the manner he intended. The Book of Genesis is the best and most complete of his work on the Old Testament. It is a pity that the Prophet did not find time to complete his work from Exodus to Malachi as well as he did Genesis. Some of these books received considerable attention, but others received little or no correction. The work done by the Prophet will prove of great interest and worth to Latter-day Saint scholars of the Old Testament.[24]

Comparative Folklore and History of Religion as Sources. The third general source, comparative folklore and history of religions, is used to a degree in the study of the Old Testament. In times past many Old Testament scholars were prone to assume that the strictly documented history of Israel began with the reign of David. Before that time it was assumed that one could depend only on very uncertain traditions. Modern archaeological discoveries have done much to change these views, at least from the days of Abraham.[25] The scholar attempts, in part, to test traditions for their historical worth by studying the laws governing the evolution of oral tradition generally. He keeps in mind the possibility that certain traditions in the Bible could be borrowed from international folklore.

The history of religions enables the scholar to make comparisons of one religion with another, which in turn makes it possible to check the scanty evidence of the Biblical texts in certain respects.

Our time has seen a great development of interest in folklore and these modern studies of the ideas and usages of the masses of the people have reached the Near East. Collections have been made of

---

[24]For a treatment of the Prophet's revision see the pamphlet by Robert J. Matthews, *Joseph Smith's Revision of the Bible* (Provo, 1969) and consult "Suggested Readings" on page 86 for other important references. Copies of the Inspired Revision of the scriptures may be secured from the Herald Publishing House, Independence, Missouri.

[25]See W. F. Albright, *The Biblical Period From Abraham to Ezra* (Harper Torchbooks, New York, 1963).

songs, proverbs, stories—popular literature in the widest sense. The modern dialects of Arabic and Aramaic have been booked in texts, lexicons and grammars. The manners and customs, the superstitions (as we call them), religious usages and beliefs, have been recorded and studied. And when all this is done, the astonishing fact comes out that these peoples today, living there in Syria, reaching back into the desert and north into the mountains and south into Egypt, are in all essentials of fundamental thinking and living, one with the masses of people in the pages of the Old Testament. The Canaanites are there; the Hebrews are there; the Arabs are there; the Arameans are there; the Phoenicians are there—still surviving, although they may call themselves by other names. Even the tremendous fact of Islam and the apparently overwhelming invasion of the Arabs have changed little but the names. In consequence, these modern folklore researches have come to be of the first importance for the interpretation of the Old Testament.[26]

Comparative folklore and history of religions as sources for Old Testament study must be used with great care and insight. Adolphe Lods is right in giving these words of caution:

It must be emphasized here that these methods must only be employed in a subsidiary fashion and with great caution. Our foundations must rest on the evidence of the monuments and the texts. Comparative methods can only prove fertile in results if they lead us along the lines of the documentary history, not if they undertake to correct it.[27]

---

[26]Macdonald, *op. cit.*, p. 1.
[27]Lods, *op. cit.*, pp. 15f.

Chapter III

GENESIS, THE BOOK OF BEGINNINGS

Origin of the Name, Genesis. The first book of the Old Testament is called Genesis in our English version of the Bible. This name is taken directly from the Greek translation of the Bible (Septuagint) which we mentioned in the first chapter of this book. The equivalent in our Hebrew Bible is *Bereshith* which is the opening word of the book. It means, literally, "in beginning". Consequently, the word Genesis is a good name for the first book of the Bible since it deals with the beginnings of things such as the earth, life, and the nations of mankind, but more especially with the beginnings of the house of Israel.

Genesis, a Literary Masterpiece. The Book of Genesis is, by common consent, one of the great books of mankind. It stands by itself in the whole of our Old Testament and produces the effect of a single great work of genius. Gauged by every worthwhile standard it must be reckoned one of the noblest literary and religious monuments ever produced by the hand of man. Thus to quote Dr. Duncan B. Macdonald, the great Old Testament scholar:

> Genesis stands thus apart not only in the literature of the Hebrews but in the entire literature of the world. It is safe to say that there is no other book which combines as it does the philosophical study of the fundamental institutes of human life, a psychological study of a family of marked characteristics, developing into a people equally marked, and a political and economic study of that people over against the rest of the world, personified in the great figure of an adventurer of their race; the whole told in clear, objective stories which can be the delight of children, yet with a depth of sheer thought behind them which has stirred and led the thinking of the world more deeply than have the speculations of Plato.[1]

---

[1]D. B. Macdonald, *The Hebrew Literary Genius*, p. 96.

In short, we can say the Book of Genesis was to the Hebrews what the Iliad and Odyssey were to the Greeks, the Aeneid to the Romans, and the Legend of Beowulf to the Nordic races. Unless this book is understood and its spirit captured it is quite impossible, in our opinion, to plumb the marvelous depths of the Old Testament. It constitutes a fine preface to the volume.

The Philosophical Basis of Genesis. To one who has read the Book of Genesis for the first time it might appear on the surface that it consists only of a series of simple stories, beautiful, but nevertheless, just a collection of stories. On the other hand, one who has studied the book more deeply will find that its stories conform to a definite philosophical scheme. As Dr. Macdonald has also pointed out they are philosophical in basis, treatment and object. The narrator or compiler of the Book of Genesis expresses in these philosophical stories the more fundamental things of life. We may sum up the philosophical basis of the book under three heads, (1) the foundations of life and its institutions, (2) the rise of the covenant people of Israel and an analysis of the more human and spiritual characteristics of Abraham and his immediate family, (3) Israel comes into contact with the world; Joseph, a highly spiritual Hebrew, is sold into the world and becomes a savior to his people.

It will be noted that the author of Genesis does not think of Israel as a conquering nation or as a nation aloof or apart from the world. He is rather thinking of Israel as a people who are to become influential by sending their sons into the world to make good and hold their own in that world by sheer force of character.[2] We gain from the book the impression that Israel has a spiritual mission in the world, namely, to leaven and refine it through righteousness and unwavering loyalty to principle. Only a covenant people—one true to God in every respect—could make good in this mission. Joseph who was sold into Egypt became a temporal savior of his people and in a sense

___
[2]Macdonald, *op. cit.*, p. 98.

typified the spiritual mission of Israel in its peaceful penetration of a world that did not know the true God.

The divisions of the Book of Genesis corresponding to the above philosophical scheme are as follows: (1) chapters 1 to 11, (2) chapters 12 to 36, (3) chapters 37 to 50. Of these three divisions it is easily perceived that the writer is more interested in the last two, since they have to do with the immediate origin of a covenant people beginning with Abraham.

The Origin of Life and Institutions, Genesis 1-11. As hinted above, the writer of Genesis (in its present form) is more interested in showing to Israel who its great ancestors were than to tell about the origin of life and its institutions. This is readily seen in the fact that the origins of life and its institutions are briefly and concisely handled in the first eleven chapters, while thirty-nine chapters are required to tell about Abraham, the father of the faithful, and his immediate family. Nevertheless, the writer is at some pains to show that Abraham, Isaac, and Jacob, and in short, Israel had a great ancestry from the days of Adam. The early patriarchs were men of God and it was entirely fitting that the righteous Abraham and his descendants have an ancestry of great men. Therefore, this people had a great tradition and responsibility to carry on. It will be noted that there are two rather long genealogies showing Abraham's descent. These are found in Chapters Five and Eleven.

Chapters One and Two give an account of the origin of this world and of man. These two chapters are masterpieces and should be carefully read by the student. The fundamental meaning of creation in the original Hebrew is to "cut" or "shape". The stories imply that the earth was created or organized out of existing materials and what is of interest to us is the fact that the world as first created seemed good in God's eye. This, in turn, gives us a clue as to why God created a physical world. He created it for the purpose of making it possible for man to exist. It is not directly stated that God was glorified thereby, but such may be deduced from the fact that man was made in the "image" of God. Man is the important thing in the stories of the creation.

In Chapter Three we find a story dealing with the origin of sin, or in other words, the fall of man. In Chapter Four we have the origin of civilization and incidentally, the first murder. The murder of Abel by Cain was so important in the eyes of the writer that he gives special attention to it. Cain and Abel are commonly supposed to be the first children of Adam and Eve, whereas, all that can honestly be deduced from the story is that they are mentioned first. Then, as now, a murderer gets the headlines. In Chapters Six to Nine we have the origin of the Flood, or in other words, how the wicked world was blotted out and how again under the leadership of Noah the earth was repopulated after the great destruction. In Chapter Nine we have the beginnings of vine culture explained. Here also is to be found an account of a weakness in a life of the Patriarch Noah. As indicated in our first chapter, the Bible is a book of life and it points out the weaknesses of men as well as their strong points. Chapter Ten gives the Hebrew account of the origin of the various nations of the world. Chapter Eleven discusses the origin of various languages and gives a genealogy from Shem to Abraham in whom the writer is especially interested. A quick reading of Genesis will show that while the matter contained in the first eleven chapters was important to the writer it was nevertheless secondary to what follows.

The Origin of the Covenant People, Israel. Beginning with Chapter Twelve we find the narrator of Genesis going more and more into detail about the lives of his subjects. Since he is so interested in the Patriarchs Abraham, Isaac, and Jacob, he tells as much about them as he possibly can— their travels, the crises in their lives, their flocks and herds, their wives and love affairs—even their relations with God are rather minutely described. What is the reason for this? *Because it was important for later Israel to know as much*

as possible about Abraham, their great ancestor who cove-
nanted with God, and Isaac and Jacob unto whom the
covenant was confirmed. It is to be noted throughout, that
these stories of the patriarchs are significantly religious.
We shall find it convenient at this point to inquire into
the nature of the covenant God made with Abraham. The
terms of the covenant may be summed up as follows: (1)
Abraham was to be made a great nation.[3] (2) in him all of
the families of the earth were to be blessed,[4] (3) his descendants were to inherit Palestine as an everlasting possession,[5] (4) his descendants were to be as numerous as
the dust of the earth or the stars of the heavens,[6] (5)
kings and nations were to come of his descendants,[7] (6)
the covenant he made with God was to be an everlasting
one, or as we would say, a gospel covenant,[8] (7) circum-
cision was to be the sign of the covenant.[9] Some modern
scriptures have given us some very interesting sidelights on
the nature of Jehovah's covenant with Abraham.

And I will make of thee a great nation, and I will bless thee above
measure, and make thy name great among all nations, and thou shalt be
a blessing unto thy seed after thee, that in their hands they shall bear
this ministry and priesthood unto all nations; and I will bless them
through thy name; for as many as receive this Gospel shall be called
after thy name, and shall be accounted thy seed, and shall rise up and
bless thee, as their father; and I will bless them that bless thee, and
curse them that curse thee; and in thee (that is, in thy priesthood) and
in thy seed (that is, thy priesthood), for I give unto thee a promise
that this right shall continue in thee, and in thy seed after thee (that is
to say, the literal seed, or the seed of the body) shall all the families
of the earth be blessed, even with the blessings of the Gospel, which
are the blessings of salvation, even of life eternal.[10]

---

[3]Gen. 12:2.
[4]Gen. 12:3.
[5]Gen. 13:14, 15.
[6]Gen. 13:15; 15:5.
[7]Gen. 17:6.
[8]Gen. 17:7.
[9]Gen. 17:10-14.
[10]See Abr. 2:9-11; D&C 110:12. Note the connection of ancient with modern
Israel.

The covenant principle of sacrifice is beautifully exemplified in the life of Abraham and is to be accepted as
one of the great teachings of the Book of Genesis. Abraham
was so faithful and anxious to serve God at any cost that he
was willing to offer up on the altar his beloved son Isaac.[11]

We shall not at this point say anything about Jacob
and his family because he is to be dealt with in the following
chapter.

Israel Contacts the World. Few stories in all the history of the race can compare in beauty and conception
with the stories of Joseph who was sold into Egypt. In
these stories it is possible for the author of Genesis to point
out in an appealing form the way in which Israel as a body
came into contact with the world.[12] Joseph is pictured as
an individual who unwaveringly sought after righteousness
and to whom character was paramount. Through him the
house of Israel is saved from destruction. Also through
him Israel is magnified in the eyes of the world for Joseph
has become a prince among men. He is a type of the true
Israelite of the covenant whose mission it is to penetrate
the world and leaven and spiritualize it. The more one
reads the Book of Genesis the more strongly do the philosophical and religious conceptions of the author appeal to
the emotions and intellect. Genesis is a book to be read
and re-read and studied and pondered over.

---

[11]Gen. 22:1-18. See Jacob 4:5.

[12]Israel was a name divinely given to Jacob. See Gen. 32:24-28. Later on it
was applied to his descendants as a whole.

Chapter IV

JACOB AND HIS FAMILY— THE TWELVE TRIBES

Jacob Foreordained to Leadership. In the previous chapter we pointed out that behind the stories in the Book of Genesis there is a definite religious philosophy prevailing. The most important lessons in the book deal with Abraham and the beginning of the house of Israel, a covenant people. In this chapter we want to pay special attention to Abraham's grandson, Jacob, who was the immediate father of the twelve men after whom the twelve tribes were named. Jacob, so the narrator of Genesis attempts to point out, has a great role to play in the history of Israel. In fact he is the one who was first named Israel.[1] In the study of Genesis some writers spend far too much time pointing out Jacob's supposed weaknesses—his deceit, guile, grasping disposition, etc.—and not enough in observing his good points, particularly his untiring efforts to find and serve God. In our opinion there has not, heretofore, been enough emphasis given to the fact that Jacob was foreordained to be the leader in his father's house and not Esau. The author of Genesis is very careful to point out that Jacob's mother, Rebekah, is told by the Lord in answer to prayer before the birth of her two sons that "the elder [Esau] shall serve the younger [Jacob]." The full answer to her petition (note the poetic form) is as follows:

> Two nations are in thy womb,
> And two peoples shall be separated
>   from thy bowels;
> And the one people shall be stronger
>   than the other people;
> And the elder shall serve the younger.[2]

[1]Gen. 32:28.
[2]Gen. 25:23.

If the above passage has any significance at all it is that the younger son, Jacob, is to "supplant"[3] his elder brother, Esau. It is not unreasonable to suppose that Rebekah made known to Jacob what the Lord had told her and this fact, as much as anything else, spurred him on to claim his blessings. Unless these facts are constantly kept in mind we are in great danger of misinterpreting the narrator's intentions in telling about Jacob's methods of obtaining leadership. The writer of Genesis wants us to understand that Jacob was a mighty man and favored by God.

Jacob Obtains the Birthright and Blessing. We should remember that those chapters of Genesis dealing with the way in which Jacob obtains the birthright and blessing from his brother Esau are meant to be deeply religious in nature—they portray the fight of a great man to obtain God's blessings due him by promise and by good living. According to ancient patriarchal customs, it appears that the eldest son in the family ordinarily fell heir to most of the material possessions of his father as well as to his spiritual calling. In the present instance Esau would have been heir to his father's estate and also to his patriarchal priesthood. Jacob, as the younger son, could not hope to obtain them except through extraordinary means. The writer of Genesis is not so seriously concerned with the shrewd and deceitful manner in which he got them as Western readers are apt to be. To the true Oriental, Jacob's methods of obtaining the blessings would not be looked upon as sinful or unethical. From the point of view of the ancient writer, Jacob was justified in being shrewd in obtaining his blessings, since God had promised them to him. Esau, on the other hand, is pictured as an individual who despises his birthright and is concerned only with his immediate creature comforts.[4] He is shown to be unworthy of the blessing because at heart he proved

[3]"Supplanter" is one meaning assigned to Jacob's name. See Gen. 27:36.
[4]Gen. 25:28-34.

himself to be murderous and bad in other respects.[5] Such an individual could not be a covenant man—one meriting the great blessings of God. Whatever view we may take of Jacob, the fact remains that he did obtain the birthright and blessing and God confirmed them upon him in the same way that he did to Isaac, his father, and to Abraham, his grandfather.[6]

The Wives and Children of Jacob. Because of the intention of Esau to slay his brother after the death of Isaac, Jacob is persuaded by his parents to leave his pleasant home and journey to Haran, far to the north, where he is to stay with his kinsfolk and take to wife one of the daughters of Laban.[7] Before the young man leaves, Isaac gives him a blessing as follows:

> And God Almighty bless thee, and make thee fruitful, and multiply thee, that thou mayest be a congregation of peoples; and give thee the blessing of Abraham, to thee, and to thy seed with thee; that thou mayest inherit the land of thy sojournings, which God gave unto Abraham.[8]

The above quotation shows that Isaac realized the blessings of God would indeed be given to his younger son. So Jacob betakes himself to Haran. One night, so we are told, he had a vision in which the angels of God ascended and descended upon a ladder set upon the earth. Finally the Lord stood before him and confirmed upon him the blessings of Abraham and Isaac. On awakening, Jacob called the place Bethel, which in the original language means "the house of God".[9] When Jacob arrives at Haran he falls in love with a beautiful girl by the name of Rachel.[10] One of his kinsfolk, Laban, her father, promises that Jacob may have her for wife if he will serve him seven years. This he does but when the marriage night arrives he is given

---

[5]Gen. 27:41-42; 27:46; 28:6-9.
[6]Gen. 28:10-15; 32:2, 24-30.
[7]Gen. 27:43-45; 28:1-2.
[8]Gen. 28:3-4.
[9]Gen. 28:10-19.
[10]A shepherdess. Incidentally, her name means "ewe".

Leah, her elder sister, and is obliged to work another seven
years in order to obtain Rachel.[11] The stories concerning
these two women and their struggles, one to win Jacob's
love and the other to be blessed with children, are full of
pathos and at times appear humorous to Western readers.
They are, however, truly Oriental in character and to be
appreciated should be interpreted from that viewpoint. It
happened that Rachel, the beloved wife, for a long time has
no children. That gave her rival, Leah, an opportunity—so
she thought—to win the favor of Jacob by bearing children.
As the story shows, Leah is not completely successful. The
names she gave to the six boys born to her are all indicative
of the strivings that she made. The boys and the meanings
of their names are given herewith in chronological order:
Reuben (see! a son); Simeon (hearing); Levi (joined);
Judah (praise); Issachar (hired); Zebulun (habitation). The
reader is advised to look over the story concerning the
birth of Leah's children with the meaning of these names
before him.[12] It will be found very enjoyable. When at
the first Rachel finds that she is to have no children, though
she is Jacob's beloved, she fears that the curse of God is
upon her. Oriental women to this day consider it a
curse of God not to have children. According to the law
of the time she could give one of her handmaidens to
Jacob, who might have children by her. She gave to him
her maid Bilhah, who bore two boys, Dan (a judge) and
Naphtali (my wrestling).[13] Leah, not to be outdone, gives
to Jacob her maid, Zilpah, who also bore two children, Gad
(fortune) and Asher (happy).[14] Finally, so the story points
out, Rachel gives birth to a son, Joseph (added), and just
prior to her death another is born to her who is called
Benjamin (son of the right hand).[15] The stories of these
women and their children are full of human interest and

---

[11]Gen. 29:16-30.
[12]Gen. 29:31-35; 30:17-20.
[13]Gen. 30:1-8.
[14]Gen. 30:9-13.
[15]Gen. 30:22-24; 35:16-19.

that is exactly what the writer of Genesis wants them to be. He wants later Israel to understand all the details of the origin of the twelve tribes because they are of such tremendous significance. After working twenty years for Laban, Jacob leads his family to the land of his nativity. The story of his meeting with Esau is dramatically narrated and shows the practical wisdom of Jacob in meeting the issues of life. Through all these stories it is to be carefully noted that Rachel, the beloved wife, and her son Joseph, received preferential treatment and indeed, if we are to understand in part the prominent role played by the tribe of Ephraim in the Old Testament, that fact must be clearly understood.[16]

Israel Prevails With God and Men. On the way back from Haran with his wives and children, Jacob is portrayed as being alone one night and wrestling with an unknown man until the break of day.[17] It would appear from the story that the man was some divine individual. Finally this supernatural individual said, "Let me go for the day breaketh." That Jacob seemed to recognize the unusual character of the man is seen in his answer, "I will not let thee go, except thou bless me." The man then asked Jacob his name and replied, "Thy name shall be called no more Jacob, but Israel;[18] for thou hast striven with God and with man and hast prevailed." Jacob asked for the man's name and while no direct answer is given it is significant that Jacob called the place where he wrestled *Peniel*. For as he said, "I have seen God face to face, and my life is preserved." Peniel does, indeed, in the Hebrew language mean "the face of God". This was, in the eyes of the writer, a most significant and sacred incident and indicated to him that Jacob was a great patriarch and man of God because he had seen God face to face. The reader of the Genesis stories is advised to pay special attention to this

---

[16]Ephraim was Joseph's son.
[17]Gen. 32:24-31.
[18]That is, *He who strives with God*.

incident and others of its kind because they are intended
by the writer to reveal the extremely close relations existing
between God and those patriarchs who covenanted with
him.

Joseph, Prince Among Men. In the Joseph stories we
have remarkable accounts of the character and work of
the favorite son of Jacob by his beloved wife, Rachel.[19]
Joseph is portrayed from the first as a visionary man and
his brethren make him the butt of their ridicule because
they think that he is attempting to show his superiority to
them. In this connection there is one phrase in Genesis,
not often referred to, that it will be well for us to quote.
Joseph's father says to him, "What is this dream that thou
hast dreamed? Shall I and thy mother and thy brethren
indeed come to bow down to thee to the earth?" The
account goes on to say, "And his brethren envied him; but
his father kept the saying in mind." The little phrase
"kept the saying in mind" shows that the writer of the
story wanted us to keep in mind the apparent prophetic
qualities of the father who seemed to have a foreboding or
forewarning of the greatness of his son. The Joseph stories
are magnificent for the simple reason that they deal with
a great man—a prince among men—and are told in a manner that befits the beautiful character of the hero. Above
everything else, we see in them the integrity, chastity,
honesty and sterling worth of Jacob's favorite son. They
will remain undimmed for all ages to come.

While in Egypt as a great ruler, Joseph marries Ase-
nath, the daughter of the priest of On. By her he has two
sons, Manasseh (forgetting), and Ephraim (fruitful).[20]
Our understanding of Genesis and of the Old Testament
would be very incomplete without an explanation of the
position of Joseph's two boys among the twelve tribes
of Israel. As we have already seen, Jacob's wives had
borne him twelve sons and yet one reads in the Old Testa-

---

[19]Gen. 37-50.
[20]Gen. 41:50-52; 46:20, 27.

ment that Joseph's two sons are reckoned among the twelve whose names are applied to the tribes of Israel. Altogether there were fourteen men to be considered. How, out of these fourteen men, do we get twelve names selected? In Genesis 48:1-6 we find that Joseph's two sons were blessed by Jacob and literally adopted by him. Verse 5 reads,

> And now thy two sons, who were born unto thee in the land of Egypt before I came unto thee into Egypt, *are mine; Ephraim and Manasseh, even as Reuben and Simeon shall be mine.* (Italics ours.)

It is clear that Joseph's two sons were literally adopted by his father. I Chron. 5:1-2 indicates that Ephraim took the place of Reuben at the head of the twelve tribes. Reuben was not displaced from the group of twelve, but his position at the head was taken away because of his wicked actions with respect to his father. Manasseh also finds his place among the twelve.[21] Joseph's place among the twelve and the blessings accompanying it were swallowed up in the blessings of his two sons so there are but thirteen left to be accounted for. Later on, as the Pentateuch[22] indicates, Levi was chosen to have the Lord for an inheritance and not to have an inheritance in the same sense as the others.[23] This leaves but twelve of the patriarchs to be formally accounted for and they are the progenitors of the so-called twelve tribes of Israel. Throughout the Old Testament the tribe of Ephraim is constantly recognized as having a preeminent position among the tribes of Israel.[24] Judah, from whence the Christ was to come, was also given a prominent place among the twelve sons of Jacob.[25]

---

[21]See Gen. 35:22; 48:15-22; 49:3, 4.

[22]The first five books of the Old Testament.

[23]Deut. 10:8, 9; see also Josh. 13:14, 33.

[24]See, e. g., Isa. 7:8, 9, 17; Jer. 31:9.

[25]Gen. 49:8-12; I Chron. 5:2. If modern Israel will keep the above facts in mind it can understand and interpret correctly its connection with ancient Israel, for the two are spiritually akin. The Ephraim of our day, by virtue of its position at the head of Jacob's family, has been chosen to carry the gospel to the world. This fact should make Genesis and the Old Testament take on meaning and vitality for us.

Chapter V

MOSES—ISRAEL'S GREAT LAWGIVER

Importance of Moses. Among Western Peoples the name of Moses is a household word. Revered and honored, his name and work have come down through the centuries. He has been spoken of as the founder of the Hebrew nation in the sense that he welded the tribes of Israel together and gave them a national self-consciousness. In fact, the Hebrews are a people still to be reckoned with. Their Jewish representatives are to be found in all parts of the world. They are making their contributions to society in numerous ways. Their religion, Judaism, which has made them what they are, is one of the great world religions. Historically, Christianity and Islam, two other great world religions, have very close connections with the Hebrew people. Thousands of Christian peoples think of Moses as the author or compiler of the first five books of the Old Testament. They especially think of him in connection with the Ten Commandments. Moses is looked upon by Christians, Jews, and Mohammedans alike, as a prophet. It is quite probable that in almost any list of the ten greatest men in the world Moses' name would be included.

The Course of Moses' Career. Moses' career may be logically divided into three periods of forty years each. The first forty years may be called the Egyptian period and is summed up in the first fifteen verses of the second chapter of Exodus. As the adopted son of Pharaoh's daughter, Moses must have been familiar with the inner circle of court life. We can presume that he was also familiar with the best in Egyptian education and diplomatic procedure of his day. His sympathies and heart, however, seemed to have gone out to his brethren, the despised Hebrews, who were in bondage. As the story in Exodus points out, this first period in the great lawgiver's life came to an end when he slew an Egyptian task-master who was abusing one of his people. He fled and came to the land of Midian.

The second period of his life could well be called the Desert Era or the Period of Preparation. During the time he was in Midian he herded sheep, meditated, became well acquainted with the desert wherein he afterwards led his people and finally received his call to the ministry. All of this is summed up in the third chapter of Exodus.

The third period of forty years deals with Moses' career as leader and lawgiver of his nation. It may not seem too presumptuous to say that the books of Exodus, Leviticus, Numbers and Deuteronomy are scarcely sufficient to give a complete outline of this last part of his life.

Divine Leadership, the Key to Moses' Career. Anyone making a careful study of the life of Moses can readily understand the reason for his great success. It is perfectly apparent in the Old Testament account that Moses subjected himself to divine guidance and leadership throughout his amazing career. As related in Exodus, we find that God, through Moses, remembers His people in bondage as He promised Abraham.[1] We find that it is God who first calls Moses to His work, who sends Moses to Pharaoh to demand the release of His people, who brings the plagues upon the Egyptians, who directs the exodus of His people from Egypt, who commands the building of the tabernacle, who thunders out from Sinai with fire and smoke, who gives the Ten Commandments and, in general, is the one who directs the battles of His people. Moses, according to tradition, seems to have been a humble and meek man.[2] He was intelligent, teachable and a good follower. These are among the most necessary qualifications for great religious leaders. It appears that when God finds a man of this type He uses him and makes a great man out of him and Moses was no exception. In the

---

[1]Gen. 15:13, 14.
[2]Num. 12:3.

hands of God he became a mighty leader and as a result commands the affection of millions at this late date.

Moses Expresses Righteous Indignation. Let us suppose that we, like Moses, had been adopted by Pharaoh's daughter and brought up at court with its luxury and pomp while our fathers and mothers, brothers and sisters, and relatives were in heavy bondage to the Egyptians. What would be our feelings and emotions as we saw our own flesh and blood beaten and abused and subjected to intolerable tasks day after day? When we ask ourselves this question we place ourselves in the position Moses was in. His mother had nursed and brought him up before he was presented at court.[3] We can be sure that she hoped her boy might someday be the instrument to bring a mitigation of the sufferings of her people. As Moses grew to manhood the early teachings of his mother remained with him and he grieved as he contemplated the lamentable state of his brethren.

> And it came to pass in those days, when Moses was grown up, that he went out unto his brethren, and looked on their burdens; and he saw an Egyptian smiting a Hebrew, one of his brethren. And he looked this way and that way, and when he saw that there was no man, he smote the Egyptian, and hid him in the sand.[4]

The real manhood of Moses is shown in the righteous indignation he expressed when he saw one of his helpless brethren being maltreated. Undoubtedly this kind of treatment had been going on for generations. No people has a moral right to subject another to bondage and ill-treatment. Sooner or later God takes a hand and in this case Moses was His instrument. The above incident was the beginning of Israel's liberation. Many have questioned the ethics of Moses' action, but we can imagine Old Testament writers would point out that it was far better for one man to die than for a whole nation to be subjected to

---

[3]Exo. 2:7-10.
[4]Exo. 2:11, 12.

slavery. There is such a thing as righteous indignation, rare in our day, and Moses could be aroused to it.

Moses, the Gentleman. After Moses had killed the Egyptian he fled to the land of Midian where there occurred an incident that vitally affected the course of his career.

But Moses fled from the face of Pharaoh, and dwelt in the land of Midian; and he sat down by a well. Now the priest of Midian had seven daughters; and they came and drew water, and filled the trough to water their father's flock. And the shepherds came and drove them away; but Moses stood up and helped them, and watered their flock. And when they came to Reuel their father, he said, 'How is it that ye are come so soon today?' And they said: 'An Egyptian delivered us out of the hand of the shepherds, and moreover, he drew water for us, and watered the flock.' And he said unto his daughters: 'And where is he? Why is it that ye have left the man? Call him, that he may eat bread.' And Moses was content to dwell with the man; and he gave Moses Zipporah, his daughter.[5]

The above incident is a very revealing one. It portrays Moses as one of those noble men whom we call in our day a gentleman. A gentleman is one who in every circumstance of life attempts to do the kindly and just thing. Moses had the courage and kindliness on this occasion to help some girls in a trying situation. It is the opinion of the writer that this incident reveals the calibre and fibre of Moses' character as well or better than anything else in the Old Testament. Nor was Moses the only gentleman in the story.

Reuel, or Jethro, as he was often called, belonged to the same class as Moses. He recognized Moses' benevolent deed and invited him to dwell with him. That he seemed to think Moses the gentleman was a preferred matrimonial risk is seen in his presentation of Zipporah to him in marriage. And we can agree with Jethro that gentlemen are always preferred.

Moses and the Covenant at Sinai. The picture given by Exodus of the circumstances under which Israel received

---

[5]Exo. 2:15-21.

the Ten Commandments is one of the most vivid and striking in the Old Testament. God is portrayed as being very near His people. Moses is shown to be in close communication with Him and the people are given great manifestations of His presence.

> And Moses went up unto God, and the Lord called to him out of the mountain, saying: 'Thus shalt thou say to the house of Jacob, and tell the children of Israel: . . . Now therefore, if ye will hearken unto My voice indeed, and keep My covenant, then shall ye be Mine own treasure from among all peoples; for all the earth is Mine; and ye shall be unto Me a kingdom of priests, and a holy nation. . . . And Moses came and called for the elders of the people, and set before them all these words which the Lord commanded him. And all the people answered together, and said: 'All that the Lord hath spoken we will do.' And Moses reported the words of the people unto the Lord. And the Lord said unto Moses: 'Lo, I come unto thee in a thick cloud, that the people may hear when I speak with thee, and also believe thee forever.'[6]

When Moses had prepared his people to hear God, Mount Sinai seemed to be on fire and smoke ascended as from a furnace.[7] In the midst of the fire and smoke God delivered instructions including what we call the Ten Commandments as found in Exodus 20.

> And all the people perceived the thunderings, and the lightnings, and the sound of the trumpet, and the mountain smoking; and when the people saw it, they trembled, and stood afar off.[8]

Moses would be forever remembered if he were responsible only for the Ten Commandments as we have them in Exodus 20. These commandments are recognized among most peoples as being absolutely necessary for a civilized society. They are given as specific commandments and are given in a negative form, as prohibitions. The higher and more fundamental laws upon which they are based are given in the Gospel of Matthew in the portion known as the Sermon on the Mount.[9] This ancient code

---

[6]Exo. 19:3-9.
[7]Exo. 19:18.
[8]Exo. 20:18.
[9]Matt. 5-7.

was, in general, superior to any code of the ancient world. Whatever people may think of it, it remains to this day the most famous code in the world, and certainly no code has been suggested that has had greater influence.

Moses, the Loyal. On one occasion, while on the Mount of Sinai, Moses was told by the Lord that the Israelites had made a molten calf and were worshiping it and in other ways dealing corruptly. The Lord said to Moses:

I have seen this people, and behold, it is a stiff-necked people. Now therefore let me alone, that my wrath may wax hot against them, and that I may consume them; and I will make of thee a great nation.[10]

This saying was a great test of Moses. Through long experience he knew the faults and failings of his people. They were none too easy to handle. And now the Lord was offering to make of him a great nation in their stead. What should he do? His answer is a wonderful tribute to another quality he possessed, namely, loyalty to his God and to his people despite the frailties of the latter.

"Lord, why doth Thy wrath wax hot against Thy people, that Thou hast brought forth out of the land of Egypt with great power and with a mighty hand? Wherefore should the Egyptians speak, saying: For evil did He bring them forth, to slay them in the mountains, and to consume them from the face of the earth? Turn from Thy fierce wrath, and repent of this evil against Thy people. Remember Abraham, Isaac, and Israel, Thy servants, to whom Thou didst swear by Thine own self, and saidst unto them: I will multiply your seed as the stars of heaven, and all this land that I have spoken of will I give unto your seed, and they shall inherit it forever."[11]

This statement of the Lawgiver is a sufficient answer to the question, Why has Moses' name and work come down through the centuries?

Moses and the Origin of Israel's Religion. The origin of Israel's religion, according to Old Testament scholars, is one of the hardest problems of Hebrew history. There

---

[10]Exo. 32:9, 10.
[11]Exo. 32:11-13.

have been several schools of thought which have differed more or less widely on this subject. Some of their views may be fairly well gathered from the following: (1) One of them assumes that Moses' and hence Israel's religion, is of Midianitish origin and that Yahweh (Jehovah) was the God of the Midianites. They base this conclusion on the assumption that when Moses went into the land of Midian and came into close contact with Jethro, the Priest of Midian, he also came into close contact with the religion of the Midianites. Moses is supposed, therefore, to have introduced the Midianite god and religion to his people. Exodus 18 is pointed to as added proof of this assumption. (2) Another holds that Moses' god was not a new god or one with which he had not been heretofore acquainted with, but the God of the Israelite fathers. He is presumed to have revealed himself, however, to Moses for the first time as Yahweh, a name not known to the early Hebrew fathers. They base their claims upon Exodus 6:2-3 which reads as follows:

> And God spoke unto Moses, and said unto him: "I am the Lord; and I appeared unto Abraham, unto Isaac, and unto Jacob, as God Almighty, but by My name Yahweh,[12] I made Me not known to them."

This group would deny the Midianitish origin of the Yahweh religion. (3) Yet another view was taken by Professor T. J. Meek of the University of Toronto, who thought that Yahweh (from an original *Yah* or *Yahu*) was originally a storm god, a personification of one of the powers of nature, of South Arabia, that was later adopted as the god of the tribe of Judah. Meek seemed to think that Moses' great work consisted in getting the Israelites in Egypt to put their trust in a Yahweh already known to them.[13] The above illustrates well enough for our purpose here some of the different views that have been held by scholars with

---

[12]The Hebrew text does not contain the vowels of this name. The above vowels are the ones generally used by scholars. The name Jehovah generally used dates back only to the fourteenth century A. D. and onward.

[13]T. J. Meek, *Hebrew Origins*, (1st Ed.) pp. 92f.

respect to the origin of Moses' religion. The present writer, however, would draw the following picture of the origin of the religion introduced to the Hebrews by Moses: Let us first consider the probable condition of the Hebrews in bondage. It is not likely that they had any strong or outstanding leaders during this period. As time went on it is not unreasonable to suppose that the Hebrew people turned, at least in part, to Egyptian religious practices. This is borne out by the fact that when Moses took them into the desert they made a golden calf and in other respects showed their liking and affinity for Egyptian religion. It would also seem doubtful that Moses, during the first forty years of his life, fully understood the high covenant religion of Abraham, Isaac, and Jacob, his forefathers. When Moses later went to Midian and met Jethro, the Priest of Midian, he, without any doubt, became well acquainted with the religion of the man who was later to become his father-in-law. To be sure, nothing direct is said about the matter in the text of Exodus. However, a careful reading of the eighteenth chapter of Exodus will reveal, so it seems to the writer, that the religion and God of Moses was essentially the same as that of Jethro.[14] Throughout the chapter there seems to be a complete harmony in views between the two men. It is not pressing the matter too far to say that the God who appeared to Moses in the burning bush was the God worshiped by Jethro, and presumably other Midianites. It appears that there was a very close relation between the Midianites and the Hebrew people. It is quite possible that the Midianites were the relatives of Abraham, Isaac, and Jacob and that consequently some of them had religious contacts and views very similar to those of the patriarchs.[15] When Moses, therefore, came into contact with Jethro he got a firsthand

---

[14]In the Hebrew text the names Elohim (God) and Yahweh (Jehovah) are both used without any clear distinction between them. The reader's attention is called especially to verses 1, 9, and 12. Even in the English version our point is apparent.

[15]Consult Gen. 25:2, 4; I Chron. 1:32, 33; Exo. 2:15, 16; 3:1, 18:1; Num. 22:4, 7; Judges 1:16; 4:11, 17; 5:24; I Sam. 15:6. The Kenites mentioned in the last few references were apparently Midianites.

knowledge of the religion and God of the early Hebrew patriarchs, of whom we have already spoken. That would readily account for the fact that there seems to be no difference between the God who spoke to Moses in the bush and the God of Jethro. They were one and the same. However, it is necessary to say something about Exodus 6:2-3, quoted above. This text does, indeed, offer a difficulty but, in the writer's opinion, not an insurmountable one. It would appear to the writer that the Hebrew of verse 3 has been misunderstood. We propose a somewhat different translation of the latter, based on the Inspired Revision of the Bible by the Prophet Joseph Smith. It is that the last clause of verse 3 be read as a question rather than as a declaration. The two verses would then read as follows:

> And God spoke unto Moses, and said unto him: "I am the Lord; and I appeared unto Abraham, unto Isaac, and unto Jacob, as God Almighty, but by My name Yahweh was I not known to them?"

The answer expected would be "Yes". There may be some objections to this translation but we think the idea contained therein has merit and brings into harmony most of the traditions concerning the God worshiped by the Hebrew people. In other words, the God of Abraham, Isaac, and Jacob, as well as the "new" God of Moses had the same name, Yahweh (Jehovah). It is quite likely that Moses received a priestly blessing from his father-in-law, Jethro, giving him the right to act and function in the religion as understood by the Midianites.[16] The call, therefore, made by God to Moses in the burning bush was a call to even greater service in which the Lord's people should be redeemed from bondage. In our opinion, the naturistic god suggested by Meek and others as the god of Israel could not have had such tremendous influence

---

[16]Latter-day Saints know from modern revelation that Jethro conferred the Holy Priesthood upon Moses. See D&C 84:6-25. This reference pretty well settles the question of the origin of Israel's religion in Moses' day.

as did the living personal God of Abraham and Moses in close communion with His people.

We believe that a distinction should be made between the teachings which Moses first gave to his people when he led them out of Egypt and those which were given after they had rejected Moses by building the golden calf. As for the first teachings, they were undoubtedly about the same as those advocated by Abraham, Isaac and Jacob. When Moses found that his people could not live up to the simple, but high ideals of the covenant religion, he gave them a lower law or one based upon the law of carnal commandments.[17] This lower law became known as the law of Moses and was in general effect among his people until the time of Christ. Even the so-called lower law was despised and abandoned by many of the people of later Israel. On the other hand, the higher form as first propounded by Moses was in all essentials the same as that proposed by the great prophets in later Israelite history.

Such in broad outline, we believe, must have been the origin of the religion of Israel.

A Summary of Moses' Work. We may summarize Moses' great work as follows: (1) He, through the inspiration of the Lord, was the author—or better, the restorer—of Israel's religion. (2) He led the tribes of Israel, twelve in number, out of Egypt into the desert. We see no reason to doubt the ancient tradition, as so many scholars have,[18] that the tribes which went down into Egypt were twelve in number. The persistent tradition is that twelve tribes went down into Egypt and that twelve came out. (3) Moses welded together the twelve tribes of Israel and gave them a national consciousness. (4) He gave them laws and a code that were binding throughout their national history and that have had a marvelous influence to this day. (5) He led them forty years in the wilderness, during

---

[17]D&C 84:19-28; Heb. 3:7-19; 4:1-11; Ezek. 20:5-11, 23, 25 (note especially verse 25); Gal. 3:7-9, 15-24; I Cor. 10:1-5 (important); John 8:56.

[18] See Meek, op. cit., pp. 29 ff.

which time he taught them and gave them wise directions relative to their future course as a nation. (6) He gave them the idea that they were to be "a kingdom of priests, a holy nation."[19] (7) By delegating authority to others, he built up a democratic organization among his people. (8) The pattern of the organization he built up was God-centered. He taught the Hebrew people to look to God in all of their affairs of life. This prophetic pattern will be seen through much of the Old Testament.

---

[19]Exo. 19:6.

Chapter VI
ISRAEL'S CLASH WITH CANAANITE CULTURE

Israel's Problem. After the Exodus from Egypt—so the Old Testament makes plain—the Lord through Moses consistently refused to allow His people to go into the land of Canaan. This was a wise decision, for in their unschooled state they would have succumbed too easily to the evils of Canaanite culture. They had little or no spiritual morale—years of bondage in Egypt had darkened their minds and perspective. Moses, at the Lord's command, therefore, took them in hand until all of the older generation, with their materialistic views of life and lack of faith had passed away. The younger generation, free from the contamination and pre-suppositions of Egyptian life and thought, would have a chance in Canaan to bring about the type of civilization desired by God. Even a new generation of Israelites would have extreme difficulties unless it was willing to root out and completely supplant the decadent, rotten and morally bankrupt civilization of the Canaanites. Incidentally, the writer of Genesis points out that in Abraham's day the Lord had said, "The iniquity of the Amorite is not yet full".[1] That is to say, Canaanite civilization was not at that time completely ripe and ready for destruction. By Moses' time it was—so the great lawgiver makes clear in unmistakable language. In many books of the Old Testament numerous references are made to the terrible immoralities and gross orgies of the Canaanites. This will be shown presently. Canaanite civilization was a symbol to Old Testament prophets and historians of all that was bad and indecent.

Since Israel did not completely uproot Canaanite civilization as Moses advised, her problem was as follows:

---

[1]Gen. 15:16.

For many centuries after their settlement in Canaan the Israelites were faced with a very serious practical problem. Could they preserve their ancestral traditions, above all their religion—the worship of Jahweh (Jehovah)—and at the same time adopt the civilization of the ancient inhabitants of Palestine, or were the two incompatible? It is becoming more and more clear that in the religious realm as in the rest, the conflict resulted in a compromise, and to a certain extent in fusion.[2]

It will now be advisable for us to look at some of the characteristics of Canaanite culture in order to understand better the significance of Israel's entrance into Palestine.

Canaan and Her Culture. Canaanite civilization was already ages old when Israel entered Palestine. The people understood the working of iron and bronze, knew much about the arts, cultivated the vine and the fig-tree, were skilled in fortifying their cities, knew much about the art of dyeing and safeguarded commerce and travel. A certain class could read and write. It appears that there was considerable wealth among the Canaanites. In respect to foreign relations it seems that the Canaanites had established over a period of centuries close contacts with other countries, particularly Babylon and Egypt.[3] These facts are all interesting and useful, but we are more particularly concerned with the morals and religious practices of the Canaanites.

The practice of human sacrifice was a feature of Canaanite religion. Archaeological excavation confirms the testimony of the Phoenician, Hebrew and classical writers. New-born children were often sacrificed; in fact, at the founding of a new house human victims of various ages were sacrificed for one reason or another. This old custom still prevails in Syria, strange to say, except that animals are sacrificed instead of human beings.

---

[2]Adolphe Lods, *Israel*, p. 2.

[3]*Ibid.*, pp. 59-63. For an up-to-date discussion of the evolution of Canaanite culture and religion consult W. F. Albright, *Yahweh and the Gods of Canaan*, Ch. III. See also Albright's, *The Biblical Period From Abraham to Ezra*, Ch. II, "The Age of Moses," and J. L. McKenzie, *The World of the Judges*, Ch. IV.

The Canaanites still practiced the foundation rite in all its primitive horror. At Megiddo there was found under the fortress the body of a girl of fifteen: the body had no ornaments and rested on the first stones of the building to which it had been fastened by a layer of cement. At Megiddo also was found in the middle of a wall a jar containing the body of an infant buried head first: the jar had been partly crushed by the stones of the wall; hence it had not been buried in the wall after it had been built.[4]

The Canaanite religion was a cruel one as is evident in the bloody rites indulged in by the priests of Baal even as late as the time of Elijah. In order to obtain an answer from their God they cut themselves "with swords and lances, till the blood gushed out upon them."[5]

During the seasons sacred to the Canaanites they indulged in orgiastic practices including sexual excesses. Such rites evidently played a considerable part in Canaanite religion. A homosexual guild was recognized in Canaanite temples.[6]

The Canaanites had certain sacred men and women (*qedeshim* and *qedeshoth*, respectively) who devoted themselves to sacred prostitution.[7] That such practice was not uncommon may possibly be deduced from the story of Tamar in the Book of Genesis.[8] Since the Canaanites were agriculturists it is quite natural to assume that they were interested in fertility cults.

Belief in magic and divination was common, as well as belief in sacred animals which were supposed to have supernatural power or knowledge.

When the Hebrews first came into contact with the Canaanites the latter were worshiping what are commonly called in the Old Testament, *baals* and *astartes*.[9] "Baals" were local divinities worshiped "on every high hill and under every green tree". The corresponding feminine title

---

[4]Lods, *op. cit.*, p. 99.
[5]I Kings 18:28.
[6]Lods, *op. cit.*, p. 102; Albright, *From Abraham to Ezra*, p. 16.
[7]Lods, *op. cit.*, p. 103.
[8]Gen. 38:13-16.
[9]Judges 10:6; I Sam. 7:4; 12:10, etc.

was "baalath". Names of these divinities are still preserved in place names in our Old Testament.[10]

In addition to local divinities the Canaanites had numerous gods who ruled over large territories. The god Dagon mentioned in Judges and Samuel was such a one with a long and interesting history in various localities of the Near East.[11]

Canaanite female deities of a general character such as Astarte, Asherah, Anath, Kadesh and the like, all representing various aspects of fertility, finally seem to have merged into one great female goddess who was called Astarte. This name finally came to mean a goddess in general. So arose the expression "the baals and astartes" among the Hebrews to denote all Canaanite gods and goddesses.[12]

The Canaanites had numerous sacred things such as caves, rivers, mountains, springs, trees and idols. The last named existed in great numbers throughout Palestine as the writer can personally testify. Archaeologists are constantly finding them in their excavations. These sacred things naturally formed centers around which the Canaanites worshiped. Hence the proscription of Deuteronomy:

> Ye shall surely destroy all the places, wherein the nations that ye are to depossess served their gods, upon the high mountains, and upon the hills, and under every leafy tree. And ye shall break down their altars, and dash in pieces their pillars, and burn their Asherim with fire; and ye shall hew down the graven images of their gods; and ye shall destroy their name out of that place.[13]

Speaking of the morals of the Canaanites, Professor Lods has said:

> Israelite writers of every period agree that among the Canaanites, family ties were lightly regarded, the paternal authority was flouted, while in the matter of sexual morality, liberty was carried to the extent of licence. . . . The depravity of the Canaanites was notorious: witness the vices attributed to the inhabitants of Sodom and Gomor-

---

[10]See Judges 20:33; Josh. 19:8; II Sam. 5:20.
[11]See Lods, *op. cit.*, pp. 127 ff.
[12]*Ibid.*, pp. 132 ff.
[13]Deut. 12:2, 3.

rah, the reason alleged for their destruction by the fire of Jahweh (Gen. 13:13; 18:20-1; 19). . . In considering these judgments, allowance must be made for the narrower outlook of a people accustomed to the severity of desert morals and easily shocked by the greater laxity of city life. But there must have been a large residue of truth in these strictures: the very religion of the Canaanites, with its bloody ritual, its female deities, its frequent ceremonial orgies, the halo of sanctity with which it surrounded prostitution, all tended to foster licence rather than to eradicate it.[14]

Even from the above meager description of Canaanite religion and morals it must be apparent, allowing to the Canaanites every benefit of doubt, that Israel faced a stiff problem in preserving her religious heritage when she invaded Canaan. This fact, well known to her leaders, helps explain in part the apparent ruthlessness of the Israelites in dealing with the Canaanites, both before and after invading Palestine.

The Effects of Canaanite Culture on Israel. The Book of Judges makes clear that Israel did not conquer all of Canaan when first she entered it. The so-called "conquest" consisted only of the Jordan valley and the eastern highlands of Ephraim.[15] For a long time during the days of the Judges many of the Israelites were essentially "hillbillies",[16] hemmed in by their enemies on every side. After the generations of Israelites who had been acquainted with Joshua passed away, the effects of Canaanite morals and religion began to be apparent upon the younger generation. For long periods of time the Canaanites conquered Israel and this fact alone would tend to disrupt her settled religious life and practice. Times were rough and banditry was rampant. As the record itself states: "In those days there was no king in Israel; every man did that which was right in his own eyes."[17] All of this seems to have taken place

---

[14]Lods. *op. cit.*, pp. 147 ff.

[15]For discussions of the "conquest" see T. J. Meek, "The Israelite Conquest of Ephraim," *Bulletin of the American Schools of Oriental Research*, No. 61, February, 1936, pp. 17-19; Albright, *From Abraham To Ezra*, Ch. III; McKenzie, *op. cit.*, Ch. V.

[16]Judges 6:2.

[17]Judges 17:6.

because Israel did not drive the Canaanites completely
out. The Lord said to the Israelites:

Ye have not hearkened to My voice; what is this ye have done?
Wherefore I also said: 'I will not drive them out before you; but they
shall be unto you as snares, and their gods shall be a trap unto you.'[18]

And a snare and a trap they were. Note the following
which is but one of numerous similar accounts.

And the children of Israel again did that which was evil in the
sight of the Lord, and served the Baalim, and the Ashtaroth, and the
gods of Aram, and the gods of Zidon, and the gods of Moab, and the
gods of the children of Ammon, and the gods of the Philistines; and
they forsook the Lord, and served Him not.[19]

Israel's conduct during this period had a lasting effect upon
her religion and morals. For centuries Israel's prophets
and wise men referred to it and denounced her allegiance
to old Canaanite practices. It is plain that Israel, during
the period of the Judges, compromised her relatively high
religious ideals with Canaanite practices and certain elements in her population must have apostatized completely.
No better illustration of compromise can be found in the
period of the Judges than that in Chapters 17 and 18 of
the book. The student is advised to read these carefully.
A man, Micah, of the hill-country of Ephraim, makes a
"graven image and a molten image"—presumably of Jehovah—has a "house of God," consecrates his son to be
his priest, but gives him up in favor of a young Levite who,
for a stipend, becomes his priest. Then certain Danites
come along seeking an inheritance. They kidnap the priest,
take Micah's "graven image of the ephod, and the tera-
phim, and the molten image." The priest goes with them
to be "a father and a priest." After arriving at their des-
tination the Danites slay the native settlers and "set them
up Micah's graven image which he made." Throughout
the story the observant reader can perceive the union of
the Canaanite religious practices with those of Israel. It

---

[18]Judges 2:2, 3.
[19]Judges 10:6.

will also be of value to read the story of the Levite's concubine in Chapters 19 and 20. We have no disposition to lighten the faults of the Israelites at the expense of the Canaanites—certainly the Old Testament does not—but the influence of Canaanite religion on Israel can scarcely be gainsaid.

Centuries later we find Elijah,[20] Isaiah,[21] Hosea,[22] Jeremiah,[23] and others of the prophets bewailing such influence. As for Ezekiel—in taunting tones, he says to Jerusalem,

> Son of man, cause Jerusalem to know her abominations, and say: Thus saith the Lord God unto Jerusalem; Thine origin and thy nativity is of the land of the Canaanite; the Amorite was thy father, and thy mother was a Hittite.[24]

It seems quite evident that without a fair degree of acquaintance with Canaanite culture and its effect upon the Chosen People it is difficult to understand properly the work of Israel's prophets.

---

[20]I Kings 18:21-40.
[21]Isa. 1:10, 29, 30, etc.
[22]Hos. 2:8, 13, 16, 17; 4:13-19.
[23]Jer. 1:16; 2:1-9, 20-28.
[24]Ezek. 16:2, 3.

Chapter VII

AN OVERVIEW OF ISRAEL'S NATIONAL HISTORY

(From the Period of the Judges to 70 A.D.)

Biblical Chronology. Students of Israel's history find it exceedingly difficult to secure accuracy in the dating of events. The following table is a tentative one.

Period of the Judges. Documentary evidence at the present time is inconclusive as to the time this period began and ended. Scholars have varied anywhere from about 1400 B.C. to 1200 B.C. for the beginning of the period and many now agree that 1020 B.C. marked the end of it.

The United Kingdom[1]

1020-1000	Saul
1000- 961	David
961- 922	Solomon

Kings of Israel	Date	Kings of Judah
Jeroboam I	922	Rehoboam
	915	Abijah (Abijam)
	913	Asa
Nadab	901	
Baasha	900	
Elah	877	
Zimri, Tibni, Omri	876	
	873	Jehoshaphat

---

[1]All dates unless otherwise specified are B.C. For many of these dates I have been heavily dependent upon W. F. Albright, *The Biblical Period From Abraham to Ezra*, pp. 116-117. The dates given for Zedekiah and the fall of Jerusalem are, I think, too low. On the basis of Book of Mormon studies, I would put Zedekiah at 601 B.C. and the fall of Jerusalem about 590 B.C. There would seem to be a constant three to four year error in regnal chronology. It can't, as yet, be proved.

Ahab	869	
Ahaziah	850	
Jehoram or Joram	849	Jehoram
Jehu	842	Ahaziah, Athaliah
	837	Joash or Jehoash
Jehoahaz	815	
Joash	801	
	800	Amaziah
Jeroboam II	786	
	783	Uzziah (Azariah)
	750	Jotham (co-regent)
Zechariah	746	
Shallum, Menahem	745	
Pekahiah	736	
Pekah	735	Ahaz
Hoshea	732	
Capture of Samaria	722/1	
	715	Hezekiah
	687	Manasseh
	642	Amon
	640	Josiah
	609	Jehoahaz, Jehoiakim
	598	Jehoiachin
	597	Zedekiah
	587	Fall of Jerusalem—Babylonian Exile.
	538	Persian Period—Return of first Jewish exiles.
	516	Jerusalem temple rebuilt.
	480	Malachi, last of Minor Prophets
	445	Nehemiah
	428	Ezra
	333	Hellenistic Period—Alexander the Great conquers Palestine.
	167	Maccabean period—Jews revolt and establish religious emancipation.

142-63 Jews politically independent
      until Pompey establishes rule
      of Rome over Jerusalem.

A.D. 170 Jerusalem destroyed by Titus.

Chapter VIII

THE NATURE OF
HEBREW LITERATURE

Some Essentials of Great Literature. The Old Testament has been almost universally recognized to be literature in the truest and best sense of the term. It contains some literature that is thought by many to be the world's greatest. It may be well, therefore, for us to consider for a few moments some of the essentials of a great literature.

All of us can agree that great literature should have a great theme or subject. A petty, trivial or commonplace theme, no matter how beautifully handled, ill adapts itself to the requirements of great literature because it is too narrow and limited in its outlook on life. Its content is too easily exhausted, it does not constantly give the exhilaration of new discovery by repeated examination.

Then, too, we may agree that in addition to having a great theme, a given piece of literature must be beautifully expressed to be called great. Its diction and imagery should be well nigh faultless. If it has these qualities it has a good chance to survive.

Great literature has the faculty of bringing into activity man's whole being. The greater the scope of any literature—that is, the greater the number, variety, color and complexity of the impulses it arouses in man—the better its quality.

We are perhaps safe in saying that the authors of the world's best literature have had such varied and wide experiences, have had so many avenues of approach, and have known human nature so well that we can never quite get away from them. Each age reads them, relives and seems never to tire of them.

Longinus, the great Greek critic of the second century A. D. was right when he said: "Nature did thus implant in our souls an invincible and eternal love of that which is great, and by our standards divine."

Some General Observations on Hebrew Literature. One of the outstanding characteristics of the Hebrew literature in the Old Testament is the way in which it expresses the close personal relationship existing between God and His people. The Hebrews claimed to be a "covenant" people, a people who had made a special agreement with God to serve Him and keep His commandments. They claimed to be in close touch with God through their seers and prophets. The Almighty talked with His servants as one man talks with another. These claims may not be received by many modern thinkers, but the fact remains that they were the foundation of the Hebrew national existence. The quiet and firm assurance of the Hebrews in the reality of God and His nearness to them is expressed in their literature. God had a real interest in all of their doings, in all of the vicissitudes of their life. For that reason Hebrew literature makes no hair-line distinctions between what we regard as secular on the one hand and sacred on the other. It is mostly God-centered. This fact is one of the prime reasons why the Old Testament is great and world famous.

Another characteristic of Hebrew literature that we must notice is its strong tendency to be ruled by ideas rather than facts. Not that the Hebrews couldn't be objective and see facts, but the latter were used mainly to press home ideas.

If it was the weakness of the Hebrew mind to be ridden by ideas, it was its strength to be able to express these so that they seemed as real and unshakable as the eternal hills.[1]

Inasmuch as most of the literature of the Old Testament was written in Hebrew we should be remiss if nothing was said about the characteristics of the language and its influence upon the English translation of the Bible.

Hebrew is essentially a farmer's language—it is close to the ground, so to speak. The vocabulary of the Hebrew

---

[1]Duncan B. Macdonald, *The Hebrew Literary Genius*, p. 11.

Old Testament is comparatively small. To be sure, many rare words occur in books like Job; but the running vocabulary of average prose is small and simple. The noun has no case-endings and the verb has only two tenses, if we may speak of them as such. Broadly speaking, Hebrew syntax, though it has many subtleties of its own, is very simple. Whereas in Greek and Latin, sentences are built together: in Hebrew they are laid together. Hebrew has the habit of co-ordinating clauses rather than of subordinating them, and one principal verb follows another with a regularity that reminds one of the simple speech of children. The very regularity of the language caused Dr. John E. McFadyen to say to the student of it the following:

> If he [the student] goes forward to the study of the language with a faith in its regularity, he will find its very phonetic and grammatical principles to be instinct with something of that sweet reasonableness, that sense of fair play, we might almost say that passion for justice, for which the Old Testament in the sphere of human life so persistently and eloquently pleads.[2]

Perhaps few people realize that many of those elements which go to make up the greatness and beauty of the Authorized Version are due to the fact that it is an attempt to give a fairly literal translation of the Hebrew original.

> I would also call attention to one feature of a really great style which our English Bible owes to its Hebrew original. This is the sense of dignity, restraint, and power which results from a sparing use of adjectives. Every student must be struck with the very small supply of these words possessed by Hebrew. We have the expression of a few elementary qualities, good, bad, big, little, holy, profane—and many of these are rather participial or nominal than strictly adjectival—bodily defects, and one or two color words. . . . It is partly the paucity of adjectives which gives stateliness and dignity to our Old Testament in the Authorized Version. There is no adjective in Ps. 23. . . .[3]

The following statement also by Professor T. H. Robinson will be apropos at this point:

---

[2]John E. McFadyen in A. B. Davidson—J. E. McFadyen, An Introductory Hebrew Grammar (Twenty-second Edition), p. 3.

[3]Theodore H. Robinson, The Genius of Hebrew Grammar, p. 23.

They [the Hebrews] possessed a concrete directness of thought, a clarity of vision, an instinct for synthesis, and an appreciation of reality, which made them ideal exponents of truth for simple people. And they had a great and stately music in their soul. I doubt not that others beside myself will feel that no better instrument than the Hebrew mind could have been found for the supreme literary revelation of God.[4]

The student of the literature of the Old Testament in English translation should be cautioned against cramping it too tightly in the shoes of the English scheme of letters and literary classification. After all, the Old Testament is an oriental literature and not an occidental one. The Hebrews were an ancient people and their language and thought patterns, their manners and customs and, in general, their psychology was different in many respects from our own. Those who will keep these facts in mind will not make the mistake of calling the Twenty-third Psalm and certain of the Proverbs sonnets, not to mention other types of mistakes that might be cited. It may be permissible to treat the Old Testament purely as English literature but it will never do to claim that such treatment always represents the spirit of the original. Hebrew literature better follows the scheme of Arabic letters, and even here it does not completely fit. Certainly Arabic literature reveals no dominating personality like the Hebrew Jehovah.

Contrary to the views of many others, the writer has the firm conviction that the Old Testament was written by a comparatively few record keepers. The Hebrew people, as stated before, were a covenant people and the keeping of their records was probably not left to chance by the prophetic leaders among them.[5] These record keepers over a long period of time revealed the many-sidedness of the Hebrews and in this sense the literature they produced is a national one.

It is the further conviction of the writer that far too much emphasis has been placed by modern critics on the

---

[4]*Ibid.*, p. 24.

[5]See Deut. 31:9, 24-26; 17:18; Josh. 24:26; II Sam. 20:24, 25; Isa. 34:16; Ezra 7:12-14.

element of folklore in the Old Testament. Some folklore
there may be, but not in the great amount claimed by certain writers who seem in so many instances unable to penetrate the spirit that permeates the ancient literature.

Speaking in terms of our own literary art, it should be
pointed out that Hebrew literature had no drama in the
absolute sense. Their lyric had to serve for that and we shall
say more about it presently.

Paronomasia or play on words is a very essential
literary device in the Old Testament. Unfortunately those
who have no knowledge of the original language are at a
great disadvantage here since puns seldom carry over well
into the English. Occasionally, by stretching a point, we
can catch the spirit of the original in English. An interesting case in point is seen in Amos 8:1, 2. As usually translated this passage reads as follows:

> Thus the Lord God showed me; and behold a basket of summer
> fruit. And He said: 'Amos what seest thou?' And I said: 'A basket of
> summer [kaiz] fruit.' Then said the Lord unto me:
> The end [kez] is come upon My people Israel.

If the reader will allow the use of the word "fall" to
be used instead of "summer" and "end" he will get an
effect that closely approximates the effect in Hebrew. The
passage will then read:

> Thus the Lord God showed me: and behold a basket of fall fruit.
> And He said: Amos, what seest thou?' And I said: 'A basket of fall
> fruit.' Then said the Lord unto me: The fall is come upon My people
> Israel.

The reader familiar with Amos will recognize at once
how tame the first translation is compared to the last where
the play on words is reasonably well duplicated in the
English. But in most cases we can't do that well.

The Hebrews used numerous figures of speech with
telling effect. Alliteration[6] was a favorite device. Note the
following in Micah 1:10 (Moffatt's translation):

---

[6]Repetition of the same letter.

> Tell it not in Tell-town,
> In Weep-town weep.

So also onomatopoeia[7] of which the following is a good example:

> Ah! the booming of the peoples, the multitudes,
> Like the booming of the seas they boom.[8]

Rhyme is not very frequently found in the Old Testament.

Characteristics of Hebrew Poetry. As with other peoples, the poetry of the Hebrews expressed their soul. Strangely enough, in the literature of the Old Testament there is no word for "poet". Much of the Hebrew wisdom and prophetic literature is poetry as any one can see for himself who possesses a modern translation of the Old Testament. There is in Hebrew literature, therefore, a very close connection between poetry and prophecy. The Hebrew poet was a singer and for that reason all Hebrew poetry in terms of English literary art is lyric poetry. Hebrew poets were spontaneous in their art. When under inspiration they wrote down or sang out immediately what was in their hearts without making any attempt to control and polish their product as did the ancient Greeks. The latter were masters of poetic form and patiently planned and polished every line of their work. Not so with the Hebrew poet. Fixed forms of literary art were not his forte. That is the reason there are no sonnets in Hebrew literature.

Hebrew poetry may be classified into three general types: (1) Didactic lyric, (2) Dramatic lyric, (3) Epic lyric.

Most of the psalms are of the first type. They are the impassioned, soul-stirring outbursts of penitent, suffering, exultant or worshipful men who give us the benefit of their inmost emotional and deeply religious experiences. For that reason they form one of the finest devotional collections in existence.

---

[7]Formation of words to imitate the sound of the thing mentioned.
[8]Isa. 17:2. (Translation of G. A. Smith).

The dramatic lyric is beautifully exemplified by the monologues in the Book of Job.

The best example of the epic lyric is to be found in the Song of Deborah in the fifth chapter of the Book of Judges.

The outstanding rhetorical characteristic of Hebrew poetry is the phenomenon called *parallelism*. This feature of the poetry was first systematically dealt with by Bishop Robert Lowth at Oxford in the year 1753. By parallelism we simply mean the rhythm or balance felt as the poetry is read. This rhythm is a balance of thought rather than of syllables. That is to say, there is a parallelism of ideas between the two halves of a line. The half-line is known as a *stichos*. There are three main types of parallelism.

(1) *Synonymous*. The second line, or *stichos*, repeats the thought of the first line.

> O Lord, rebuke me not in Thine anger;
> Neither chasten me in Thy wrath.
>> Ps. 38:1.

> Oh that my vexation were but weighed,
> And my calamity laid in the balances altogether.
>> Job 6:2.

(2) *Antithetic*. The second line is in contrast to the first.

> For the Lord regardeth the way of the righteous;
> But the way of the wicked shall perish.
>> Ps. 1:6.

> A soft answer turneth away wrath,
> But grievous words stir up anger.
>> Prov. 15:1.

(3) *Synthetic*. The sense of the first line is completed or continued in the second.

> O Lord my God, in Thee have I taken refuge;
> Save me from all them that pursue me, and deliver me.
>> Ps. 7:1.
> Wine is a mocker, strong drink is riotous;
> And whosoever reeleth thereby is not wise.
>> Prov. 20:1.

In reference to the above it may be remarked that while synonymous parallelism may at times be monotonous it nevertheless has the advantage of being emphatic. It should also be noted that a knowledge of parallelism often helps in determining the meaning of a passage otherwise obscure.

What is the meaning of the following lines in Amos 4:6?

> And I also have given you
> Cleanness of teeth in all your cities.

The next line gives the clue.

> And want of bread in all your places.

"Want of bread" is synonymous with "cleanness of teeth" so the latter means hunger or famine.

Another good illustration occurs in Gen. 4:23 where Lamech says:

> For I have slain a man for wounding me,
> And a young man for bruising me.

Query: How many men were slain? The answer is *one*, because the second line is synonymous with the first.

Another kind of parallelism that some think is a special type is known as "emblematic". Examples follow:

> Where no wood is, the fire goeth out;
> And where there is no whisperer, contention ceaseth.
> Prov. 26:20.

> As the hart panteth after the water brooks,
> So panteth my soul after Thee, O God.[9]
> Ps. 42:1.

Still another kind is what may be called "stair-like" parallelism where a part of the first line is repeated, and the sense continued therefrom.

> Ascribe unto the Lord, O ye sons of might,
> Ascribe unto the Lord, glory and strength,
> Ascribe unto the Lord the glory due unto His name.
> Ps. 29:1, 2.

---

[9]Certainly this passage is more emblematic than synthetic.

There are varieties of parallelism, but behind them all the same principle exists. Thus we have the triplet, quatrain, introverted quatrain, introverted triplet, double triplet, etc. To some of these varieties the writer has applied the name of "eccentric" parallelism and "concentric" parallelism. The concentric variety is so called because the segments of circles joining lines paralleling each other in thought are concentric. Note the following example using an introverted quatrain:

> 1. My son, if thy heart be wise,
> 2. My heart will be glad, even mine;
> 2. Yea, my reins will rejoice,
> 1. When thy lips speak right things.
>
> Prov. 23:15, 16.

The eccentric variety is so called from the fact that segments of circles joining lines parallel in thought are out of center and cross each other. The following is an example:

> 1. The Lord is my light and my salvation;
> 2. Whom shall I fear?
> 1. The Lord is the stronghold of my life;
> 2. Of whom shall I be afraid?
>
> Ps. 27:1.

By combining lines of Hebrew poetry in certain ways stanzas and strophes may be formed somewhat analogous to those in English poetry.

Characteristics of Hebrew Prose. We may ask at the outset the difference between Hebrew prose and Hebrew poetry. Professor Duncan B. Macdonald has, in our opinion, given a splendid answer.

It is emotion and the emotion always goes with the song. The sequence appears to be this: The Hebrew artist can tell a story straight and clear in prose; his brain is cold; he can think about his creation and develop it and shape it. It may be a creation of pathos or of terror, of repentance or of joy, but, so long as it is not the poet's pathos, repentance, terror, joy, he creates in prose and his creation is not himself. But should his brain be fired by the situation in which his character is and his own emotion roused; should he feel this situation

as his own; then the thread of narrative breaks; he bursts into song; he
and his character melt together and for that moment he can render
only himself, how he felt and reacted to it all. It may be that after
his outburst he will recover his self-possession and resume his narrative, but it will be in prose.[10]

Most of the Old Testament from Genesis to II Kings
is prose. Occasionally a little poetry is met with. The
prophetic books contain great amounts of poetry, but a
large amount of prose is also to be found among them. We
estimate that Jeremiah is nearly sixty per cent prose, Ezekiel about eighty-five per cent, Jonah seventy-five per cent.
Haggai is nearly completely so; and Zechariah is about sixty-
five per cent. The other prophets contain much less.[11] The
remaining books, the Writings according to the Jewish classification,[12] contain prose and poetry as follows: The books
from Esther to II Chronicles are almost solid prose. Most
of the remaining books are poetry with the exception of
the Prologue and Epilogue of Job, Ruth, and about sixty-
five per cent of Ecclesiastes.

How is this prose to be classified? Authorities often
differ greatly as to how it should be done. Thus Moulton
would classify the prose of Genesis as epic stories, epic
cycles and epic history. He also classifies as epic portions
of Exodus, Numbers, Joshua, Judges, Samuel and Kings.
Ruth and Esther are classified as epic history.[13] The writer
has no particular objection to this if the literature of the
Old Testament is viewed purely as English literature, that
is, if it can honestly be viewed as such. But he strenuously
objects to the term "epic" if the literature is regarded as
Hebrew literature for the reason that true epic is quite
foreign to Semitic peoples.

---

[10]Macdonald, op. cit., p. 22.

[11]These estimates are made on the basis of the classification in the Jewish Publication Society Edition of the Old Testament and may differ from other editions. It is
not always easy to distinguish prose from poetry and vice versa.

[12]See Chapter I.

[13]Richard G. Moulton, The Literary Study of the Bible (Revised and Partly Rewritten Edition) pp. 480-485.

We have here but little space in which to discuss the prose of the Old Testament. For our purposes we may classify it briefly as follows:

1. The Story.
2. History.
3. Oratory. (Prose portions.)

To the above we might have added prophetic prose but have refrained from doing so since, as we have seen above, in the literature of the prophets it is often difficult to determine the dividing line between prose and poetry. Then, too, prophetic literature needs a distinctive treatment.

The story has, of course, numerous examples in the Old Testament. Nearly all of Genesis would be classed as such. These stories can well be classed as philosophic in treatment and approach. (See Chapter III.) The Abraham and Isaac stories are admirably done and meet the requirements of good short stories, but they are not done with the consummate skill and artistry of the Joseph stories. The religious element in these stories is, of course, usually of a very high order.

The stories in Exodus are not nearly so well told as those in Genesis. Some of them remind one of historical romance.

The Book of Ruth may be classed as the first true "short story" known to literature.[14] By nature it is a story that can best be put in short form. It is a gem of its kind.

The Book of Jonah which is classed among the prophetic books, is in form a religious story. The stories in the Book of Daniel may be classed in the same category. Those in Daniel are, however, not so well told as the one in Jonah.

The Book of Esther is a story of foreign origin.

There are but two fables in the Old Testament. These are found in Judges 9:7-15 and II Kings 14:8, 9. It should be remarked that fables are not native to the Hebrews and

---

[14]Macdonald, *op. cit.*, p. 121.

the two mentioned must have been derived and adapted from foreign sources.

The parable is also to be classed under story. The stories given in II Sam. 12:1-6 and II Sam. 14:4-9 may be called parables.

The Hebrews never attained to the writing of history in our modern scientific sense. That is, they did not write history which could be considered the product of unbiased investigation. Nevertheless, there is preserved in the Old Testament a fairly reliable key to the history of the Near East. The Hebrew records are worthy of a respectful hearing before any modern court.

The Book of Genesis may be spoken of as a philosophy of history. So also the Book of Judges. The general view taken by Judges may be found condensed in 2:11-23.

Such professedly historical books as Samuel, Kings, and Chronicles are interesting to examine for the purpose of ascertaining their methods. The stories in Samuel are fresh, vigorous and picturesque, and seem so true to life that we can easily believe that they are trustworthy and told with little purpose other than to reveal the facts. The Books of Kings are more formal in arrangement. The author or compiler had something to teach and seems somewhat biased against the kings of the Northern Kingdom. The compiler of Chronicles covers essentially the same period of time as in Kings, but he emphasizes the theological aspects more than the latter. He has a tendency to moralize a great deal and attempts to show that blessings follow those who keep the law of the Lord and that punishment befalls the sinner.

Not all orations in the Old Testament are prose, but the following examples are sufficient for our purpose:

Deut. 1:6-4:40. ⎫
    5:1-11:32. ⎪
    28.   ⎬   Orations of Moses.
    29:2-31:8. ⎭

I K. 18:20-40.—Elijah on Mt. Carmel.

The Hebrew Prophetic Literature. The literature of the prophets is so distinctive in spirit that it ought to be described as a separate type. Some of the forms of prophetic literature with examples according to the English classification of Moulton[15] are given herewith:

1. Prophetic Discourse. Isa. 1:2-4; Ezek. 34.
2. Lyric Prophecy. Isa. 9:8-10:4.
3. Symbolic Prophecy.
   a. The Emblem. Jer. 13; 18:1-17; 24.
   b. The Vision. Ezek. 37:1-14.
   c. The Parable. Isa. 5; Ezek. 15-17, 23.
4. Prophetic Intercourse.[16]
   a. With God.
   b. With Enquirers.
   c. With the World.
5. Dramatic Prophecy. Micah 6:1-8; 6:9-16.
6. The Doom Song. Jer. 25:15-31; Gen. 9:25; Isa. 21-22:14; Ezek. 26-28.
7. The Rhapsody. Hab. 1-3; Joel 1-3; Isa. 40-66.

This is as much space as can be allotted to the Old Testament as literature, but studied purely from that point of view the Hebrew scriptures will give a lifetime of delight and satisfaction.

---

[15]See Moulton, *op. cit., pp. 363-456.*
[16]*Ibid.,* pp. 383 ff.

Chapter IX

THE WISDOM OF THE SAGES— KOHELETH AND PROVERBS

The Scope and Nature of Wisdom Literature. The so-called Wisdom literature of the Old Testament includes Koheleth (Ecclesiastes), Proverbs, Job and the following from the Book of Psalms: 1; 19:7-14; 32:8-11; 34:12-23; 37; 49; 73; 94:8f.; 111; 112; 119; 127; 128; 133.

Outside of the Old Testament the following works should be included in Hebrew Wisdom literature: The Wisdom of Jesus Sirach (200 B.C.-180 B.C.); the Book of Tobit 4:13 f.; 12:6-11; 14:9 f. (circa 200 B.C.); I Esdras 3:1-4:63 (circa 300 B.C.).; The Letter of Aristeas, paras. 187-294 (circa 40 B.C.); The Wisdom of Solomon (circa 30 B.C.); IV Maccabees (circa 30 A.D.); The Book of Baruch 3:9-4:4 (after 70 A.D.); Pirque Aboth (Sayings of the Fathers, from 150 B.C. to 250 A.D.); the didactic poem of 250 hexameters of Pseudo-Phocylides (150 B.C.-70 A.D.).[1]

The origin of Wisdom literature is usually explained as follows: At an early period of time, short, pithy sayings became popular when they expressed something which seemed to be true to life. Among the Hebrews, who had strong religious instincts, these sayings frequently took on a decidedly religious turn. At a later time when used in literature they became more complex and acquired an extended sense. Thus, the utterances of Balaam (Num. 23:7, 18, etc.) are a supposed example. It is assumed that collections of popular sayings were eventually made by

---

[1]See O. S. Rankin, *Israel's Wisdom Literature*, p. 9. Rankin's dates have not been followed in every instance. This material is given for the sake of completeness. A recent book which discusses Wisdom and the Wisdom books is Sellin - Fohrer (tr. D. Green), *Introduction to the Old Testament*, Part Three, pp. 304-341. For an excellent survey of Proverbs as wisdom literature see R.B.Y. Scott, *Proverbs* (Anchor Bible), pp. xv-liii and 3-30. For a discussion of Canaanite literary influence on Israel, including Wisdom, see W. F. Albright, *Yahweh and the Gods of Canaan*, especially pp. 220-229.

different individuals who added to them proverbs of their own. Finally, these collections were written down, and in this way their literary form began. Once the literary form had been attained, there gradually evolved a guild or group of Wisdom writers, *Chakamin*, "Wise men," or "Sages", who developed the Wisdom literature. It is supposed that the "Sages" came originally from the ranks of the learned scribes who often held important positions of state. The attention of the reader is called to II Sam. 8:17, where mention is made of Seraiah the *Sopher* or scribe, an officer of David's; reference may also be made to I Kings 4:3; II Kings 19:2; 22:3-7; Jer. 36:20, 21. These Scribes may have been trained in a town like Kiriath-sepher which means "the book city", or, as the Septuagint reads it, "the Scribe city".[2]

Professor S. R. Driver speaks of Hebrew Wisdom in the following terms:

Wisdom, among the ancient Hebrews, was a term which was used in special connections, and hence acquired a special limitation of meaning. It was applied to the faculty of acute observation, shrewdness in discovery or device, cleverness of invention.[3]

And of the Hebrew "Wise Men" he says:

"Wise men" are alluded to in the Old Testament in terms which appear to show that they must have formed, if not a school, yet a tolerably prominent class in ancient Israel (cf. Jer. 18:18; Prov. 1:6; 22:17; 24:23; Job. 15:18). The interest of these "wise men," however, did not center in the distinctively national elements of Israel's character or Israel's faith; and hence, for instance, the absence in the Proverbs of warnings against idolatry, and of most of the favorite ideas and phraseology of the prophets (as "Israel," "Zion," "my people," "saith Jehovah," etc). The wise men took for granted the main postulates of Israel's creed, and applied themselves rather to the observation of human character as such, seeking to analyze conduct, studying action in its consequences, and establishing morality, upon the basis of principles common to humanity at large. On account of

---

[2]See W. O. E. Oesterley and T. H. Robinson, *An Introduction to the Books of the Old Testament*, pp. 150, 151, 157.

[3]S. R. Driver, *An Introduction to the Literature of the Old Testament* (New Edition, Revised 1913), p. 392.

their prevailing disregard of national points of view, and their tendency to characterize and estimate human nature under its most general aspects, they have been termed, not inappropriately, the *Humanists*, of Israel.[4] Their teaching had a practical aim: not only do they formulate maxims of conduct, but they appear also as moral advisers, and as interested in the education of the young (Prov. 1-9; cf. Ps. 34, 37). The observation of human nature, however, naturally leads on to reflection on the problems which it presents; hence Job and Ecclesiastes form part of the Hebrew *Chokhmah* (Wisdom)—literature. Nor is the observation of nature, especially in so far as it affords evidence of providential arrangements or designs, alien to the lines of thought which the wise men of Israel pursued. . . .[5]

The above views of Wisdom literature have been for years the usually accepted orthodox, scholarly, variety. But they have been vigorously assailed by the very competent Semitist, Professor Duncan B. Macdonald, who protests against the prevailing ideas that the Hebrew mind was unphilosophical and that Wisdom took its place.

We come now to a more systematic consideration of the philosophy of the Hebrews. Such a study is made difficult by the prevailing prejudice that the Hebrews had no philosophy—that the Hebrew mind was essentially unphilosophical—and the whole subject is further obscured by a myth which has been built up that, instead of philosophy, the Hebrews had something called Wisdom which is expressed in a part of their literature commonly called the Wisdom Literature.[6]

Macdonald shows how the whole temper of the Hebrew mind was Platonic. He points out how the substitution of the word "reason" or the cognate words, "rational," or "rationality" for the word "wisdom" in the Wisdom literature of the Old Testament will often cause the meaning to flash out in new reality.[7] Macdonald makes a strong case and the writer is inclined to believe that he is right in many respects.[8] At any rate, the student is entitled to know

---

[4]Rankin, *op cit.*, p. 3, says: "The Wisdom literature may be called the documents of Israel's humanism, not in the sense of a rejection of the supernatural, or even as intending a concern chiefly with man's welfare, but because its general characteristic is the recognition of man's moral responsibility, his religious individuality and of God's interest in the individual life."

[5]Driver, *op cit.*, p. 393.

[6]Duncan B. Macdonald, *The Hebrew Literary Genius*, p. 171.

[7]*Ibid.*, pp. 171 f. Those interested should read completely Chapters 13 and 14 of his work.

[8]See Macdonald's, *The Hebrew Philosophical Genius*.

that the older views respecting the Wisdom literature have been disputed.

After this general discussion of the literature we may now proceed to a consideration of Koheleth (Ecclesiastes) and Proverbs. The Book of Job will be treated in the next chapter.

KOHELETH

The Meaning of Koheleth. It has been commonly supposed that Solomon, the wise king of ancient Israel, wrote the book we are now to consider. In fact, the first verse of the book says:

THE WORDS OF KOHELETH, THE SON OF DAVID,
KING IN JERUSALEM.

The Hebrew title of the book is Koheleth and we would do well to use it instead of Ecclesiastes. The word is a feminine participle, derived from a root meaning "assemble." At first used to designate an activity or office, the word was finally extended to the man who held the office. So the participle probably has reference to one who convenes or addresses an assembly. Hence "Speaker" or "Preacher" are approximately correct renditions of the word.

Some Facts About the Book and Its Author. The Jewish scholars at the synod held in Jamnia, Palestine, in 90 A.D. were undecided as to whether or not Koheleth should be accorded a place in the canon of scripture. Only the reputed Solomonic authorship and the last two verses in the book seem to have fixed a place for it. The scholars were much perplexed by its contradictions[9] and distressed by the skeptical spirit and apparent heretical tendencies that pervaded it.

Martin Luther rejected the tradition that Solomon wrote the book and now only a few conservative scholars hold that he did so.[10] Those who reject the Solomonic authorship date the book late[11] for linguistic, historical and

---

[9]Cf. 4:2 with 9:4.
[10]See Robert D. Wilson, A Scientific Investigation of the Old Testament, p. 12.
[11]300 B.C.—250.

philosophical reasons. In respect to the last point, scholars have variously argued that Babylonian, Greek and even Egyptian influence pervade the book. The writer believes that none of their general claims can be proved beyond reasonable doubt. Modern scholarship differs as to whether the book is the product of a single person or many. One scholar held that at least eight persons had a hand in its composition. The writer sees no good reason to doubt the essential unity of the book though aware that a number of difficulties present themselves in doing so. But it will also be found difficult to explain certain facts about the book on the basis of multiple authorship.

The author—let us call him Koheleth—seems to have come from an old and noble family and was the possessor and cultivator of large estates—the gentleman-farmer type with much worldly experience. Though an aristocrat by family connection, he was also such in feeling and appreciation for his fellow men, because he said:

> But I returned and considered all the oppressions that are done under the sun; and behold the tears of such as were oppressed, and they had no comforter; and on the side of their oppressors there was power, but they had no comforter.[12]

How true that statement rings today!

After a long experience in all classes of society and amid all kinds of living, Koheleth comes to certain conclusions or rules concerning life. He carefully weighs the points for and against each—reason will be found ruling throughout his formulations. Koheleth points out that something can be said for almost every course of action except folly—and even a fool may have certain satisfactions in his own way. The author seems to be writing in his old age,[13] and one of the high points of his teaching is the admonition to enjoy life with a beloved partner.

> Enjoy life with the wife whom thou lovest all the days of the life of thy vanity, which He hath given thee under the sun.[14]

---

[12]Eccles. 4:1.
[13]See Eccles. 11:9; 12:1.
[14]Eccles. 9:9.

The book has a thoroughly pessimistic tone in many parts of it, nevertheless, men still read and enjoy it. Said Professor Macdonald:

> Every age has found itself in his book and yet there is no end. It is safe to say, that of the Hebrew literature that has reached us, this book is the fullest and most perfect flowering of the essential Hebrew genius in its strength and in its weakness.[15]

Some Teachings of Koheleth. The teachings in the book are seldom developed in any systematic way and, in fact, many of them are inconsistent with each other, thus revealing the changing moods and temperament of the author.

One of the outstanding teachings of the book is the fact that we live in a changing world and that it is constantly "becoming" and not "being". The changes that constantly go on in the world, Koheleth observed, could be put into a table of opposites such as we find in Chapter 3.

> A time to be born, and a time to die;
> A time to plant, and a time to pluck up that which is planted;
> A time to kill, and a time to heal;
> A time to break down, and a time to build up.[16]

Koheleth in the same way would express the doctrine that there is no good without evil.

Another teaching of Koheleth is that God has given man labor to do so that ultimate reality behind events in the world remains a mystery to him.

> I have seen the task which God hath given to the sons of men to be exercised therewith. He hath made everything beautiful in its time; also He hath set toil[17] in their heart, yet so that man cannot find out the work that God hath done from the beginning to the end.[18]

---

[15]Macdonald, *The Hebrew Literary Genius,* p. 199. The writer does not agree completely with this statement, but cites it as an example of the favor in which the book is held.

[16]Eccles. 3:2, 3, etc.

[17]The will to toil is what is meant. In the usual English translations, "the world," or "eternity" which render the present Hebrew text, are meaningless in this context. The simple interchange of two Hebrew letters gives the above excellent result.

[18]Eccles. 3:10, 11.

Under these circumstances there can be nothing better for man to do than enjoy life as best he can by making proper adjustments to events as they occur in the world. Because of the will to work placed in man, he will enjoy labor; in fact, find it to be his only real enjoyment in life.

> I know that there is nothing better for them, than to rejoice, and to get pleasure so long as they live. But also that every man should eat and drink, and enjoy pleasure for all his labor, is the gift of God.[19]

By means of labor and toil man can achieve a transitory happiness. Since old age will surely come, men should enjoy its opposite when the opportunity is at hand.[20] We can now understand what is meant in the first chapter of Koheleth where the usual translations say:

> Vanity of vanities, saith Koheleth;
> Vanity of vanities, all is vanity.[21]

In the words of Dr. Macdonald, to whose brilliant insights we owe so much in this discussion of Koheleth:

> The world was very far from being "vain" or "empty" to Ecclesiastes; it was very full of the most worthwhile things in the doing of which was joy. But they did not abide; they were in perpetual flux; and man had to toil after them. In that toiling there was joy, but he had to keep it up; the accomplished work was always escaping him. So he could say, "Oh, how transitory; all things are transitory!" and go on to describe the groaning, travailing universe in its perpetual circlings. There was no progress in it and man was carried with it, round and round. But man by giving himself to it; by laboring at each thing as it came could snatch a joy.
>
> But we must never forget that this round of events was not ultimate. Behind it was God, and it was only a kind of screen that God had erected between man and Himself that He Himself, behind it, might remain inscrutable.[22]

Koheleth points out that successful work makes a man an object of jealousy. Peaceful poverty, he thinks, is better than troubled and profitless wealth.[23] He also shows that

---

[19]Eccles. 3:12, 13.
[20]See Eccles. 11:9.
[21]Eccles. 1:2.
[22]Macdonald, *The Hebrew Literary Genius*, pp. 207 f.
[23]Eccles. 4:4, 6.

wealth does not satisfy its owner, for others "eat it". The sleep of a laboring man is sweet, but not that of the rich man. Riches are often kept by the owner to his hurt; or perhaps they perish and his son has nothing left. A rich man can not take his wealth with him at death.[24]

The author pleads with one not to be self-righteous or to be over-wise; neither on the other hand to be over-wicked or a fool.[25] "Why should you die before your time?"

It is a good thing to be conveniently deaf at times, lest you hear your servant curse you; for you know in your own heart that you have cursed others.[26]

Koheleth comes to the conculsion that, since the work of God is inscrutable from beginning to end, the only course left to man is to make the most of the present.

Such are a few of Koheleth's teachings. It is impractical to summarize them all here. With many of them we may disagree, but a careful reading of the book will make us enjoy the calm and steadfast courage with which the author faced life.

The end of the matter, all having been heard: fear God, and keep His commandments; for this is the whole man.[27]

THE BOOK OF PROVERBS

The Authorship of Proverbs. The authorship of this Wisdom book is commonly ascribed to Solomon. The superscription of the book reads:

The proverbs of Solomon the son of David, king of Israel.

Again in 10:1 we have another title:

The proverbs of Solomon.

At the head of another collection, beginning at 22:17, there

---

[24]Eccles. 5:9-16.
[25]Eccles. 7:15-17.
[26]Eccles. 7:21, 22.
[27]Eccles. 12:13. The translation "the whole man" is much deeper and more significant than the usual one, "the whole duty of man." The words "duty of" were added by the Authorized Version translators. It is possible that "the duty of all men" is meant by the Hebrew text.

is now no title in our Hebrew text, but the Septuagint has preserved it.

> Sayings of the Wise.

The collection beginning at 24:23 has the title:

> These also (belong) to the Wise men.

Then the collection beginning with 25:1 has the interesting title:

> These also are proverbs of Solomon, which the men of Hezekiah, king of Judah copied out.

And no less interesting is the superscription of Chapter 30:

> The words of Agur the son of Jakeh; the burden.

Finally, at the head of Chapter 31 there appears:

> The words of king Lemuel; the burden wherewith his mother corrected him.

Looking back over these titles it is evident that not all of the Book of Proverbs is claimed to have been written by Solomon. However, a goodly portion of it would appear to be so.

According to the Book of I Kings, Solomon was a very wise man who was the author of a large number of proverbs.

> And God gave to Solomon wisdom and discernment abundantly, and largeness of understanding, as the sand that is on the sea shore. And Solomon's wisdom was greater than the wisdom of all the sons of the East, and all the wisdom of Egypt. And he was wiser than all men . . . and his name was in all the nations around. And he spoke three thousand proverbs. . . .[28]

But in spite of the apparently strong testimony of the above citations, most modern scholars have a tendency to doubt or deny Solomon's authorship of the sections ascribed to him. The writer can not help feeling that their strongest arguments are based on rather slender threads of evidence. They do not actually prove anything. We can see no real

---

[28] 1 Kings 4:29-32.

reason to doubt that a good proportion of the proverbs ascribed to Solomon are really his, though at the same time admitting that they were collected, or "copied out," edited, and put into various collections at a later time.

Let us now proceed to a consideration of the form and teaching of the Book of Proverbs.

An Analysis of Proverbs and Some of Its Teachings. It is usual to discuss Proverbs under eight divisions. We shall point these out to the student and indicate the trend of teaching in each. Space prevents a detailed discussion.

1. Chapters 1-10. These chapters have been called the "Praise of Wisdom". The author, who speaks like a father to a son, admonishes that "The fear of the Lord is the beginning of knowledge" and warns against temptations and dangers. A strong appeal is made to obtain wisdom and avoid folly, particularly when she appears in the guise of the strange woman.

> Say unto wisdom: 'Thou art my sister,'
> And call understanding thy kinswoman;
> That they may keep thee from the strange woman,
> From the alien woman that maketh smooth her words.[29]

2. Chapters 10:1-22:16. This division contains proverbs in the strict sense of the term. Their form is regular and each verse, with the exception of one (19:7), contains a complete proverb consisting of two members only. The proverbs in this division are so miscellaneous in content as almost to prevent general characterization. They are usually bright in tone and the happy aspects of life are generally stressed. There are some very fine religious proverbs in this collection, but generalizations are usually drawn from secular life. An occasional flash of humor adds interest:

> As a ring of gold in a swine's snout,
> So is a fair woman without discretion.[30]

---

[29]Prov. 7:4, 5.
[30]Prov. 11:22.

3. Chapters 22:17-24:22. This division is really a collection of maxims in which proverbs are interwoven. Instead of the two member proverbs as in the previous collection, we find them generally with four members and occasionally even more. Chapter 23:29-35 is really a short poem on wine drinking. The division warns against drunkenness, gluttony, undue pursuit of wealth and indulgence to excess.

4. Chapter 24:23-34. This collection is considered generally to be an appendix to the previous collection. There are a variety of forms as in the other. Verses 30-34 satirize the slothful man.

5. Chapters 25-29. This division is a series of loosely connected sayings resembling the second division above. It is an appendix to that division. Chapters 25-27 contain the most proverbs without any specific moral bearing. In this division religious proverbs are few. The "fool" is satirized,[31] the sluggard derided[32] and care in agricultural pursuits is urged.[33]

6. Chapter 30. This division contains the skeptical and enigmatical words of Agur. The form of the proverbs in this division is peculiar and sometimes they are called "numerical" proverbs. Among other matters, the author calls attention to the four insatiable things,[34] the four incomprehensible things,[35] the four intolerable things,[36] the four wise animals[37] and the four things comely in their going.[36]

7. Chapter 31:1-9. Contains the words of advice to King Lemuel by his mother. No one knows who Lemuel was. He is warned against women and wine, exhorted to judge righteously and to plead the cause of the poor.

---

[31]Prov. 26:1, 3-12.
[32]Prov. 26:13-16.
[33]Prov. 27:23-27.
[34]Prov. 30:15, 16.
[35]Prov. 30:18-20.
[36]Prov. 30:21-23.
[37]Prov. 30:24-28.
[38]Prov. 30:29-31.

8. Chapter 31:10-31. An alphabetic poem describing and praising the good housewife.

Unfortunately, the Book of Proverbs has been much neglected. It deserves a wider reading than it usually gets. To be sure it has its limitations, but is in certain respects of special interest and value to our modern world. It has a simple creed throughout, the fear of Jehovah, and this point is driven home with many practical examples. The appeal of the book is to experience and in this sense it is "in the Land of Us." (Job 1:1)

Its appeal is therefore one which cannot be evaded, as it commends itself, without the support of revelation, to the universal moral instincts of mankind.[39]

---

[39]John E. McFadyen, *Introduction to the Old Testament* (New Edition, Revised), p. 299.

Chapter X

JOB AND THE PROBLEM
OF SUFFERING

Estimates of the Book of Job. The test of time and human experience have demonstrated that the Book of Job is one of the greatest masterpieces of the world's literature, if not the greatest.

The author of it was beyond all question an individual of superb literary genius and possessed a penetrating, rich, daring, and creative mind. He had a profound knowledge of the deep problems of human life and seems almost to have run the complete gamut of suffering and sorrow. In its range of imagination and beauty of diction the book has few, if any, equals. With these qualities it combines also a sense of dignity and nobility that set it apart as a sublime monument to the powers of the human spirit. It is poetry in the highest sense of the term.

The great Carlyle said of it: "Such living likenesses were never since drawn. There is nothing written, I think, in the Bible or out of it of equal literary merit."

Characteristics of the Book. A careful reading of the Book of Job shows that it consists of five parts:

1. Chapters 1 and 2. The Prologue, in prose.
2. Chapters 3-31. Three cycles of speeches between Job and his friends, Eliphaz, Bildad and Zophar, in poetry. (Chaps. 3-14; 15-21; 22-31.)
3. Chapters 32-37. The Elihu speeches, in poetry with the exception of 32:1-6.
4. Chapters 38:1-42:6, also in poetry.
5. Chapter 42:7-17. The Epilogue, in prose.

The book is part of that group of Hebrew writings known as Wisdom Literature, a little of which we have already studied. Certain writers regard it as a philosophical discussion, others as a religious discussion of the problem: Why do the righteous suffer? Dr. S. R. Driver called it a work of *religious philosophy*.[1] Many scholars have looked upon the Book of Job as a work by more than one hand and think that it is the result of a growth in which several stages can be distinguished. Some, however, have maintained that it is a unity and a very small number have thought it to be an imitation of a Greek tragedy.

The date of the Book of Job is not known, but it is generally assumed to be between 600 and 400 B. C.; some authorities assign it to Solomon's era, and a very few to patriarchal times.

Job, the Conventional Pious Hebrew. The story opens with a view of Job as a model of piety and righteousness. In accordance with a philosophy that obtained in ancient Hebrew society, Job was a prosperous—yes, a rich —man, for does not God prosper the righteous and bring misfortune to the wicked?

> For the Lord regardeth the way of the righteous;
> But the way of the wicked shall perish.[2]

So said the Psalmist. And did not Moses say:

> And it shall come to pass, if thou shalt surely obey the voice of Jehovah thy God, to observe to do all His commandments, which I command thee today, that Jehovah thy God will set thee supreme above all the nations of the earth. . . . Blessed shall be the fruit of thy body, and the fruit of thy ground, and the fruit of thy beasts, the offspring of thy cattle, and the young of thy flock. . . . If thou wilt not observe to do all the works of this law that are written in this book, that thou mayest fear this glorious and fearful name, Jehovah thy God; then Jehovah will make thy plagues wonderful, and the plagues of thy seed, plagues great and lasting, and sicknesses severe and lasting.[3]

Even in the matter of children Job had seven sons and three daughters—twice as many sons plus one as daughters —and what more could a good Oriental ask for? Thus Job fulfilled the Hebrew ideal of a righteous man. And

---

[1]S. R. Driver, *An Introduction to the Literature of the Old Testament* (New Edition, 1913), p. 409.

[2]Ps. 1:6.

[3]Deut. 28:1, 4, 58, 59.

let us not forget that in a large number of cases the old
Hebrew doctrine is true.

> Society being organized as it is, the habits which go to constitute
> righteousness are such as to win a man respect from his fellow-men,
> and to command success; on the other hand, wickedness paralyses the
> moral energies, blinds an individual and a nation alike to the real
> conditions upon which prosperity depends, and often overreaches
> itself. The doctrine was deeply impressed on the ancient Hebrew
> mind; and all exceptions were a source of great perplexity to it.[4]

The Lord Utters a Challenge. One day when the
sons of God came to present themselves before the Lord
a certain individual, Satan by name, also showed up. In
the Prologue of Job he seems to be regarded as a kind
of prosecuting attorney or "FBI" man whose function it is
to test whether good men are really genuine.

> And the Lord said unto Satan: 'Hast thou considered My servant
> Job, that there is none like him in the earth, a wholehearted and
> an upright man, one that feareth God, and shunneth evil?'[5]

The Lord's question shows He is so sure of Job's righteousness that He can well afford to put him to a test. There
is a note of challenge and pride in His words. It is immediately taken up by Satan.

**Is There Such a Thing as Disinterested Righteous-
ness?** Satan propounds in answer to the Lord a question
that has become famous:

> Doth Job fear God for nought?[6]

Satan thinks not and insinuates that any man would
be righteous if God hedged him about and gave him great
possessions. Every man has his price. If Job had everything taken away there would be a different story to tell.

> But put forth Thy hand now, and touch all that he hath, surely
> he will blaspheme Thee to Thy face.[7]

---

[4]Driver, *op cit.*, p. 409.
[5]Job 1:8.
[6]Job 1:9.
[7]Job 1:11.

The writer of Job thus brings to the foreground the question as to whether or not there is such a thing as righteousness for its own sake, and sets the stage to test the validity of the common Hebrew doctrine that "suffering is a sign of the Divine displeasure, and presupposes sin on the part of the sufferer."[8]

Jehovah assents to the test and in the words of Professor McFayden, "grants the Satan permission to deprive Job of all that he *has* in order that he may discover what he *is*."[9] In a series of disasters, Job loses all of his material possessions and even his children are slain. But through it all he is faithful and resigned.

> The Lord gave, and the Lord hath taken away;
> Blessed be the name of the Lord.[10]

Satan is thus checkmated. He insists, however, that Job's test has not been searching enough. True enough, he has passed the property test, but his person has not been touched.

> Skin for skin, yea, all that a man hath will he give for his life. But put forth Thy hand now, and touch his bone and his flesh, surely he will blaspheme Thee to Thy face.[11]

Jehovah consents to a second trial and Job is smitten with a painful and loathsome disease. Even his wife tells the patriarch to blaspheme God and die. But Job nobly answers:

> What? shall we receive good at the hand of God, and shall we not receive evil?'[12]

Again Satan loses. Three of Job's old friends then come to comfort Job and express their sorrow. Three cycles of speeches then follow between Job and his sheikh

---

[8]Driver, *op cit.*, p. 409.
[9]John E. McFadyen, *Introduction to the Old Testament,* (New Edition, Revised), p. 302.
[10]Job 1:21.
[11]Job 2:4.
[12]Job 2:10.

friends. These speeches as indicated above, are written in
poetry.

Job Breaks With Tradition, Cycle One. The Job
we have been dealing with thus far in the Prologue is
the patient and righteous Job of tradition—the one known
to Ezekiel[13] and others to the present time. But with the
opening speech of the poems we are dealing with a changed
man. In an outburst amazing for its vehemence and power,
Job laments the days of his birth and wishes for death.
This is not the voice of tradition, it is the voice of humanity
crying out against the pain, suffering and apparent injustice
in the world. Job, who had been acquainted with a God
who smiled upon him and blessed him, is reeling under
the terrible blows of a Being that smashed him and cast
him about so cruelly. He is forced to ask himself which of
the two manifestations is that of Jehovah. If not from
Jehovah, why does the latter permit his pain and suffering
to go on? At any rate, Job has learned a primal fact of life,
that righteousness is no guarantee against pain and suffering. In facing his friends who subscribed to the old Hebrew
philosophy described above, Job had the advantage of
knowing the facts. But the problem of his own soul was
not an easy one to meet.

The author of the book has shown in the case of Job
that there is such a thing as disinterested righteousness in
this world. However, the question arises, Is God justified
in bringing pain and suffering upon a righteous and innocent person in order to prove him such? A good portion
of the poem is devoted to an examination of this question.
The author of it is, therefore, seeking a justification of God.

After hearing Job's ringing lament, Eliphaz, the Te-
manite, oldest and most kindly disposed of the three comforters, answers him that those who sow mischief reap the
same, that man is born unto trouble as the sparks fly up-
ward, that man cannot be pure before his Maker, that
he (Job) should commit his cause to God and not despise

---

[13]Ezek. 14:14, 20.

His chastening. Job would be assured of his restoration under these conditions.[14]

Job turns aside this optimistic speech, pleads that his cause is righteous, points out that man's life on earth is like that of a hireling, and hopes for a quick death.[15]

Bildad, the Shuhite, less sympathetic than Eliphaz, is much put out because of Job's charges against God, and assures his friend that retribution awaits the wicked. Job is also assured that if he is righteous he will have a happy future.[16]

In ironical vein, Job concedes that since might is right, God is almighty, destroying the innocent and wicked alike. He prays God not to condemn him, but wants to know why He contends with him. Why at the first did God favor him, only at the last to thrust torment upon him?[17]

Zophar, the Naamathite, the youngest and most impetous of Job's friends, feels that he can state the truth without aid of revelation or tradition. He very bluntly points out that Job's multitude of words should be stopped, that he has boasted and mocked with none to make him ashamed.

> But oh that God would speak,
> And open His lips against thee.[18]

If, however, Job would only set his heart right and stretch out his hands toward Him, there would dawn a better day.[19] At the end of his speech he ominously warns:

> But the eyes of the wicked shall fail,
> And they shall have no way to flee,
> And their hope shall be the drooping of the soul.[20]

With withering sarcasm Job replies:

---

[14]Job 4, 5.
[15]Job 6, 7.
[16]Job 8.
[17]Job 9, 10.
[18]Job 11:5.
[19]Job 11.
[20]Job 11:20.

> No doubt but ye are the people,
> And wisdom shall die with you.[21]

He then goes on to point out that his wisdom and understanding are not inferior to his friends, and proceeds to challenge the moral order of the world.

> The just, the innocent man is a laughing-stock,
>
> . . .
>
> The tents of robbers prosper,
> And they that provoke God are secure,
> In whatsoever God bringeth into their hand.[22]

Job wants his friends to be honest—God does not need any man to distort facts for Him.

> But ye are plasterers of lies,
> Ye are all physicians of no value.
>
> . . .
>
> Will ye speak unrighteously for God,
> And talk deceitfully for Him?[23]

Job longs for an opportunity to reason with God, but since he gets no answer he laments the sadness of life which ends so completely in death.[24]

The friends' appeals to God's universal goodness, His discriminating justice, and His omniscient insight, fail to convince Job. He still contends that his sufferings are absolutely unmerited. So his friends now take another tack.

The Second Cycle. Eliphaz once more opens the debate. He is much more severe than before because Job seems to despise religion and arrogate to himself superior wisdom. He, therefore, describes in forceful terms the evil conscience and the fate of the sinner.[25]

Job replies by telling what "sorry comforters" his friends are, and then proceeds to complain of his luckless

---

[21]Job 12:2.
[22]Job 12:4, 6.
[23]Job 13:4, 7.
[24]Job 12-14.
[25]Job 15.

and pitiable condition. He points out that, despite his innocence, God seems to be his relentless adversary and man an arch foe. Nevertheless, he still appeals to the righteous God in heaven who he feels is still his Witness, as against the unintelligible God of punishment, and then falls back again into despondency and gloom.[26]

Bildad, much angered by Job's hard words against the friends and his heretical charges concerning God, answers him very pointedly by describing the fate of the wicked and their dishonor after death.[27]

Job, whose soul is vexed, answers with even a more pathetic description of his woes. But through it there shoots a flitting gleam of assurance that someday God will vindicate him.[28] In the magnificent language of the Authorized Version he declares:

> For I know that my Redeemer liveth,
> And that He shall stand at the latter day upon the earth:
> And though after my skin worms destroy this body,
> Yet in my flesh shall I see God.[29]

Zophar replies that the triumph of the wicked is short and the joy of the godless but for a moment; the greed of the rich man is eventually swallowed up in the wrath of God's judgments.[30]

In a devastating speech, Job arraigns the doctrine of retribution held up by his friends for his special benefit, and challenges the justice of God's moral order in the world. The homes of the wicked are safe, they prosper in all they do, and peacefully go to their graves. To Job the world is turned topsy-turvy.[31]

The Third Cycle. Not having as yet moved Job from his views, the friends proceed now to accuse Job of

[26]Job 16, 17.
[27]Job 18.
[28]Job 19.
[29]Job 19:25, 26. Unfortunately, the Hebrew text of these verses is corrupt and commentators disagree as to the exact meaning.
[30]Job 20.
[31]Job 21.

specific sins which before were only hinted at. Eliphaz points out that his wickedness is great: he has stripped men of their clothing, held bread from the hungry, sent widows away empty, and in other ways abused his power.[32]

Job is driven to despair by these charges, and he again wishes that he might come to God's seat and argue his cause. Why does not the Almighty interpose? Again Job questions the moral order.[33]

By this time the arguments of Job's comforters are very nearly exhausted, and Bildad in a very short speech asks how man, a worm, can be just with God or clean in the face of His majesty.[34]

Zophar fails to come forward, and the rest of the speeches are by Job. He rises to the heights in describing his past prosperity and his present humiliation. Some of the noblest elevations of Old Testament morality are reached in Chapter 31 when Job depicts the principles that determine his past conduct and character. He concludes with a desire for the Almighty to listen to him.[35]

> Oh that I had one to hear me!—
> Lo, here is my signature, let the Almighty answer me—[36]

At this point a very self-sufficient young man, an evident bystander who has not hitherto been mentioned, steps forward and takes part in the debate.

The Speeches of Elihu.

Then was kindled the wrath of Elihu the son of Barachel the Buzite, of the family of Ram; against Job was his wrath kindled, because he justified himself rather than God. Also against his three friends was his wrath kindled, because they had found no answer, and yet had condemned Job. Now Elihu had waited to speak unto Job, because they were older than he. And when Elihu, saw that there was no answer in the mouth of these three men, his wrath was kindled.[37]

---

[32]Job 22.
[33]Job 23, 24.
[34]Job 25.
[35]Job 26-31.
[36]Job 31:35.
[37]Job 32:2-5.

This is a clever attempt on the part of the author to display the rashness and confidence of youth. The young man speaks at length, but all to no purpose. He adds practically nothing to the solution of the problem and, what is more, the literary art of his speeches is considerably below the level of the rest of the book. However, Professor Sellin of the University of Berlin holds that the only solution of the book is to be found here—namely, that the purpose of suffering is to purge the righteous of spiritual pride.[38] Professor C. H. Cornill also believes this section holds the key to the solution of the problem.[39] Many others dissent.

The Almighty Listens to Job. In answer to Job's impassioned plea, Jehovah does answer him. He does this by means of questions which call Job's attention to His Almighty wisdom, power and love, and to the corresponding ignorance and impotence of man.[40]

He had not before realized, the *comprehensiveness* and *infinite resource* of the Divine intelligence; it fills him with a vivid and overpowering sense of the transcedent majesty of the Creator, in the presence of which his doubts vanish, and he owns his presumption in having dared to contend with God.[41]

With Job's humble admission of his inadequate estimation of God the poem ends.[42]

The Epilogue.[43] After Job's troubles are over and his friends properly condemned by Jehovah for their rebuke of him, the epilogue gives a picture of his final prosperity. He has twice as many material possessions given him as at first, and seven sons and three daughters are born to him. The author slyly points out that all his brethren,

---

[38]See John E. McFadyen, *op cit.*, pp. 309ff.

[39]*Ibid.*, p. 311. "If a man recognizes the educative value of suffering and takes it to heart, the suffering becomes for him a source of infinite blessing, the highest manifestation of divine love." But imagine how Job would deal with the educative advantages his children would have in being killed!

[40]Job 38:1-40:2, 6-26; 41.

[41]Driver *op cit.*, p. 426.

[42]Job 40:3-5; 42:1-6.

[43]Job 42:7-17.

sisters, and friends who had deserted him in the day of his trial, "did eat bread with him in his house" and gave him money and rings of gold.

> And after this Job lived a hundred and forty years, and saw his sons, and his sons' sons, even four generations. So Job died, being old and full of days.[44]

The Solution of the Problem. The book seems to offer no final solution to the problem of unmerited suffering in the world. But, as Professor D. B. MacDonald observes, it does strike a "hard blow to the doctrine that all's well with the world."[45] The Prologue would seem to suggest that earthly sufferings find an ultimate explanation in the heavenly councils. It seems also to suggest that suffering is the test of fidelity to God.[46] We should rather expect to find the solution in Jehovah's pronouncements to Job (chs. 38ff.), but such is not the case.

> God simply presents Himself as He is, and Job is cowed, and abhors himself in dust and ashes. This is no solution of the problem, and the poet cannot have intended it to be understood as one. In other words, it looks as though he had deliberately told his readers that there was no solution—at least none that the human mind could appreciate.[47]

Apparently the book leaves us to trust in God—in Him who understands the universe, with its innumerable wonders and reaches—for man who cannot as yet understand the simpler facts of the physical world is not likely to be able to understand the more subtle mysteries of the eternal realm.[48]

---

[44]Job 42:16, 17.

[45]Duncan B. Macdonald, *The Hebrew Literary Genius*, p. 28.

[46]McFadyen, *op. cit.*, p. 307.

[47]W. O. E. Oesterley and T. H. Robinson, *An Introduction to the Books of the Old Testament*, p. 176.

[48]See McFadyen, *op. cit.*, p. 308.

Chapter XI

THE BOOK OF PSALMS

The Importance of the Psalms. The Book of Psalms is the greatest book of devotional literature in existence. It is a sounding board of the heart and soul of the Hebrew people. In fact, it reflects the soul experiences of the whole race of mankind.

Its language is that of the heart, and its thoughts are of common interest to worshipful humanity. It reflects almost every phase of religious feeling: penitence, doubt, remorse, confession, fear, faith, hope, adoration, and praise. Even the unlovely emotion of hatred is frankly expressed in certain of the imprecatory psalms. The Psalms appeal to mankind in every age and land because, being so divine and yet so human, they rest on the foundations of universal experience. Whenever a heart is breaking with sorrow or pulsating with thanksgiving and adoration, its strongest emotions find adequate expression in the simple and yet sublime language of the Psalter.[1]

In the days of the early Church the Psalms were on the tongues of all Christians and Jews. Of the scriptures they were the best known and most used and it is said that many Christians knew the Book of Psalms by heart.

It is, of course, well known that through the centuries the Psalms have had an enormous influence upon literature in many lands and amid many tongues. The universality of the Psalms naturally makes a great appeal to those who are interested in literature.

Again, the Psalms have been much used in hymns because of their elevated thought and the relative ease with which they can be set to music. Martin Luther used them extensively and his enemies complained that the people were singing themselves into Lutheranism. This fact is, of course, an excellent illustration of the tremendous influence that has been exerted by the Psalms.

---

[1]Charles F. Kent, *The Origin and Permanent Value of the Old Testament*, p. 191.

The Psalm Titles. We have already pointed out (Chapter I) that the Book of Psalms is the first in the "Writings" of the third division of the Hebrew canon.

In the Hebrew Bible the whole collection of psalms is entitled *Tehillim,* the plural of *Tehillah,* which means "praise", a "song of praise", "hymn", etc. In the New Testament it is stated that Jesus and His apostles sang a "hymn" at the Last Supper just before going to the Mount of Olives.

And having sung a hymn, they went out to the Mount of Olives.[2]

It is very probable that the hymn they sang was from the Psalms. Psalm 118 could well have been the one selected, or at least parts of it (see especially vss. 17ff.).[3]

Unfortunately, the Hebrew title for the whole body of psalms is inappropriate because most of the psalms are not songs of praise; in fact, only one is actually called a *Tehillah* (Ps. 145). The title given by the Septuagint, depending on the manuscripts, is usually *Biblos Psalmon* or *Psalmoi* ("Book of Psalms" or "Psalms"). Hence the title of the book in English. One Greek manuscript has the title *Psalterion* ("Psalter"). This accounts for another title we sometimes give the book. The Greek title is probably a translation of the Hebrew word *mizmor,* "psalm," which occurs in fifty-seven individual psalm titles. The Hebrew word comes from a root which means to "pluck" and would seem to imply that the psalms in question were sung to the accompaniment of some stringed instrument.

Thirty-four psalms have no title at all and are called for that reason "Orphan" psalms.

A full discussion of the technical terms in the remaining psalm titles is beyond the purview of this book, but we may notice some general classifications: (1) Titles having musical directions, (2) Titles containing names of popular melodies, (3) Titles containing refer-

---

[2]Matt. 26:30; Mark 14:26.
[3]See Gustaf Dalman, *Jesus-Jeshua,* pp. 131 f.

ences to episodes of David's life, (4) Some other terms used in the titles of the Psalms.[4]

The Fivefold and Threefold Divisions of the Psalms. The Book of Psalms is divided, most scholars think artificially, into five books. Each of these books closes with a doxology, and in the case of the last one, the whole of Psalm 150 is itself a doxology. The five books follow:

Book 1. Psalms 1-41.
Book 2. Psalms 42-72.
Book 3. Psalms 73-89.
Book 4. Psalms 90-106.
Book 5. Psalms 107-150.

The break between Psalms 106 and 107 seems to be very artificial indeed. It will be observed that Book 3 contains seventeen psalms and it appears that a deliberate attempt was made to have Book 4 contain the same number by creating a break at the end of Psalm 106. The suspicion is further deepened by the fact that the doxology at the end of Psalm 106 is somewhat different from the others. Apparently it was originally intended for that Psalm only, and not to indicate the end of a book.[5] Furthermore, Psalm 107 which begins the last book goes naturally with Psalms 105 and 106. Probably Books 4 and 5 were originally one book, and so also Books 2 and 3.

Several psalms are practically duplicates. Thus 14 = 53; 40:13-17 = 70; 108 = 57:7-11 and 60:5-12. If a careful comparison is made of these duplicates, with reference to the number of times the name of Deity is used in each one, it must evoke some surprise. Further inquiry will demonstrate that in Book 1 the name of Jehovah (Lord) is greatly preponderant, while in Books 2 and 3 that of Elohim (God) prevails; again, in Books 4 and 5 Jehovah

---

[4]See W. O. E. Oesterly, *A Fresh Approach to the Psalms*, pp. 76-90.

[5]The five books of the Psalms were evidently in existence when the Book of Chronicles was composed because Psalm 106 is partly quoted in I Chron. 16:8-36. The doxology (vs. 36) of 106 would probably not have been quoted if it were intended to close a psalm collection.

is used. Accordingly, in view of the use of the name of Deity, the Psalter may be divided into three divisions:

1. Psalms 1-41. The Jehovistic Psalter.
2. Psalms 42-89. The Elohistic Psalter.
3. Psalms 90-150. Another Jehovistic Psalter.

The motive behind the use of the names Jehovah and Elohim in the manner described above remains obscure to us.

Collections of Psalms in the Psalter. Sometime in the history of the Psalms there must have been a number of small independent collections. These were eventually gathered together to form the fivefold division mentioned above. Note the following:

1. The *David* Psalms: 3-9, 11-32, 34-41, 51-65, 68-70, 86, 101, 103, 108-110, 124, 133, 138-145. A total of 72.
2. The *Korahite* Psalms: 42, 44-49, 84, 85, 87, 88. A total of 11.
3. The *Asaphite* Psalms: 50, 73-83. A total of 12.
4. The *Ma'aloth,* or "Songs of Ascents": 120-134. A total of 15.
5. The *Hallelujah* Psalms: 104-106, 111-113, 115-117, 135, 146-150. A total of 15.

A number of psalms not mentioned above are obviously parts of the psalm just preceding. Thus 10 and 33 are really sections of 9 and 32 respectively.

The above collections, if carefully studied, will in turn show interesting peculiarities pointing to their gradual growth and to the fact that many psalms are out of their original positions. The reader will be particularly interested to note that later psalms were ofttimes made up of earlier ones. Thus Psalm 96 cites 24, 47, 48; 97 cites 30, 32; 102 cites 69; 135 uses 115 and 134; 143 is a mosaic of earlier psalms, 27, 28, 69, 84; 147 makes use of 33 and 104.[6] A very instructive sample of psalm composition is shown in I Chronicles 16:8-36. This psalm, which was used by Asaph and his brethren to give thanks to Jehovah, is made up of Psalms 105, 96, and 106 in the following way:

---

[6]John P. Peters, *The Psalms as Liturgies,* p. 6, note.

I Chron. 16:8-22 = Ps. 105:1-15; I Chron. 16:23-33 = Ps. 96: I Chron. 16:34-36 = Ps. 106:1, 47, 48.

This method of combining psalms to make new ones seems to have been much used.

Psalm Classes or Types. The Psalter is almost completely religious in nature, but there is a great variety of religious moods displayed in it as anyone may determine by making his own attempt at classifiying its contents. No system of classification can ever hope to be completely successful because of the nature of the Hebrew poetry (lyric) in which the Psalms are composed. These lyrics are often characterized by swift changes of feeling, from grief and sorrow to the most glowing expressions of hope and gladness.

Perhaps one of the most scientific attempts at classification ever made was that by Hermann Gunkel, the great German scholar. He divided them into the following types:

1. Hymns, or songs of praise; a special class is formed by the "Enthronement" psalms.
2. Laments of the community.
3. Royal psalms.
4. Laments of the individual.
5. Thanksgiving of the individual.

To these larger groups several smaller classes have to be added:

6. Blessings and curses.
7. Pilgrim psalms.
8. Thanksgiving of the Israelite nation.
9. Legends.
10. Psalms dealing with the Law.
11. Prophetic psalms.
12. Wisdom psalms.[7]

A classification of the Psalms that will probably meet with more general public favor is the following by Mc-Fadyen:

---

[7]As given in W. O. E. Oesterley, *The Psalms*, I, 6. See also Sellin-Fohrer (tr. D. Green), *Introduction to the Old Testament*, pp. 260-272, for a discussion of the literary types of the psalms and their traditions.

1. Psalms of Adoration.
   a. Adoration of God for His revelation in nature, 8; 19:1-6; 29; 104.
   b. Adoration of Him for His love to His people, 33; 103; 111; 113; 115; 117; 147.
   c. Praise of His glorious kingdom, 145; 146; ending with the call to universal praise, 148; 150.
2. Psalms of Reflection.
   a. Upon the moral order of the world, 9; 10; 11; 14; 36; 37; 39; 49; 52; 62; 73; 75; 82; 90; 92; 94.
   b. Upon Divine Providence, 16; 23; 34; 91; 112; 121; 125; 127; 128; 133; 139; 144:12-15.
   c. On the value of scripture, 1; 19:7-14; 119.
   d. On the nature of the ideal man, 15; 24:1-6; 50.
3. Psalms of Thanksgiving, most of them for historical deliverances, 30; 40; 46; 48; 65; 66; 67; 68; 76; 116; 118; 124; 126; 129; 138; 144:1-11; 149.
4. Psalms in Celebration of Worship, 5; 24:7-10; 26; 27; 42-43; 84; 122; 134.
5. Historical Psalms.
   a. Emphasizing the unfaithfulness of the people, 78; 81; 106.
   b. Emphasizing the love or power of God, 105; 114; 135; 136.
6. Imprecatory Psalms, 58; 59; 69; 83; 109; 137.
7. Penitential Psalms, 6; 32; 38; 51; 102; 130; 143.
8. Psalms of Petition.
   a. Prayers for deliverance, preservation or restoration, 3; 4; 7; 12; 13; 17; 25; 31; 35; 41; 44; 54; 55; 60; 64; 71; 74; 77; 79; 80; 85; 86; 88; 120; 123; 131; 140; 141; 142.
   b. Answered prayers, 22; 28; 56; 57.
9. Royal Psalms.
   a. King's coronation, 21.
   b. Marriage, 45.
   c. Prayers for his welfare and success, 20; 61; 63.
   d. His character, 72; 101.
   e. Dominion, 2; 18; 110.
   f. Yearning for the Messianic King, 89; 132.
10. Psalms concerning the universal reign of Jehovah, i. e., Messianic psalms in the largest sense of the word, 47; 87; 93; 95; 96; 97; 98; 99, 100.[8]

The Psalms in the New Testament. It is really remarkable the number of times the New Testament writers allude to or make direct quotations from the Psalter. A

---

[8]Adapted from John E. McFadyen, *Introduction to the Old Testament*, pp. 272 f.

careful study of the facts fully justifies the conclusion that the Book of Psalms was the most loved and used Old Testament book in the early Christian Church. Bishop Perowne makes the following striking statement about the use of the Psalms in the New Testament:

It is a remarkable fact, that of all the citations in the New Testament, from the Old, which have a Messianic reference, nearly one-half is made from the Psalms.[9]

It ought to be especially noted that the Book of Psalms was quoted and used more by the Savior than any other Old Testament Scripture. His love of it must have been greatly responsible for the use made of the Psalms by New Testament writers other than the authors of the Gospels.[10] In the later Christian Church the same great use of this Book continued.

The prophetic use of the Psalms as applied to the life of our Lord by the New Testament is interesting and instructive. Two or three examples of this use will suffice.

In John 15:25 the Savior shows that the Jews in hating Him only fulfilled their own Scripture.

But this comes to pass, that the word may be fulfilled that is written in their law. *They hated me without cause.* (Ps. 35:19; 69:4. In italics.)

On another occasion He said:

I am not speaking of all of you. I know whom I have chosen, but things are as they are in order that the Scripture may be fulfilled, which says *He who eats my bread has lifted up his heel against me.* (John 13:18. Ps. 41:9 in italics.)

Just before His death on the cross the Christ quoted a psalm, apparently in fulfillment of it.

---

[9]See J. J. Stewart Perowne, *The Book of Psalms* (Third London Edition, Revised) I, 39, note.

[10]I Cor. 14:26 illustrates the common use. "When you come together, each one hath a psalm, hath a teaching, hath a revelation. . . ." So Eph. 5:19: ". . . speaking one to another in psalms and hymns, and spiritual songs. . . ."

And crying with a loud voice, Jesus said, Father, *into thy hands I commit my spirit.* (Luke 23:46. Ps. 31:5 in italics.)[11]

Very often the manner in which New Testament writers use and interpret psalms is strange and forced to us in this day of strict and scientific canons of interpretation. A discussion of the point is, however, too far afield for our purposes here.

A Brief Study of a Representative Psalm. We shall first study a psalm that is not often quoted, but which is a good example of one of the classes mentioned above. Let us begin with Psalm 47, a psalm of the universal reign of Jehovah, in Class 10 according to McFadyen's classification. In Gunkel's classification it would be an "Enthronement" psalm, (1).

For the Leader; a Psalm of the sons of Korah.
1. O clap your hands, all ye peoples;
    Shout unto God with the voice of triumph.
2. For the Lord is most high, awful;
    A great King over all the earth.
3. He subdueth peoples under us,
    And nations under our feet.
4. He chooseth our inheritance for us,
    The pride of Jacob whom He loveth.
                                                            Selah.
5. God is gone up amidst shouting,
    The Lord amidst the sound of the horn.
6. Sing praises to God, sing praises;
    Sing praises unto our King, sing praises.
7. For God is the King of all the earth;
    Sing ye praises in a skilful song.
8. God reigneth over the nations;
    God sitteth upon His holy throne.
9. Let the princes of the people be gathered together,
    The people of the God of Abraham;
    For unto God belong the shields of the earth;
    He is greatly exalted.

---

[11]Note also the following references: Ps. 8:5, 7 cf. Heb. 2:5-9; Ps. 22:7, 8, 18 cf. Matt. 27:35, 39-48; Ps. 22:22 cf. Heb. 2:11, 12; Ps. 40:6 cf. Heb. 10:5-10; Ps. 45:6 cf. Heb. 1:8, 9; Ps. 68:18 cf. Eph. 4:8; Ps. 69:9 cf. John 2:17; Ps. 110 cf. Matt. 22:43, Acts 2:34, I Cor. 15:25; Ps. 118:22, 23 cf. Matt. 21:42, Eph. 2:20; Ps. 132:11 cf. Acts 2:30.

First of all, let us find a name for this psalm. This is not easy to do in the case of every psalm. The name given should be representative of the intention of the author in writing it, and different readers may vary in their interpretation of what that intention is. The reader should bring to the task of interpretation all of the resources and background of Bible reading possible. In the present psalm it will be noted that verse 1 indicates a time of rejoicing and triumph. Verses 2, 7, and 8 present a scene in which God reigns over all the earth. The festive joy and triumph evinced in the psalm would indicate that prior to this time God and His cause were not triumphant. Verses 3 and 4 clearly indicate a time when wicked peoples and nations have been subdued and placed under the power of a righteous Israel. This is the glorious time foreseen by Israel's prophets. Joel saw it for he prophesied:

> I will gather all nations,
> And will bring them down into the valley of Jehoshaphat;
> And I will enter into judgment with them there
> For My people and for My heritage Israel,
> Whom they have scattered among the nations.
> . . .
> But the Lord will be a refuge unto His people.
> And a stronghold to the children of Israel.[12]

Micah also foresaw this time.

> In that day, saith the Lord, will I assemble her that halteth,
> And I will gather her that is driven away,
> And her that I have afflicted;
> And I will make her that halted a remnant,
> And her that was cast far off a mighty nation;
> And the Lord shall reign over them in Mount Zion from thence-
>   forth even for ever.
> . . .
> And the remnant of Jacob shall be among the nations, in the
>   midst of many peoples,
> As a lion among the beasts of the forest,
> As a young lion among the flocks of sheep,
> Who, if he go through, treadeth down and teareth in pieces,
> And there is none to deliver.[13]

---

[12]Joel 3:2, 16.

[13]Micah 4:6, 7; 5:8; see also 3 Nephi 21:11-21.

The great Isaiah saw the event and sang of it in beautiful language. All of Isaiah 60 deals with the theme and should be read by everyone. Others of the prophets might be cited.

Verses 3 and 4 do not destroy or tarnish the universalism of the psalm as certain commentators have declared, neither do they portray a lust for dominion and worldly glory. Such views show a lack of insight and appreciation for what the psalmist is trying to do. The writer is very evidently portraying the final triumph of God's kingdom upon the earth. It is a triumph for righteousness which the Lord's covenant people, the descendants of Father Abraham, shall share and enjoy. (Verses 4, 9). Verse 9 brings to mind the statement in Genesis 18:18, 19:

> Abraham shall surely become a great and mighty nation, and all the nations of the earth shall be blessed through him. For I have known him, to the end that he may command his children and his household after him, that they may keep the way of the Lord, to do righteousness and justice.

In verse 9 the word "shields" should perhaps be supplanted by "rulers" which gives much better sense. It is not necessary to emend the Hebrew text.

Those who hold this psalm to be in part narrow and particularistic should remember that a poet does not specify in detail everything he wishes to carry over to his readers or listeners. He leaves something to the imagination of his public. It isn't necessary for him to point out, as we have done in the exposition, that the nations God subdues are "wicked" or that the Israel which finally achieves its inheritance is the "righteous" remnant. That is all taken for granted according to prophetic teachings. The Psalmist sees a better day coming in the world when the people thereof are united together in a common faith and ruled over by Jehovah, the God of Abraham and Jacob. This psalm is a great gem if understood in that spirit. It has no reference to any definite part of Israel's past history that we know of despite the assertions of several commentators to the contrary. It is a poem of the future.

Now, in the light of our exposition, what shall we name the poem? Certainly "God is King" is too tame. Perhaps "The Final Triumph of Jehovah and His People" is nearer our goal, but the writer is sure better titles can be found.

The poem may be divided into two strophes. The first will include verses 1-5 and the second, verses 6-9.

At a later time this psalm became known and used by the Jews as the New Year's Psalm.

The reader will do well in the study of the Psalms to watch the varieties of parallelism present in each case.

Who Wrote the Psalms? This is one of the most difficult problems in the Old Testament. Seventy-three psalms are ascribed to David, one to Moses (90), two to Solomon (72, 127), twelve to Asaph (50, 73-83), etc. But the superscriptions of the Psalms give great difficulty to scholars, because they are seldom demonstrably reliable. Some doubt attaches to the meaning of the Hebrew preposition in the phrase "Psalm *of David.*" The same preposition is used to express *for* in the phrase, "For the chief musician", and in this case it would seem extremely doubtful that the "chief musician" is the author. Consequently, one wonders whether authorship is implied in the case of David. The same doubt attaches in the phrase "Psalms of the sons of Korah". Certainly not all the sons of Korah must have cooperated in the writing of psalms. It would seem more natural to suppose that the psalms were a collection of the Korahitic temple-singers. However, at a later time the superscriptions came to be regarded as evidence of authorship. But they are thought by many scholars not to be original and integral parts of the psalms as they stand. In the Septuagint psalm superscriptions sometimes differ from the Hebrew in assigning psalms. Thus Psalms 146-148 are assigned to Haggai and Zechariah whereas these psalms in the Hebrew are anonymous.

Certain authorities have differed as to whether or not David wrote *any* psalms. Some have doubted that psalms were written before the Exile. In the midst of this confusion what course shall we take? When the doctors disagree among themselves perhaps the truth will be found between the extremes adopted by them. It is conceivable that one will not be found far wrong if he assumes that the ancient traditions are at least partly right, that David did write some of the Psalms as did others also whose names are written in the superscriptions. Nor, on the other hand need we suppose that still others did not write psalms in the course of Israel's long history. Talent is not confined to any one man or age.

Chapter XII

THE BOOK OF PSALMS (Continued)

Psalms of Adoration. We shall now proceed to become acquainted with some of the great psalms in a few of the classes mentioned in the previous chapter. Of the first class, according to McFadyen's classification, we select two, Psalms 8 and 19:1-6. We shall give each psalm a name as was done in the psalm studied in Chapter XI. It is hoped that the reader will disagree with the name given and proceed to give it a better one.

Psalm 8
The Divine Immanence of God.
For the Leader; upon the Gittith.
A Psalm of David.

1. O Lord, our Lord,
    How glorious is Thy name in all
        the earth!
    Thou hast set Thy glory above
        the heavens.

2. Out of the mouth of babes and
        sucklings hast Thou founded strength,
    Because of Thine enemies;
    That Thou mightest still the enemy
        and the avenger.

3. When I behold Thy heavens, the
        work of Thy fingers,
    The moon and the stars, which
        Thou hast established;

4. What is man, that Thou art mindful
        of him?
    And the son of man, that Thou
        visitest him?

5. Yet Thou hast made him but little
        lower than the Gods,
    And hast crowned him with glory
        and honor.

6. Thou hast made him to have
   dominion over the works of Thy
   hands;
   Thou hast put all things under
   his feet:

7. Sheep and oxen, all of them,
   Yea, and the beasts of the field;

8. The fowl of the air, and the fish of
   the sea;
   Whatsoever passeth through the
   paths of the seas.

9. O Lord, our Lord,
   How glorious is Thy name in all
   the earth!

This psalm is one of the most inspiring and beautiful
in the Book of Psalms. The poetry is good and metrically
well organized. The writer justifies the title given above
because the psalm treats of the glory and power of God
which is manifested throughout all His creations.[1] The
Psalmist contemplates how glorious God's name is over
all the earth, but when he beholds the planets and stars
at night he wonders how the Almighty can take notice of
man who seems in comparison so weak and insignificant.
Yet he realizes that man was created in the image of God,
belonging, in fact, to the same race. Man's creative power
and his desire to achieve righteousness in the world make
him the greatest revelation of God. Even in his humble,
mortal state he is "little lower than the Gods." (So the
Hebrew text.) The dignity and supreme worth of man have
been seldom better taught than in this poem.

Professor Oesterley calls attention to a significant
point in this psalm:

Unique in the Psalter is the teaching that within the hearts of
little children lies enshrined divine strength which has the power to
subdue everything; the deep significance of this is only realized when

---

[1]"He comprehendeth all things, and all things are before him, and all things are
round about him; and he is above all things, and in all things, and is through all things,
and is round about all things; and all things are by him, and of him, even God, forever
and ever." D&C 88:41.

our Lord's words are recalled: "Whosoever shall not receive the kingdom of God as a little child, he shall in no wise enter therein." (Mark 10:15; Luke 18:17).[2]

Psalm 19:1-6.
The Heavenly Bodies Testify
For the Leader. A Psalm of David.

1. The heavens declare the glory of God,
    And the firmament showeth His handiwork;
2. Day unto day uttereth speech,
    And night unto night revealeth knowledge;
3. There is no speech, there are no words,
    Neither is their voice heard.
4. Their line is gone out through all the earth,
    And their words to the end of the world.
    In them hath He set a tent for the sun.
5. Which is as a bridegroom coming out of his chamber,
    And rejoiceth as a strong man to run his course.
6. His going forth is from the end of the heaven,
    And his circuit unto the ends of it.
    And there is nothing hid from the heat thereof.

Readers may at once ask why only six verses are given of this psalm. It is thought by many authorities that verses 7-14 originally formed a separate psalm. Certainly the subject matter of these verses seems to have little in common with what precedes. Neither is the poetry of as good quality as in the earlier verses. At any rate, verses 7-14 are reflective in type, not belonging to the classification we are at present considering.

This psalm, like the one preceding, is in adoration of God for His revelation in nature. Many commentators have attempted to connect it with pagan mythology, expecially of the Babylonian variety. Such procedure is errant nonsense. The psalm is very deeply spiritual and in a very vivid, picturesque style tells how the heavenly bodies, particularly the sun, testify of God's majesty and glory.

The reader's attention is called to verse 4 where the word "line" is hard to understand. Note that the dif-

---

[2]W. O. E. Oesterley, *The Psalms*, I, 141.

ficulty is cleared up by the synonymous parallelism in the
next line. (See Chapter VIII.)

Psalms of Reflection. In this group we select Psalms
15; 23; 24:1-6; 90.

Psalm 15

Who May Commune With God?

A Psalm of David.

1. Lord, who shall abide in Thy tabernacle?
   Who shall dwell on Thy holy mountain?
2. He who walketh uprightly, and worketh righteousness,
   And speaketh truth in his heart;
3. And slandereth not with his tongue,
   Nor doeth evil to his friend,
   Nor taketh up a reproach against his neighbor;
4. In whose eyes a vile person is despised,
   But he honoreth them who fear the Lord;
   Nor sweareth falsely to do harm,[3] and changeth not;
5. He that putteth not out his money on interest,
   Nor taketh a bribe against the innocent.
   He that doeth these things shall never be moved.

This psalm gives an answer to the question, Who
may acceptably commune with God? The poem has received rather shabby treatment at the hands of a number
of commentators who fail to see its high spiritual and
moral values. The Psalmist very simply and effectively
describes the character of him who can draw near to God
and abide in His presence; or as we would say, worship
effectively. This psalm ought to be more widely read and
taken to heart than it is today. It breathes the true
prophetic spirit throughout.

The last line, "He that doeth these things shall never
be moved," means that he who lives in accordance with
what precedes is fortified against the evils and temptations
of life. In New Testament terms, such a person is built
upon a rock.[4]

---

[3]The text is corrupt at this point. "He that sweareth to his own hurt" does not make
sense. Commentators have tried in various ways to emend the clause. The writer thinks
that three Hebrew words have dropped out of the text. Restore *lô* . . . *'al-sheqer* . .
and we get the satisfactory result above.

[4]See Matt. 7:24.

The Epistle of James and Isa. 33:13-16 may profitably be read in connection with this psalm.

Psalm 23.
The Lord is My Shepherd.
A Psalm of David.

1. The Lord is my shepherd; I shall not want.

2. He maketh me to lie down in green pastures;
    He leadeth me beside the still waters.

3. He restoreth my soul;
    He leadeth me in the paths of righteousness for His name's sake.

4. Yea, though I walk through the valley of the shadow of death,
    I will fear no evil,
    For Thou art with me.
    Thy rod and Thy staff, they comfort me.

5. Thou preparest a table before me in the presence of mine enemies;
    Thou anointest my head with oil; my cup runneth over.

6. Surely goodness and mercy shall follow me all the days of my life;
    And I shall dwell in the house of the Lord forever.

This exquisite and beautiful psalm is probably the best known and loved in the Book of Psalms. It breathes a spirit of calm, peace, and serenity. Through the psalm there is felt an absolute assurance and trust that all is well, that the Lord is at the helm. To appreciate it completely one ought to spend some time in Palestine. The writer has had the privilege of watching Palestinian sheep and shepherds in many parts of that land. There the shepherd leads the sheep from place to place. They know his voice and follow him. The shepherd's life is the inspiration of this poem.

In reference to the anointing with oil in verse 5 the reader may consult Dan. 10:3; Amos 6:6; Micah 6:15; II Sam. 12:20; Deut. 28:40, with profit. In connection with the psalm as a whole, Ezek. 34; John 10:1-16; 21:15-17 will be found valuable supplementary reading as will also modern accounts of the shepherd's life in Palestine.

Psalm 24:1-6.

Who Shall Stand in God's Holy Place?

A Psalm of David.

1. The earth is the Lord's, and the fullness thereof;
   The world and they who dwell therein.
2. For He hath founded it upon the seas,
   And established it upon the floods.
3. Who shall ascend into the mountain of the Lord?
   And who shall stand in His holy place?
4. He who hath clean hands, and a pure heart;
   Who hath not lifted up his soul unto vanity,
   And hath not sworn deceitfully.
5. He shall receive a blessing from the Lord,
   And righteousness from the God of his salvation.
6. This is the generation of them who seek Him,
   Who seek Thy face, O Jacob.

Selah.

As with Psalm 19, so it is necessary to divide Psalm 24 into two parts. The last part of this psalm (verses 7-10) is different in content and treatment from the portion printed above and belongs to a different classification.[5]

The reader will at once perceive that this psalm is similar in many respects to Psalm 15. But it surpasses the latter in general treatment and poetic excellence. The spirituality of this psalm is very high and it deserves a careful reading. The essence of the good life is defined briefly and inclusively.

The last clause in verse six should possibly read, with some manuscripts, "O God of Jacob." The meaning of "Selah" is unknown. Some scholars think it is a term having reference to the music used, whether vocal or instrumental.

Psalm 90.

Lord, Be Merciful to Us.

A Prayer of Moses the Man of God.

1. Lord, Thou hast been our dwelling place in all generations.

---

[5]It does not necessarily follow that the same author was not responsible for both parts of the psalm. Authorities are divided upon this question.

2.   Before the mountains were brought forth,
Or ever Thou hadst formed the earth and the world,
Even from everlasting to everlasting, Thou art God.

3.   Thou turnest man to contrition;
And sayest: "Return, ye children of men."

4.   For a thousand years in Thy sight
Are but a yesterday when it is past,
And as a watch in the night.

5.   Thou carriest them away as with a flood; they are as a sleep;
In the morning they are like grass which groweth up.

6.   In the morning it flourisheth, and groweth up;
In the evening it is cut down, and withereth.

7.   For we are consumed by Thine anger,
And by Thy wrath are we confounded.

8.   Thou hast set our iniquities before Thee,
Our secret sins in the light of Thy countenance.

9.   For all our days are passed away in Thy wrath;
We spend our years as a thought.

10.   The days of our years are three-score years and ten,
Or even by reason of strength four-score years;
Yet is their pride but travail and vanity;
For it is speedily gone, and we fly away.

11.   Who knoweth the power of Thine anger,
Even according to Thy fear so is Thy wrath.[6]

12.   So teach us to number our days,
That we may gain a heart of wisdom.

13.   Return, O Lord; how long?
And have pity upon Thy servants.

14.   O satisfy us in the morning with Thy mercy;
That we may rejoice and be glad all our days.

15.   Make us glad according to the days wherein Thou hast afflicted us,
The years wherein we have seen evil.

16.   Let Thy work appear unto Thy servants,
And Thy glory unto their children.

17.   And let the favor of the Lord our God be upon us;
And establish Thou the work of our hands upon us;
Yea, the work of our hands establish Thou it.

This psalm is one of the best-known and loved selections in the Psalter. Isaac Taylor said of it:

> The ninetieth Psalm might be cited as perhaps the most sublime of human composition, the deepest in feeling, the loftiest in theological

---

[6]This line is apparently corrupt. The writer finds no emendation that is satisfactory.

conception, the most magnificent in its imagery. True is it in its report of human life as troubled, transitory, and sinful. True in its conception of the Eternal,—the Sovereign and the Judge, and yet the refuge and the hope of men who, notwithstanding the most severe trials of their faith, lose not their confidence in him; but who, in the firmness of faith, pray for, as if they were predicting, a near-at-hand season of refreshment. Wrapped, one might say, in mystery, until the distant day of revelation should come, there is here conveyed the doctrine of immortality; for in this very plaint of the brevity of the life of man, and of the sadness of these his few years of trouble, and their brevity and their gloom, there is brought into contrast the divine immutability; and yet it is in terms of a submissive piety; the thought of a life eternal is here in embryo.[7]

Herder calls it "that ancient Psalm, that hymn of eternity."[8]

Many critics who have denied Moses the authorship of the psalm,

Nevertheless admit, that in depth and loftiness of thought, in solemnity of feeling, and in majesty of diction, it is worthy of the great lawgiver and prophet.[9]

This psalm is used as a burial chant by the Anglican Church.

Psalms of Thanksgiving. In this group of psalms we should like to have printed three, Psalms 46, 76 and 118, but due to the limitations of space the first-mentioned must suffice.

Psalm 46

A Song of Faith.

For the Leader; [a Psalm] of the sons of Korah;
upon Alamoth. A Song.

1.   God is our refuge and strength,
     A very present help in trouble.
2.   Therefore will we not fear, though the earth do change,
     And though the mountains be moved into the heart of the seas;
3.   Though the waters thereof roar and foam,
     Though the mountains shake at the swelling thereof.
                                                    Selah.

---

[7]As quoted by J. J. Stewart Perowne, *The Book of Psalms* (Third London Edition, Revised), II, 157.

[8]*Ibid.,* p. 159.

[9]*Ibid.,* p. 158.

4. There is a river, the streams whereof make glad the city of God,
   The holiest dwelling-place of the Most High.
5. God is in the midst of her, she shall not be moved;
   God shall help her, at the approach of morning.
6. Nations were in tumult, kingdoms were moved;
   He uttered His voice, the earth melted.
7. The Lord of hosts is with us;
   The Lord of Jacob is our high tower.

                                        Selah.

8. Come, behold the works of the Lord,
   Who hath made desolations in the earth.
9. He maketh wars to cease unto the end of the earth;
   He breaketh the bow, and cutteth the spear in sunder;
   He burneth the chariots in the fire.
10. "Let be, and know that I am God;
    I will be exalted among the nations, I will be exalted in the earth."
11. The Lord of hosts is with us;
    The Lord of Jacob is our high tower.

                                        Selah.

This beautiful psalm is really a psalm of the future and envisages a day when wars shall cease and deadly weapons be abolished. The universalism of the poem is shown in the hope that God will be exalted among the nations, among all men everywhere. It is full of faith and hope. The simplicity, warm emotion, and depth of thought which characterize this psalm have made it famous. Not without good reason has it been called "the grandest song of faith" ever written.

Psalm 46 was Martin Luther's favorite and upon it he based his noble hymn, "Ein' feste Burg ist unser Gott" (A Strong Fortress is Our God).

The Imprecatory Psalms. Of these psalms we select but one, the famous one hundred thirty-seventh.

Psalm 137.
A Lamentation of the Captivity.

1. By the rivers of Babylon,
   There we sat down, yea, we wept,
   When we remembered Zion.

2. Upon the willows in the midst thereof
    We hanged up our harps.
3. For there they that led us captive asked of us words of song,
    And our tormentors asked of us mirth:
    "Sing us one of the songs of Zion."
4. How shall we sing the Lord's song
    In a foreign land?
5. If I forget thee, O Jerusalem,
    Let my right hand forget her cunning.
6. Let my tongue cleave to the roof of my mouth,
    If I remember thee not;
    If I set not Jerusalem
    Above my chiefest joy.
7. Remember, O Lord, against the children of Edom
    The day of Jerusalem;
    Who said: "Rase it, rase it,
    Even to the foundation thereof."
8. O daughter of Babylon who art to be destroyed;
    Happy shall he be, who repayeth thee
    As thou hast served us.
9. Happy shall he be, who taketh and dasheth thy little ones
    Against the rock.

This psalm evidently dates from the Babylonian Captivity. In beautiful language the writer laments the sad state and despondency of captive Israel among her Babylonian foes. As he broods over her wrongs and the memory of the past he grows resentful and vindictive as verses 7-9 show.

Perowne says of the Psalm:

What a wonderful mixture is the Psalm of soft melancholy and fiery patriotism! The hand which wrote it must have known how to smite sharply with the sword, as well as how to tune his harp. The words are burning words of a heart breathing undying love to his country, undying hate to his foe. The poet is indeed
    "Dowered with the hate of hate, the scorn of scorn,
    The love of love."[10]

This psalm is a human document of the first rank.

The Penitential Psalms. We choose from this group the profound Psalm 51. With it should be read Psalm 130, another of the great penitentials.

---

[10]Perowne, *op. cit.*, II, 407.

Psalm 51

Cleanse Me From Sin.

For the Leader. A Psalm of David; when Nathan the prophet came unto him, after he had gone in to Bath-sheba.

1. Be gracious unto me, O God, according to Thy mercy;
And according to the multitude of Thy compassions blot out my transgressions.
2. Wash me thoroughly from mine iniquity,
And cleanse me from my sin.
3. For I know my transgressions;
And my sin is ever before me.
4. Against Thee, Thee only, have I sinned,
And done that which is evil in Thy sight;
That Thou mayest be justified when Thou speakest,
And be in the right when Thou judgest.
5. Behold, I was brought forth in iniquity,
And in sin did my mother conceive me.
6. Behold, Thou desirest truth in the inward parts;
Make me, therefore, to know wisdom in mine inmost heart.
7. Purge me with hyssop, and I shall be clean;
Wash me, and I shall be whiter than snow.
8. Make me to hear joy and gladness;
That the bones which Thou hast crushed may rejoice.
9. Hide Thy face from my sins,
And blot out all mine iniquities.
10. Create me a clean heart, O God;
And renew a stedfast spirit within me.
11. Cast me not away from Thy presence;
And take not Thy holy spirit from me.
12. Restore unto me the joy of Thy salvation;
And let a willing spirit uphold me.
13. Then will I teach transgressors Thy ways;
And sinners shall return unto Thee.
14. Deliver me from bloodguiltiness, O God, Thou God of my salvation;
So shall my tongue sing aloud of Thy righteousness.
15. O Lord, open Thou my lips;
And my mouth shall declare Thy praise.
16. For Thou delightest not in sacrifice, else would I give it;
Thou hast no pleasure in burnt-offering.
17. The sacrifices of God are a broken spirit;
A broken and a contrite heart, O God, Thou wilt not despise.
18. Do good in Thy favor unto Zion;
Build Thou the walls of Jerusalem.

19. Then wilt Thou delight in the sacrifices of righteousness, in burnt-
     offering and whole offering;
     Then will they offer bullocks upon Thine altar.

This psalm is perhaps the most heart-searching of the penitential psalms. A sense of guilt and sinfulness seems to have penetrated the very soul of the writer, and he pleads with God to purge him and deliver him with all the fervor and power at his command. It is a marvelous plea of a penitent man for forgiveness. He throws himself wholly and completely upon God's mercy.

This psalm is one of the four reckoned by Martin Luther as being the best psalms. It was read to Henry V on his death-bed at his own request. Thomas More, Lady Jane Grey and Count Egmont each recited it prior to their execution. Numerous other famous persons have quoted it in times of trouble, not to mention thousands of others less well known but deeply mournful individuals.

Despite the fact that many leading commentators deny this psalm to David, the writer cannot help but feel that it could have come from him when the dire consequences of his sin were explained by Nathan, the prophet. (See II Sam. 12:1-14.)

Royal Psalms. Of this type we select Psalm 63.

Psalm 63.
A Soul's Yearning for God.
A Psalm of David, when he was in the wilderness of Judah.

1. O God, Thou art my God, earnestly will I seek Thee;
    My soul thirsteth for Thee, my flesh longeth for Thee,
    In a dry and weary land, where no water is.
2. So have I looked for Thee in the sanctuary,
    To see Thy power and Thy glory.
3. For Thy loving kindness is better than life;
    My lips shall praise Thee.
4. So will I bless Thee as long as I live;
    In Thy name will I lift up my hands.
5. My soul is satisfied as with marrow and fatness;
    And my mouth doth praise Thee with joyful lips;

6. When I remember Thee upon my couch,
   And meditate on Thee in the night-watches.
7. For Thou hast been my help,
   And in the shadow of Thy wings do I rejoice.
8. My soul cleaveth unto Thee;
   Thy right hand holdeth me fast.
9. But those that seek my soul, to destroy it,
   Shall go into the nethermost parts of the earth.
10. They shall be hurled to the power of the sword;
    They shall be a portion for foxes.
11. But the king shall rejoice in God;
    Every one that sweareth by Him shall glory;
    For the mouth of them that speak lies shall be stopped.

Psalm 63 is without question one of the most beautiful and exquisite psalms in the Psalter. It is the outpouring of a soul who earnestly seeks communion and rest with his God.

Unfortunately, space forbids our printing other great psalms in their different classifications, but it is hoped that the reader will find added joy and satisfaction in seeking still others that will appeal to his religious and esthetic sensibilities.

Chapter XIII

THE NATURE AND SCOPE
OF PROPHECY

Men of God. From time to time "holy men" have appeared in various religions and have exerted much influence upon their people, but few have produced so profound an effect upon our civilization as have the Hebrew prophets. The Greeks had their "oracles"; the Babylonians had their "astrologers" and "diviners"; others had "wise men" or "crystal gazers", but none had a "prophet" in the Hebrew connotation of the word. The eminent Hebraist, C. von Orelli, says: "We come to the conclusion that no phenomenon analogous to Biblical prophecy, even in form, is anywhere to be found in the world of nations."[1]

The great religions of Christianity, Judaism and Islam owe much to the prophets of Israel. Moses was a prophet and is also considered one of the three great lawgivers of ancient times, the others being Hammurabi of Babylon and Solon of Greece. He and many other Hebrew prophets such as Isaiah, Jeremiah, Amos and Ezekiel are in the limelight of religious history. Therefore, let us inquire more thoroughly into the mission of a prophet and the nature of prophecy.

What Constitutes a Prophet? Before we can answer that interrogation, we must define our terms and clarify our position in order to come to grips with the problems involved. First of all, our word "prophet" is derived from the Greek word "prophetes." The term usually denoted "one who, uttering or interpreting an oracle, was believed to speak not his own thoughts but a revelation 'from without'."[2] According to Macdonald, the Hebrew "nabhi"

---

[1]C. von Orelli, *Old Testament Prophecy*, p. 24. For a fuller discussion of prophecy and the prophets see Sperry, *The Voice of Israel's Prophets*, pp. 1-13.

[2]*Encyclopedia Britannica*, 14th Edition, XVIII, 586.

which is translated prophet means " 'a giver of information' or 'a recipient of information', i. e., as to the Unseen
World . . ."[3] A prophet is therefore one who receives a
message from God and who gives it to the people "as one
having authority." The prophet does not arrogate to himself
the spiritual prerogative, but he is commissioned and sent
of God, and what he says is as binding as if the Lord Himself
had spoken audibly to the people. The Hebrew prophets
never say "I saw," or "I know," but "The Lord shewed
me," "Thus saith Jehovah."[4] In other words, he is an
intermediary between God and His people. And while
the prophet is the mouthpiece of Jehovah to the group
that does not alter the fact that each member of the group
may receive individual inspiration or revelation.[5]

This brings us to the point where we must consider
the term "seer" in relation to prophecy. In I Sam. 9:9 it
is recorded, "he that is now called a Prophet was before-
time called a Seer," but it is highly probable that this
statement is a "gloss" added by a commentator who did
not fully comprehend the fundamental difference between
a "prophet" and a "seer". There is, however, a real difference both in the meaning of the words and in their use.
"Ro'eh" means literally "one who sees" or "one who per-
ceives by the eye," whereas "nabhi" means a recipient
or a giver of information. Another word for "seer", denoted by "chozeh," is also used in contradistinction to
prophet. A "chozeh" is literally a "gazer" or one who

---

[3]Duncan B. Macdonald, *The Hebrew Literary Genius*, p. 69. See also Albright,
Yahweh and the Gods of Canaan, pp. 181-2, where the word is defined as "one who
was called by God for a special purpose, or who believed that he had received such a
call." The etymology of the word seems to be uncertain; but see Torczyner in the
reference to Albright.

[4]*Encyclopaedia Britannica*, 14th Edition, XVIII, 589. Some may be inclined
to take exception to this statement of Rev. William Alexander Leslie Elmslie since there
are cases of the use of "I saw" as in Isa. 6:1. Rev. Elmslie evidently wished to stress the
fact that the prophet does not set himself in the foreground as the "authority"; instead,
the prophet emphasizes his dependence upon God and gives his message a more authoritative tone by saying, "The Lord shewed me," or "Thus saith Jehovah."

[5]For instance, such was the case with Hagar, Gen. 16:7-12; and Solomon, I
Kings 3:5-14.

looks intently at an object. Dr. Macdonald says in reference to the three words "nabhi", "ro'eh" and "chozeh":

These three words, apparently, had different applications and suggested different ideas. One of many puzzling and tantalizing references to the older, and lost books of the Hebrews is in I Chronicles 29:29. There for the details of David's reign we are referred to three books: the Book of Samuel, the Seer (ro'eh)—probably our Book of Samuel; the Book of Nathan, the Prophet—the word is nabhi; the Book of Gad, the Gazer (chozeh). . . . it is tolerably plain from this reference that the terms "seer," "prophet," "gazer," were not exactly synonymous. It is plain, too, that the "gazer" was the equivalent of our "scryer" or "crystal gazer," whatever were the material of the smooth, shining surface at which the Hebrew gazer looked in order to make contact with the Unseen. As to the methods of the "prophet" and the "seer" we can only guess. . . .[6]

There is not only a distinction in the meaning but also in the use of the terms "seer" and "prophet". Why do we find "Samuel the seer" and "Nathan the prophet" or "Shemaiah the Prophet" and "Iddo the seer"?[7] In II Kings we find:

. . . the Lord testified against Israel and against Judah, by all the prophets, and by all the seers. . . .[8]

We see, therefore, that the sacred writers did not use "prophet" and "seer" synonymously.

It would appear that a seer was one who beheld the unseen, and, if so instructed, he declared what he had seen to the sons of men. His was not a mere dream but a "waking" experience in which all of his physical senses were under control, though his "seeing" was spiritual. He

---

[6]Macdonald, op. cit., p. 70. Some may prefer to believe that "crystal gazing" originated in the use of the "Urim and Thummim" which were in the possession of the Hebrews and even possibly in the custody of their patriarchal ancestors. It is true that the Urim and Thummim are first mentioned in relation to Aaron, but it does not follow that no one used them before that time. The term "chozeh" may possibly have been coined to denote a user of these sacred instruments. Albright, op. cit., p. 187, refers to the "ro'eh" or seer of I Sam. 9:9 as a "diviner," and to the tradition that the synonym hôzîm was applied to archetype poet-musicians."

[7]I Chron. 25:5; 29:29; II Chron. 9:29; 12:15; 29:25, 30.

[8]II Kings 17:13. See also Isa. 29:10; 30:10.

saw what lay hidden in the past or what the present and future held for the children of God, and this he could reveal; whereas a prophet could speak of such things only by inspiration or verbal instruction from some authorized source. When a prophet began to see the events of which he spoke, he was to that extent a seer also.

The Prophetic Calling. A prophet was never one to assume so important a responsibility unless he was called of God. As a rule, God Himself called the prophet on a mission to mankind though, in rare instances a prophet acting by authority called another as did Elijah.[9] Some were evidently foreordained to the office as in the case of Jeremiah.[10] In the majority of cases, however, mature men were called on prophetic missions to deliver the word of God.[11] Now we may ask, Is a prophet always a prophet? It might be said that a man is a prophet only when he is acting as such; nevertheless, we have no recorded instance where a man has ever been recalled from the prophetic ministry.

Would one be justified in saying that a prophet operates only in the prediction of future events? The fact is that this is only one and, in many instances, the least significant of prophetic functions. Certainly, some never left any notable prediction on record. John the Baptist, Elijah, Elisha, Nathan, Iddo and many others are believed to be great prophets but we find little or no prediction by them. The prophets were teachers, statesmen, and counselors of the people. Moses gave to man his great law code, including the "Ten Commandments" which he received on Mount Sinai.[12] These form the essence of our law system and represent the type of prophetic function which is to give laws and principles for the society and progress of man. The prophets were concerned not alone with the spiritual life and the future but also with the mundane

---

[9]I Kings 19:19-21; II Kings 2:9-15.
[10]Jer. 1:4,5.
[11]Jonah is a typical example.
[12]Exo. 20:1-17.

activities of the people. They seemed to have labored
with the idea that what we are to be, we are now becoming; and, if the conditions of society are not favor-
able, men cannot achieve the spiritual status the Lord desires, for the children of God cannot live the "abundant
life" in war, in ignorance, in poverty, in illness or in sin.
The prophets were the great champions of human rights,
for they evidently realized that no society can rise higher
than the level of the vast majority of its component members.

Another function was to reveal God to man. Jehovah
is so portrayed as to make him more comprehensible to
the finite minds of His people. The Lord is represented
as possessing attributes much in common with man; therefore, He spoke to the people according to their understanding and weaknesses. He was described as being jealous[13]
of the reverence paid to truth and righteousness and to
Him who exemplified all good. As a result of sin and
rebellion against Jehovah, He was angry[14] with men since
that which they rejected was designed for their welfare.
He punished for wrong doing;[15] nevertheless, He was
merciful[16] in judgment. Jehovah was above all a God of
love. This group of teachings may be summed up in the
first great commandment: "Thou shalt love the Lord thy
God with all thy heart, and with all thy soul, and with
all thy mind."[17]

The worth of personality and the brotherhood of man
was emphasized again and again. The social teachings of
the prophets are one of the prominent features of our
Old Testament. Likewise the basic principles of character
were stressed in the messages of God. Jonah was taught
responsibility; Amos[18] made honesty a cardinal virtue, while
Micah emphasized the qualities of justice, kindness, mercy

---

[13]Exo. 20:5; Deut. 4:24; Nahum 1:2.
[14]Isa. 30:27; Jer. 7:19, 20.
[15]Exo. 20:5; Nahum 1:2, 3.
[16]Neh. 9:17, 31; Deut. 4:31.
[17]Deut. 6:5; cf. Matt. 22:37.
[18]Amos 8:4-6.

and humility.[19] Others condemned hypocrisy,[20] pride, undependability, worldliness, backsliding, idolatry,[21] oppression,[22] and dishonesty.[23] Again, brotherhood is the great element in the prophets. In fact, "Thou shalt love thy neighbor as thyself" is the heart of their teachings.[24]

Besides teaching the "gospel" to their contemporaries, the prophets entered other phases of life. Many seemed very close to the king, undoubtedly due to the fact that the first king of Israel, Saul, was chosen and anointed by Samuel, the seer and prophet.[25] Notable examples of prophets who acted as counselors to kings may be found in the cases of Nathan and David,[26] or Isaiah and Hezekiah.[27] Amos was a social reformer; many others championed the cause of the people. As is evident, the prophets entered into every phase of Hebrew social life; therefore, we may conclude that their work was as broad as the needs of the people.

False Prophets. All prophets were not of God. The wicked prophets of Baal held a very prominent position in Israel in the reign of Ahab. They officiated in the orgiastic Canaanite religion with all its lewd and repelling practices. There was also the professional school of the prophets which may have been just and reputable at its inception but finally degenerated into an unscrupulous guild that divined for money and power. With these the true prophets had to compete for the people's attention; in the case of Elijah it needed a supernatural demonstration to convince men that the prophets of Baal were unreliable.

---

[19]Micah 6:8.
[20]Jer. 2:11; Hos. 4:6-19; Micah 3:5-7.
[21]Hosea 5:5; 6:4; 7:8; 9:9; 11:7; 13:2. See also Hos. 4:16, 17.
[22]Isa. 3:13-15; Amos 4:1.
[23]Amos 8:4-6.
[24]Lev. 19:18; cf. Matt. 22:39.
[25]I Sam. 10:1, 24, 25.
[26]II Sam. 12.
[27]II Kings 19:20.

What is the Nature of Revelation? Prophecy. Prophecy includes the idea of revelation. The word revelation means to unveil, or make known something that is hidden or kept secret, whether that be in the past, present, or future sense. Such revelation may be given in a dream which is sometimes called apocalyptic as in the Book of Daniel.[28] Again it may be in waking vision such as Moses[29] or Isaiah[30] experienced. Some messages Jehovah dictated word for word;[31] others were inspired but the prophet was left to express them in his own language.[32] In such cases, the Lord, through the medium of the Holy Spirit, planted the ideas in the mind of the prophet and these were expressed as the word of God. In still another way the prophet, being inspired, reasoned from already established facts and persuaded the people to righteous living. Being the representative of God, the will of the prophet in such cases is also the will of Jehovah. Under inspiration, the intellect and spiritual faculties are quickened beyond the natural tempo, and with penetrating insight the inspired can unveil the unknown and make clear the obscure. The principal difference between inspiration and revelation lies in degree rather than in kind.

The Predictive Element of Prophecy. Many biblical scholars are in disagreement as to whether there exists a predictive element. There is one school which holds that a prophet must speak out of a definite concrete situation and cannot see beyond the historical horizon of his own times. Anything that was predicted and fulfilled was either the result of keen insight or was written after the prophet's time and attributed to him. This position is opposed by a number of well known and equally competent scholars. Orelli, for instance, says:

---

[28]Dan. 7:1.

[29]Exo. 33:9-11.

[30]Isa. 6:1.

[32]Isa. 7:3-9.

Undoubtedly the prophets, whose writings we still have, owed their high reputation in great part to the fulfilment of their oracles in reference to the future.[33]

The popular concept of a prophet's message has been focused upon the predictive element often to the exclusion of equally important phases. Isaiah prophesied concerning Cyrus of Persia;[34] Jeremiah of the Babylonian captivity,[35] and Micah of the Christ;[36] and each was fulfilled. The Old Testament predictions which deal with the advent of the Messiah are referred to repeatedly in the Gospels.[37] There are also many unfulfilled prophecies which deal— so many believe—with a yet future period, especially regarding the last days and the millennium.[38] These are regarded rather lightly by some; nevertheless, to many spiritually minded individuals a prophecy is regarded as a transcript of the annals of eternity to be fulfilled when all the conditions warrant it.

Repentance in the Prophetic Message. We must take cognizance of the fact that the prophets did not carry a message to their people for the mere pleasure of doing so.

---

[32]Dan. 2:27-45. George Reynolds expressing his views of the Bible said:
"There are in the Bible the words of God, the words of angels, of men, and of the devil. Some parts of the Bible are simply history, written from the writer's standpoint and according to his knowledge. Then again all servants of the Lord were not equally inspired, and even the same prophet was not equally inspired at all times and on all occasions. Consequently we have in the sacred Scriptures revelations which the Lord dictated word by word; revelations, equally binding, in which the will of the Lord is directly expressed, but clothed in the language of a prophet, who was, for the occasion, His mouthpiece; and again we have the divine word given under some general law of heaven in which not only the words but the argument was that of the speaker, but the 'word of the Lord,' nevertheless." *Mill. Star,* LXIV, 181.

[33]Orelli, *op. cit.,* p. 7. See also pp. 27, 50, 51; John E. McFadyen, *A Cry for Justice,* p. 88 f.; Alfred Guillaume, *Prophecy and Divination,* p. 111, says: "There is no prophet in the Old Testament who was not a foreteller of the future . . . When a prophet ceases to prophecy in this sense he ceases to be a prophet and becomes a preacher."

[34]Isa. 44:28; 45:1 ff., cf. Ezra 1:1-3. Dr. C. C. Torrey believes, however, that the mention of Cyrus is of late date and was not found in the original manuscript.

[35]Jer. 25:8-13; cf. IIChron. 36:5ff; Dan. 9:2.

[36]Micah 5:2; cf. Matt. 2:6. This interpretation is not accepted by some scholars.

[37]For instance, see Matt. 1:23; cf. Isa. 7:14; Matt. 3:3 cf. Isa 40:3.

[38]See Joel 3:15-17; Zech. 14:3-5; Mal. 3:1-3; 4:5, 6; Isa. 11:6-9; 65:17-25.

There is a real need behind every prophetic injunction to mankind. In most cases, men are upbraided for their low standards of conduct and are called to repentance. Unless they turn to the Lord, the penalties resulting from broken laws shall be visited upon them. If the people repent, they may escape as did Nineveh, otherwise, the penalties must come. May we affirm that repentance is one of the most prominent elements in Old Testament prophecy.[39]

Promise of Hope. We must not conclude that the prophets could see only the dark and unpleasant side of affairs. Beyond every rebuke there is a ray of hope for the repentant. Israel is to be punished but is also to be redeemed; and with the prediction of the dispersion came also the prediction of the gathering. Psychologically, this method is powerful; to rebuke, but to show that the offender is chastised only for his own good and that he is still loved by the Lord.[40]

The Test of Prophecy. Now that we have defined prophecy, within certain limits, and have noted the more outstanding features of this great spiritual medium, let us consider the ways in which we may determine what is true prophecy and what is false. Moses gives the key to determine the veracity of the prophetic oracles.

When a prophet speaketh in the name of the Lord, if the thing follow not, nor come to pass, that is the thing which the Lord hath not spoken, but the prophet hath spoken it presumptuously: thou shalt not be afraid of him.[41]

Professor Orelli states:

The contents of prophecy are, consequently, not something thought out, inferred, hoped, or feared by the prophets, but something directly perceived. This explains the categorical certainty with which they announce their oracles. They know these oracles to be independent of their own subjectivity. The revelation comes before their gaze as something independent, nay, belonging to another.

---

[39]The Book of Jonah is a good illustration of this point.

[40]Joel, Amos, Obadiah and Zechariah may be studied for this element. See D&C 121:41-44.

[41]Deut. 18:22. See also Deut. 13:1-3; Jer. 28:9.

It is God who discloses these things to them—things withdrawn from human gaze. . . . The fundamental assumption always is, that the attitude of the genuine prophet to the contents of his discourse, if not passive, is primarily receptive. Only false prophets announce what they themselves have thought out or inferred on grounds of probability.[42]

Truly Moses gives the key to the predictive element of a divine message, but one would probably want to know if a man were a prophet before his prediction was fulfilled. This desire might not in every instance be easy of fulfilment. And generally speaking, prophets are not acknowledged as such by those whose outlook and actions are not on the same high spiritual plane as their own. The history of prophecy shows that to be true. Probably only through revelation or inspiration can one determine whether or not a man is a prophet. In other words, the observer must himself have in some degree the spirit of prophecy.

The Interpretation of Prophecy. When we refer to the interpretation of prophecy we mean primarily the predictive element, but the same criteria may be applied to the whole prophetic message. First of all, one needs to analyze the prophecy into its component parts and to determine, so far as possible, what the fulfillment of such a prediction would be. Secondly, one needs to study the time element involved, and this can be done only by taking the whole composition or logical division of a composition into consideration. Thirdly, one should study as many pertinent religious and secular records as possible to find the elements that fulfill the prophetic requirements, but the true scholar will weigh all factors, even those opposite to his hypothesis, and accept tentatively only that which has a preponderance of evidence. The historical setting for prophecies is most significant. Too often we try to interpret a message without understanding the need that gave it birth, the factors which would effect it, the purpose for which it was uttered, or finally, whether it achieved that

---

[42]*Op. cit.*, p. 6.

aim. There is a great tendency to interpret the scriptures from an Occidental rather than an Oriental point of view, and such deductions in which we incorporate our ideas instead of the prophets' are very often worthless. A study of Biblical languages, geography, history, manners and customs, as well as the contents of the message, are necessary to the interpretation of most of the prophets.

The foregoing may suffice for a rational interpretation, but one cannot fully comprehend a prophet's message unless it be through the eyes of inspiration as the prophet first saw it. Paul emphasized this principle to the Corinthians:

> For what man knoweth the things of man, save the spirit of man which is in him? even so the things of God knoweth no man, but the Spirit of God.
>
> Now we have received, not the spirit of the world, but the spirit which is of God; that we may know the things that are freely given to us of God.
>
> Which things also we speak, not in the words which man's wisdom teacheth, but which the Holy Ghost teacheth; comparing spiritual things with spiritual.
>
> But the natural man receiveth not the things of the Spirit of God: for they are foolishness unto him: neither can he know them, because they are spiritually discerned . . . for the Spirit searcheth all things, yea, the deep things of God.[43]

If one can combine the rational approach with the spiritual, he indeed has the fundamental requirements for the true interpretation of a prophetic message. May we say, however, that the rational approach cannot be developed without much systematic, technical study, and that the spiritual comes only by righteous living and much meditation.

Prophecy Is Conditional. Perhaps some of us are like Jonah in that we are disappointed if a prediction is not fulfilled as we desire. Prophecy is conditional as is well illustrated in respect to Nineveh.[44] The people repented, as

---

[43]I Cor. 2:10-14.
[44]Jonah 3.

a result, the city was spared. Had they not repented, the destruction decreed upon it must surely have come to pass. The Lord sent Jonah to warn the people, not because He wished to destroy them, but because He wished to save them from the error of their ways. In another instance, the Lord sent Jeremiah to warn Zedekiah, but Zedekiah rejected the message and met his doom at the hands of the Babylonians.[45] Had Zedekiah repented, he might have avoided the great disaster which befell him.

Prophecy Is Not A Mechanical Process. When a man prophesies he is by no means a mere recording instrument. Truly, the Lord may move him to say the thoughts desired, but the voice and words are those of the prophet. He may either utter the message or keep silent. The prophet in such cases thinks, under the Holy Spirit, the thoughts of God and these he repeats in the vocabulary and language at his command. Were that not so, we would not have all the diversities of vocabulary, sentence structure, figures of speech, and style that are found in the Old Testament.

---

[45]Jer. 32:1-5; cf. II Chron. 36:11-21.

Chronology of the Prophets

The birthdates given here must be considered as only approximate.

Names of Prophets	Date (B. C.)
Samuel	1080
Gad	1020
Nathan	1010
Elijah	890
Elisha	870
Joel	810(?)[1]
Jonah	800(?)[2]
Amos	785
Hosea	770
Isaiah	765
Obadiah	765(?)[3]
Micah	765
Nahum	655
Jeremiah	645
Zephaniah	645
Ezekiel	626
Daniel	625(?)[4]
Habakkuk	620
Haggai	545
Zechariah	545
Malachi	480

---

[1] The Book of Joel has been dated anywhere from 900 B.C.—350.

[2] The book named after the prophet is dated by some as late as 300 B.C.

[3] The date of Obadiah is more or less of a guess. Scholars have dated the book anywhere from about 900 B.C.—300.

[4] The Book of Daniel is thought by many authorities to have been written about 167 B.C. Others deny this, holding to a date in the sixth century B.C.

Chapter XIV

ELIJAH THE PROPHET

The Man and His Times. In Chapter I it was pointed out that the first group of the prophetic books as classified by the ancient Hebrews was the *Former Prophets,* comprising Joshua, Judges, Samuel, and Kings. Although these books do mention a number of prophets we shall discuss but one of them in this book, namely Elijah. This prophet left such an impress upon his times that the legends and stories about him are legion. Even to this day the Jews make much of him and look forward to his coming. Elijah was one of the greatest of the prophets, but the reasons for this are best understood by the Latter-day Saints. Rudolf Kittel, a great German specialist in the Old Testament, once said:

> What Moses had been to their ancestors, Elijah was to his time. Indeed after Moses, Elijah was the greatest man in Israel's religious life.[1]

Elijah is commonly known as the "Tishbite," having been born perhaps at Tishbeh in Galilee; but he seems later to have dwelt in Gilead.[2] The ministry of Elijah is most prominent during the reign of Ahab, king of Israel, the date of whose reign is usually placed at 869-850 B.C. Ahab's father, Omri, had earlier usurped the throne of Israel when that kingdom had sunk into virtual anarchy. A brave, successful soldier, he proved to be a strong, capable ruler, and made a notable impression on history outside of Israel. The Moabites were conquered by him, and even after his death and the destruction of his family the Assyrian records for a time continue to refer to him as *Humri.* Omri transferred the seat of Israelite government from Tirzah to Samaria which he built for the purpose.[3] He followed the

---

[1]*Great Men and Movements in Israel,* p. 171.
[2]1 Kings 17:1.
[3]1 Kings 16:24.

idolatrous practices of Jeroboam and acted even more wickedly than those who had preceded him on the throne of Israel.[4] Thus the father set the stage for the actions of his son, Ahab, who inherited the throne after his death.

Ahab continued his father's political successes. He continued to rule the Moabites with a firm hand and brought the long-drawn wars with Judah to an end. He sealed the treaty of peace by a marriage between his daughter Athaliah and Joram, the heir to Jehoshaphat's (of Judah) crown.[5] Ahab succeeded in taking his formidable rival, Benhadad of Damascus, as a prisoner, and thereafter stood side by side with him as ally in the great battle of Karkar (853 B.C.), which signalled the first movement of Assyrian arms in force against the West.

Ahab's military successes went to his head; but his vaulting ambition over-reached itself and in time brought about his ruin. His marriage to the terrible idolatress, Jezebel, daughter of Ethbaal, king of Sidon, was a tragedy to Israel as King Solomon's marriages to foreign women had been at an earlier time.[6] Jezebel was an oriental princess with extraordinary force of character, whose aim was to win absolute authority for herself and her own notions of rule. She worshiped Baal, and finding her husband as putty in her hands, she made him a Baal worshiper also.[7] Jezebel was not content merely to find recognition and toleration of her oriental cult; she made up her mind to secure for her god Melcarth, more than equal acceptance with Jehovah, Israel's god. Accordingly, as the scripture makes clear, Ahab built her a temple of Baal, with its customary pillar and Asherah, the pole or tree-trunk which was dedicated to the licentious rites of Ashtarte. Not only that, he allowed his unholy siren of a wife the privilege of wreaking vengeance on all who opposed her evil designs. She attempted to force all of the people

---

[4] 1 Kings 16:25-26; Micah 6:16.
[5] 2 Kings 8:18.
[6] 1 Kings 11:1-10.
[7] 1 Kings 16:30-33.

to adopt the worship of Baal. And with such force and determination did she carry out her foul purpose that not only were most of the prophets of the Lord slain, but also the four hundred and fifty prophets of Baal openly "ate at Jezebel's table."[8] The Lord's prophets who escaped were hidden in a cave by a high functionary, Obadiah, who fed them with bread and water.[9]

The Baal worship espoused by Jezebel had its origin in the belief that all tracts of ground owed their productivity and fertility to supernatural beings, or *baals*, that dwelt there. Baal worship was frequently associated with lewd rites (cf. 1 Kings 14:24), the sacrifice of children by fire (Jer. 14:5), and kissing the image.[10]

The faith of Israel was in dire plight under the circumstances described above. It could hardly be otherwise, because Jezebel, uncompromising champion of Baal-worship, sat on the throne; the true prophets of Jehovah were either dead or in hiding, and the masses of the people were wavering or halting "between two opinions" (1 Kings 18:21), scarcely able to judge whether Jehovah or Baal was the true god they ought to worship.

Such was the religious scene in Israel when the brave Elijah came on the stage to do battle for Jehovah.

Elijah Begins Work of Stemming the Tide in Jehovah's Favor. Elijah was one of the non-writing prophets. If he wrote anything, it has not come down to us. His deeds have been recorded by others. When the religious situation in Israel seemed hopeless as a result of the tyranny of Jezebel and Ahab, the Lord's great prophet stepped forward to stem the tide. Using the keys of the sealing powers of the Priesthood vested in him, Elijah stood before Ahab and said:

As the Lord God of Israel liveth, before whom I stand, there shall not be dew nor rain these years, *but according to my word*.[11]

---

[8]1 Kings 18:19.
[9]1 Kings 18:4.
[10]1 Kings 19:18; Hos. 13:2.
[11]1 Kings 17:1; italics ours.

On certain occasions the Lord in His mercy has used the persuasive powers of hunger, drought, war, and pestilence in an endeavor to guide His people into righteous paths. Witness the testimony of Amos the prophet (4:6-11) and the appeal of the great prophet Nephi to the Lord.

> O Lord, do not suffer that this people shall be destroyed by the sword; but O Lord, rather let there be a famine in the land, to stir them up in remembrance of the Lord their God, and perhaps they will repent and turn unto thee.[12]

During the ensuing drought, the Lord directed Elijah to the brook Cherith, near the Jordan. There he had water to drink and ravens brought him food (1 Kings 17:2-6) to miraculously sustain him.

When the brook Cherith dried up during the extended drought, the Lord sent Elijah to a widow woman in Zarephath in Zidon near the sea. This woman had been commanded to sustain the prophet during the continued drought in Israel. The scriptural account of how Elijah, through his marvelous powers, caused her barrel of meal and cruse of oil to fail not are too well known to repeat here.[13] Nor is it necessary to repeat the famous account of how he raised the widow woman's son from the dead.[14] These miracles only emphasize the power of the keys the Lord had vested in His servant Elijah.

Elijah Tests the Powers of Baal and of Jehovah. In the third year of the drought, the Lord instructed Elijah to go and show himself to Ahab; moreover, He promised to send rain upon the earth.[15] The ensuing account (vss. 2-18) tells how the prophet met Obadiah, one of the king's servants, and instructed him to notify Ahab to come and meet him. This Ahab did.

> And it came to pass, when Ahab saw Elijah, that Ahab said unto him, Art thou he that troubleth Israel. And he answered, I have not

---

[12]He. 11:4.
[13]1 Kings 17:9-16.
[14]1 Kings 17:17-24.
[15]1 Kings 18:1.

troubled Israel; but thou, and thy father's house, in that ye have forsaken the commandments of the Lord, and thou has followed Baalim.[16]

Then follows the famous narrative of how Elijah had Ahab gather the prophets of Baal together in order to test their powers and that of Jehovah in the presence of the people. Both Elijah and the prophets of Baal were to put a dressed bullock upon separate altars as for sacrifice. Then Elijah said:

And call ye on the name of your gods, and I will call on the name of the Lord: and the god that answereth by fire, let him be God.[17]

The people gave their assent to the test. The prophets of Baal cried and called from morn until evening, but their gods did not answer or burn their sacrifice. Elijah taunted and mocked their efforts. However, when his turn came he called upon the God of Israel to show to His people that He was the only true God.

Then the fire of the Lord fell, and consumed the burnt sacrifice, and the wood, and the stones, and the dust, and licked up the water that was in the trench. And when all the people saw it, they fell on their faces: and they said, The Lord, he is the God; the Lord, he is the God.[18]

Elijah had gone far in stemming the tide of pagan religion in Israel. Jehovah had shown His hand to the satisfaction of the people. Not only that, but the prophets of Baal were all slain at the brook Kishon, which flows at Mount Carmel's base. Elijah prayed for the rain, which came in torrents, and Ahab drove back to Jezreel with the prophet running before him.[19]

Elijah Forced to Flee Discouraged. Although Elijah had won an important round in his battle with paganism, the war was not yet over. When the wicked Jezebel heard what Elijah had done, and how he had slain the prophets of Baal, she sent a messenger to him with a threat on his

[16]1 Kings 18:17-18.
[17]1 Kings 18:24.
[18]1 Kings 18:38-39.
[19]1 Kings 18:44-46.

life. The prophet fled beyond Beer-sheba to the south of Judah where he sat under a juniper tree and wished that he might die.[20] In the ensuing account we find that the discouraged prophet made his way to a cave in Mount Horeb where he complained to the Lord.

> I have been very jealous for the Lord God of hosts: for the children of Israel have forsaken thy covenant, thrown down thine altars, and slain thy prophets with the sword; and I, even I only, am left; and they seek my life, to take it away.[21]

In the midst of spiritual experiences in the wilderness, the Lord commanded the prophet to go and anoint Hazael to be king over Syria, Jehu as king over Israel, and Elisha, the son of Shaphat, to be prophet in his stead. Then the Almighty assured Elijah that there were seven thousand in Israel who, like himself, had not bowed unto Baal or kissed him. Elijah cast his mantle upon Elisha who arose and followed him.[22]

The Episode of Naboth's Vineyard—Jehovah Hates Iniquity. The judicial murder of Naboth by Jezebel in order to obtain a coveted vineyard for Ahab was quite typical of the arbitrary deeds of oriental monarchs of the time.[23] Such an atrocity would have aroused little or no comment, still less moral condemnation, among neighboring states. But the God of Israel was a righteous God before whose bar of justice murder was murder, whether it was committed by king or the common man. The Divine penalty was announced by Elijah who was sent by the Lord to Ahab:

> Thus saith the Lord, In the place where dogs licked the blood of Naboth shall dogs lick thy blood, even thine. And Ahab said to Elijah, Hast thou found me, O mine enemy? And he answered, I have found thee: because thou hast sold thyself to work evil in the sight of the Lord. Behold, I will bring evil upon thee, and will take away thy posterity.[24]

---

[20] 1 Kings 19:1-4.
[21] 1 Kings 19:10.
[22] 1 Kings 19:11-21.
[23] 1 Kings 21:1-16.
[24] 1 Kings 21:19-21; cf. 22:37-38.

Not only had Jehovah won a decisive battle with Baal, but He had now upheld to all Israel His standard as a righteous and moral God, supreme in goodness as in power. It is one of the glories of the Old Testament that it proclaims high moral and ethical standards of conduct in a world too often guided by low ideals and pagan standards of conduct. Ancient Israel bequeaths to us a great legacy in this literature.

Elijah Taken into Heaven as a Translated Being. 2 Kings 2:1-12 gives the account of how Elijah in the company of Elisha, who refused to leave his side, proceeded from Gilgal to Jericho. It appears that not only did Elisha know that Elijah was to be taken from the earth, but that the "sons of the prophets" along the way knew also. Elijah and Elisha went to the banks of the Jordan where the former struck the waters with his mantle, and the two of them went across on dry ground. When on the other side, Elijah asked his companion what he could do for him, before he was taken. Elisha asked that a double portion of his (Elijah's) spirit be upon him. Elijah replied that he had asked a hard thing: nevertheless, if he saw Elijah when he was taken, his request should be granted; but if not, it should not be so. As the two of them went on, and talked, a marvelous thing happened.

> Behold, there appeared a chariot of fire, and horses of fire, and parted them both asunder; and Elijah went up by a whirlwind into heaven. And Elisha saw it, and he cried, My father, my father, the chariot of Israel, and the horsemen thereof.[25]

Elijah's public ministry was ended. He became a translated being. To the uninitiated the accounts of the prophet in 1 Kings and 2 Kings do not betray the sealing powers of the priesthood, but to those who understand the gospel his powers are more readily understood.

We speak of Elijah as having become a "translated" being. What is meant by this? The Prophet Joseph Smith gives this explanation:

---

[25]2 Kings 2:11-12.

Now the doctrine of translation is a power which belongs to this [Melchizedek] Priesthood. . . . Many have supposed that the doctrine of translation was a doctrine whereby men were taken immediately into the presence of God, and into an eternal fullness, but this is a mistaken idea. Their place of habitation is that of the terrestrial order, and a place prepared for such characters He held in reserve to be ministering angels unto many planets, and who as yet have not entered into so great a fullness as those who are resurrected from the dead.[26]

It will be remembered that Elijah and Moses, as translated beings, appeared upon the Mount of Transfiguration with the Savior and Peter, James, and John. (Matthew 17) On that occasion, Elijah probably conferred the keys of the sealing powers of the priesthood upon our Lord's apostles. Joseph Smith said:

The Priesthood is everlasting. The Savior, Moses, and Elias [Elijah], gave the keys to Peter, James, and John, on the mount, when they were transfigured before him.[27]

The sealing powers of the priesthood held by Elijah were also conferred, it will be remembered, upon the Prophet Joseph Smith and Oliver Cowdery in the Kirtland Temple, April 3, 1836. The resurrected Elijah himself said to them:

Behold, the time has fully come, which was spoken of by the mouth of Malachi [Malachi 4:5, 6]—testifying that he [Elijah] should be sent, before the great and dreadful day of the Lord come—to turn the hearts of the fathers to the children, and the children to the fathers, lest the whole earth be smitten with a curse—therefore, the keys of this dispensation are committed into your hands; and by this ye may know that the great and dreadful day of the Lord is near, even at the doors.[28]

The mission of Elijah has to do with the higher spiritual functions of the gospel of Jesus Christ. Elijah was the last prophet to hold the keys of the sealing powers of the Priesthood—that is, to seal in heaven what is bound upon the earth. The spirit of Elijah implies the power to invoke

[26]Joseph Fielding Smith, *Teachings of the Prophet Joseph Smith*, p. 170.
[27]*Ibid.*, p. 158.
[28]D&C 110:14-16.

a fullness of priesthood. The Prophet Joseph Smith explained it in this way:

> The spirit, power, and calling of Elijah is, that ye have power to hold the key of the revelation, ordinances, oracles, powers and endowments of the fullness of the Melchizedek Priesthood and of the kingdom of God on the earth; and to receive, obtain, and perform all the ordinances belonging to the kingdom of God, even unto the turning of the hearts of the fathers unto the children, and the hearts of the children unto the fathers, even those who are in heaven.[29]

Through the powers of the priesthood given to Elijah, men and women may be sealed to each other in marriage for time and eternity in the temples of God. Children born of these unions may be claimed by their righteous parents forever, since the latter are united by an everlasting covenant. The family organization thus continues beyond the grave, and one generation is thus sealed to another back to the days of Adam. Families that have passed into the spirit world without a knowledge of the gospel, and hence without being sealed to each other, must have the work done vicariously for them in the temples of the Lord. All of the gospel ordinances that are necessary to be performed for a living person to obtain salvation must also be performed for the dead. The Lord has made no exceptions other than for children who die under the age of eight years. That is the reason why the fathers (the dead) spoken of in Malachi 4:6 turn to their children, their living descendants, to have all the gospel ordinances from baptism to marriage, performed vicariously for them in the temples. If the children do not turn their hearts to their ancestors and perform this necessary work for them, it will make it impossible for the Lord to accomplish his purpose of making this earth the celestial abode of the righteous. Said the Prophet Joseph Smith:

> I wish you to understand this subject, for it is important; and if you will receive it, this is the spirit of Elijah, that we redeem our dead, and connect ourselves with our fathers which are in heaven,

---

[29]DHC 6:251.

and seal up our dead to come forth in the first resurrection; and here we want the power of Elijah to seal those who dwell on earth to those who dwell in heaven. This is the power of Elijah and the keys of the kingdom of Jehovah.[30]

It should be quite obvious why Elijah, ancient prophet that he was, should awaken our interest in this modern age.

---

[30]DHC 6:252; see Sperry, *Book of Mormon Compendium*, pp. 426-429.

Chapter XV

HOSEA—PROPHET OF LOVE

Some Facts Concerning the Prophet's Person. Hosea's name means "help" or "deliverance" and it is the prevailing opinion among scholars that he was a prophet of the Northern Kingdom. According to the superscription[1] of the book he was the son of Beeri, of whom we know nothing. We are further informed that Hosea was a prophet "in the days of Uzziah, Jotham, Ahaz, and Hezekiah, kings of Judah, and in the days of Jeroboam the son of Joash, king of Israel." Jeroboam II, king of Israel, reigned from 786 B. C. until at least 746, and Hezekiah, king of Judah, the last named of the others, did not begin to reign until 715 B. C. Hosea could, therefore, have had a long ministry, but we shall be reasonably conservative if we assign his work and labors to the years 750 B.C.—715. He was, therefore, a contemporary of the prophets Amos, Isaiah, and Micah and may have been personally acquainted with each of them.

All questions as to Hosea's home life depend upon the interpretation accorded Chapters 1-3 in the book. Since these have been so warmly discussed and differently interpreted by very able commentators, we shall have to lay aside the question of the prophet's domestic status for the moment.

Concerning Hosea's personal characteristics Professor G. L. Robinson writes:

> He was gentle, pensive, and inclined to melancholy, but frank, affectionate, and full of domestic feeling. He was the Jeremiah of the northern kingdom, and, like him, was little less than a martyr, prefiguring Christ. Both were ardent patriots, possessed of finely sensitive religious natures. Jeremiah was the more studied and self-conscious in his grief; Hosea, the more artless and passionate. Jeremiah was more of a theologian; Hosea, more of a poet.[2]

---

[1]Hos. 1:1.

[2]G. L. Robinson, *The Twelve Minor Prophets*, pp. 15 f.

The Times of the Prophet. In the days of Hosea the Northern Kingdom had been elevated to a position of great power by Jeroboam II. This elevation to power brought in its wake wealth and luxury with all their attendant vices. What was true of the vices of the Northern Kingdom was in the main true also of the Southern Kingdom under Uzziah. The rich oppressed the poor, politicians looked to their own interests rather than to the nation's they were supposed to serve, women became debauched and thus seriously weakened the moral fiber of the country. While Jehovah was worshiped, it was done under the symbols of oxen or calves as a state-religion. This was essentially Baal-worship, for though He was outwardly confessed, and His feasts observed (Hos. 2:13), yet Jehovah was Himself made into a Baal, so that the people even called Him their Baal (Hos. 2:16), and observed "the days of Baals" (Hos. 2:13).[3]

All of this constituted an inward apostasy from Jehovah, notwithstanding that the people still continued to worship Him outwardly. Such worship was bound to have a devastating effect upon the nation.

With the breach of the fundamental law of the covenant, viz. of the prohibition against making any likeness of Jehovah, or worshipping images made by men, more especially in consequence of the manner in which this prohibition was bound up with the divine authority of the law, all reverence not only for the holiness of the law of God, but for the holy God Himself, was undermined. Unfaithfulness towards God and His word begot faithlessness towards men. With the neglect to love God with all the heart, love to brethren also disappeared. And spiritual adultery had carnal adultery as its inevitable consequence, and that all the more because voluptuousness formed a leading trait in the character of the idolatry of Hither Asia. Hence all the bonds of love, of chastity, and of order were loosened and broken, and Hosea uttered this complaint: "There is no truthfulness, and no love, and no knowledge of God in the land. Cursing, and murder, and stealing, and adultery; they break out and blood reaches to blood." (Ch. 4:1, 2.) No king of Israel could put an effectual stop to this corruption. By abolishing the worship of the calves, he would have rendered the very existence of the kingdom doubtful.[4]

---

[3] C. F. Keil and F. Delitzsch, *Biblical Commentary on the Old Testament* (The Twelve Minor Prophets), I, 19 f. Note the influence of Canaanite religion upon Israel.

[4] *Ibid.*, p. 20.

Hosea's sketch of the state of Israel is a very gloomy one from beginning to end. Whilst offensive Canaanite religious influence and practice still continue, the nation thus persisting in its ingratitude and infidelity to God, great violence and cunning have gained the upper hand; rebellions follow one upon the other, and the kingdom advances steadily toward the ruin predicted for it by the prophets. Alliances with foreign nations such as Egypt and Assyria would be of no avail. In fact, these lands, whose friendship is courted by the nation, would only prove to be its prison. Hosea dreaded appeals to foreign governments for aid.[5] Outside aid could be no effective remedy for Israel's decay, morally and politically.

With the moral decay of Israel the thing that seems to have impressed and saddened Hosea most is the state of family life. It had become dissolute, and accordingly the prophet lays upon it his heaviest indictment. The word "whoredom," distasteful to us as it is, is used by the prophet some sixteen times to express his opinion of the situation.[6]

Such were the times in which Hosea prophesied. A knowledge of them will help us materially in understanding the prophet's message.

The Book of Hosea. It is a peculiar coincidence that the Book of Hosea, which deals with such a corrupt society as we have described, has suffered more from textual corruption than any other book of the Old Testament. It is not too much to say that certain parts of it defy successful translation and there is hardly a verse of which one can be sure is in the form it left the pen of the original writer.

The book consists of two sections, very unequal in length, Chapters 1-3 and Chapters 4-14. The first section, which is a fairly compact unit, and which contains much narrative, purports to tell the tragic domestic life of Hosea. Whether regarded as a symbolic action, or otherwise, the prophet is commanded by God in the narrative to "take

---

[5]See Hos. 8:9; 10:6.
[6]Robinson, *op. cit.*, p. 18.

a wife of harlotry" for the purpose of begetting children whose significant names were to set forth to Israel the disastrous fruits of her spiritual whoredom.

In the second section we have, as Sir George A. Smith has said, "a stream of addresses and reflections, appeals, upbraidings, sarcasms, recollections of earlier history, denunciations and promises, which, with little logical connection and almost no pauses or periods, start impulsively from each other, and for a large part are expressed in elliptic and ejaculatory phrases."[7]

Israel's spiritual adultery, which the prophet has described in the first section, is more elaborately dealt with here. He tells of Israel's religious apostasy and moral decay and of the consequences that must inevitably follow. Even Judah is referred to occasionally. Finally, he appends a solemn appeal to return to Jehovah and promises that the Lord will show compassion to the penitent and heal their apostasy.

The Story of Hosea's Unfaithful Wife. Immediately following the superscription of Hosea's book we are startled to find these lines:

> When the Lord spoke at first with Hosea, the Lord said unto Hosea: 'Go take unto thee a wife of whoredom, and children of whoredom; for truly the land plays the harlot instead of following Jehovah.'[8]

After reading these surprising lines, we ask ourselves the question: "Can it be possible that God, who hated Israel's licentious ways and moral depravity, would ask one of His own servants to marry a profligate woman?" The answer would obviously seem to be in the negative, but we read on and find that the woman Gomer, bore the prophet two sons and one daughter. The names of the sons were Jezreel, "Whom God sows," and Lo-ammi, "Not my people"; the name of the daughter was Lo-ruhama, "That hath not obtained compassion." The first name, Jezreel, was given probably because of the historical importance the plain of

---

[7]G. A. Smith, *The Book of the Twelve Prophets* (New and Revised Edition), I, 219.
[8]Hos. 1:2.

Jezreel had in Israel's history. There Israel had contracted blood-guiltiness which was now to be speedily avenged upon the house of Jehu.[9] Lo-ammi was a reminder that God would no longer call Israel "My people"[10] and Lo-ruhamah meant that He would no longer have compassion upon her.[11]

Perhaps it is not to be wondered at that commentators have put very different interpretations on Hosea's marriage. We shall not take the space to consider these in detail. Mere mention of the leading theories must suffice.[12]

1. It is thought to be allegory or a parable used by Hosea to symbolize the relation existing between Jehovah and Israel.
2. The story is assumed to be an account of actual facts. This theory has several variations.
3. A third interpretation, now very popular, insists that "Gomer was a pure woman when he (Hosea) married her, and continued pure till after the birth of her first child."[13]

Despite the heavy attack made upon the first view in modern times, the writer is inclined to think it the correct one.[14] The problem is admittedly difficult.

In spite of the various interpretations given to Hosea's marriage as related in Chapters 1-3, the religious message conveyed therein is fairly clear. Gomer, the wife of Hosea, represents Israel, the disloyal and harlotrous bride of Jehovah. Israel is, of course, unworthy of Jehovah's great love. For her gross sins she must go into exile and learn by bitter experience that her husband means more to her than she at first supposed. Jehovah steadfastly loves her throughout the long years of her wayward career and finally attempts to woo her again:

---

[9]See Hos. 1:4, 5. Jehu was one of the earlier kings of Israel (circa 842 B.C.).
[10]Hos. 1:9.
[11]Hos. 1:6.
[12]See Smith, *op. cit.*, pp. 246-252 and J. M. P. Smith, *The Prophets and Their Times*, pp. 56-60, for discussion and relevant literature.
[13]Smith, op. cit., p. 250.
[14]For a fine defense of this view see Keil and Delitzsch, *op. cit.*, pp. 27-36, 66-68.

> Therefore, behold, I will allure her,
> And bring her into the wilderness,
> And speak tenderly unto her.[15]

His tender and compassionate wooing will result in the wife's eventual return to the fold. No longer will she indulge in-the vicious Canaanite immoralities mentioned so frequently in Chapter 2.

> And it shall be at that day, saith the Lord,
> That thou shalt call Me Ishi,[16]
> And shalt call Me no more Baali.[17]
> For I will take away the names of the Baalim out of her mouth,
> And they shall no more be mentioned by their name.[18]

Note the wonderful promises God makes to Israel in the following lines:

And I will betroth thee unto Me forever;
Yea, I will betroth thee unto Me in righteousness, and in justice,
And in loving kindness, and in compassion.
And I will betroth thee unto Me in faithfulness;
And thou shalt know the Lord.
And it shall come to pass in that day,
I will respond, saith the Lord, I will respond to the heavens,
And they shall respond to the earth;
And the earth shall respond to the grain, and the wine, and the oil;
And they shall respond to Jezreel
And I will sow her upon Me in the land;
And I will have compassion upon her that had not obtained compassion;[19]
And I will say to them that were not My people:[20] 'Thou art My people';[21]
And they shall say: 'Thou art my God.'[22]

The above lines are a marvelous description of Jehovah's loving kindness to Israel. In the last days,[23] after

---

[15]Hos. 2:14.
[16]Hebrew for *My husband.*
[17]Hebrew for *My master.* Note the word play. See Baalim in following line.
[18]Hos. 2:16, 17.
[19]That is, Lo-ruhamah.
[20]That is, Lo-ammi.
[21]That is, Ammi.
[22]Hos. 2:19-23.
[23]So we take the reference to "that day" in Hos. 2:18, 21 to mean.

Israel has gone through the furnace of affliction, God will remember her and listen to her prayers. No wonder Hosea has been called the prophet of love. Some writers have called him the St. John of the Old Testament. The love that God has for His people, and patience He has in reclaiming them from their sins, are amply brought out in the story of Hosea's domestic life.

Israel to be Destroyed for Lack of Knowledge. In the second section of Hosea's prophecy, we shall take notice of a number of his teachings that expand on what is pointed at in the first section. One of the finest teachings of Hosea is that lack of knowledge—religious knowledge—is the thing that is destroying his people. We shall have occasion later to note that the prophet Isaiah emphasized the same thing.

> Hear the word of the Lord, ye children of Israel!
> For the Lord hath a controversy with the inhabitants of the land,
> Because there is no truth, nor mercy,
> Nor knowledge of God in the land.[24]

Notice *truth, mercy, knowledge.* What a trilogy!

> Truth and love are mutually conditions, the one of the other. "Truth cannot be sustained without mercy; and mercy without truth makes men negligent; so that the one ought to be mingled with the other" (Jerome). They both have their roots in the knowledge of God, of which they are the fruit (Jer. 22:16; Isa. 11:9); for the knowledge of God is not merely "an acquaintance with His nature and will" (Hitzig), but knowledge of the love, faithfulness, and compassion of God, resting upon the experience of the heart. Such knowledge not only produces fear of God, but also love and truthfulness towards brethren. Where this is wanting, injustice gains the upper hand.[25]

Another fine passage follows:

> Yet let no man strive, neither let any man reprove;
> For thy people are as they that strive with the priest.
> Therefore shalt thou stumble in the day,
> And the prophet also shall stumble with thee in the night;

---

[24]Hos. 4:1.

[25]Keil and Delitzsch, *op. cit.*, pp. 74 f.

And I will destroy thy mother.
My people are destroyed for lack of knowledge;
Because thou hast rejected knowledge,
I will also reject thee, that thou shalt be no priest to Me;
Seeing thou hast forgotten the law of thy God,
I also will forget thy children.[26]

The prophet is here pointing out that the priests and professional prophets of Israel are without knowledge. The common people, guilty as they are, are not so guilty or responsible as their religious counselors who live upon their (the people's) fines, and sin-offerings. Priests and prophets alike have given themselves over to formal ritual and have forgotten that they have an intellectual and moral responsibility to the nation. Let us never forget that the true prophets of Israel always kept their eyes open to the fact that priesthood is an intellectual, as well as a moral, trust. The prophet Malachi in a later day made a noble statement that is pertinent at this point.

For the priest's lips should keep knowledge,
And men seek law from his mouth;
Because he is a messenger of Jehovah.[27]

Hosea adds another statement that is well worth quoting.

Harlotry, wine, and new wine take away the heart.[28]

The word "heart" in Hebrew is often equivalent to our English words "brains" or "understanding". So, again, Hosea is administering an intellectual rebuke. He means here that sexual immorality and strong drink (anciently they went hand in hand as now), weaken the mental power and show themselves in the idolatry and folly of which the nation is guilty.

A Warning Against Entangling Alliances. Many people still entertain the idea that George Washington was

---

[26]Hos. 4:4-6. The word *mother* in this passage has reference to the whole nation and kingdom as in Chapter 2:2.
[27]Mal. 2:7.
[28]Hos. 4:11.

the first to sound warnings against "entangling alliances" with other nations. But in the case of Hosea we find a Hebrew prophet, centuries before Washington's time, sounding somewhat similar warnings to Israel against entangling alliances with Egypt and Assyria.

> And Ephraim is become like a silly dove, without understanding;
> They call unto Egypt, they go to Assyria.[29]

Hosea, like Isaiah in this respect, wanted his people to avoid making covenants with nations whose sole reliance was on force. Let the big nations fight their own wars. Little nations that elected to mix up with them were sure to be worsted. The big nations, furthermore, had religious practices that were totally and utterly opposite to prophetic ideals. Their immoralities, added to those Israel already had, would, in time, wreck the nation. So Israel would spread the net of destruction over herself. Instead of courting God's love and protection, her courting of the nations would only put her in a trap—and it did.

Even as they go, I will spread My net upon them;
I will bring them down as the fowls of the heaven;
I will chastise them, as their congregation hath been made to hear.
Woe unto them! for they have strayed from Me;
Destruction unto them! for they have transgressed against Me.[30]

God's Love For His People. As we have already seen, God's love for His people is such that He cannot give them up completely.

> How shall I give thee up, Ephraim?
> How shall I surrender thee, Israel?
> How shall I make thee as Admah?
> How shall I set thee as Zeboim?
> My heart is turned within Me,
> My compassions are kindled together.
> I will not execute the fierceness of Mine anger,
> I will not return to destroy Ephraim;

---

[29]Hos. 7:11.
[30]Hos. 7:12, 13.

> For I am God, and not man,
> The Holy One in the midst of thee,
> And I will not come in fury.[31]

The above passage is the greatest in Hosea. It is the heart and key of the book. It breathes the spirit of the Man of Galilee whose mercy and love for His brethren transcend all understanding. The passage does not mean that Israel shall escape the due consequences for all her sins. But it does foreshadow the long arm of Jehovah's love reaching for her in the day of redemption, the latter day, and rescuing the little righteous remnant of which Isaiah and other prophets also speak.[32]

> Whoso is wise, let him understand these things,
> Whoso is prudent, let him know them.
> For the ways of the Lord are right,
> And the just do walk in them;
> But transgressors do stumble therein.[33]

---

[31]Hos. 11:8, 9. Admah and Zeboim were two cities of the valley of Siddim which were destroyed by fire from heaven along with Sodom and Gomorrah. See Gen. 19:24; Deut. 29:23.

[32]See Hos. 14 for promise of pardon to those who turn to the Lord.

[33]Hos. 14:9.

Chapter XVI

AMOS—PROPHET OF SOCIAL JUSTICE

Early Life and Times of Amos. The early life of Amos, and for aught we know most of his life, was spent at Tekoa, a small town located on a hill at the edge of the Judaean plateau six miles south of Bethlehem. The writer spent considerable time at this place, and a more desolate site for a town or village can scarcely be imagined. It is necessary to walk the six miles from Bethlehem or ride one of the poor donkeys that can be hired for a small sum from Arab owners. Little remains of the buildings that were constructed at various times on the site of the town. To the south, north, and west limestone hills obscure the view, and eastward the even more barren desert stretches out for eighteen miles to the Dead Sea. Here Amos, one of the greatest religious reformers of all time, herded sheep (an ugly variety known as *noked*, but prized for their fine wool) and dressed sycomore trees that produced a small inferior fig, having a sweet but watery taste. His shepherd profession made him appreciate the open country with its freshness and vigor, as compared with the cities to which he doubtless carried wool. The prophecy under his name indicates that he was a very thoughtful and discerning observer of the religious and social state of his times. The superscription of his book sets forth that Amos entered on his ministry "in the days of Uzziah, king of Judah, and in the days of Jeroboam, the son of Joash, king of Israel, two years before the earthquake." We do not know exactly when the earthquake—it must have been severe—took place, but we can, with some confidence, date Amos at about 785 B. C.

Israel, the kingdom to the north of Judah, against which his preaching was mainly directed, was prosperous—yes, even wealthy.[1] Greed, corruption, and vice reigned

---

[1] The prosperity was very similar to that in America during and after the first World War.

supreme in the so-called upper classes of society. The social lot of the poor classes was pitiful. Religion had little real vitality and the dishonesty, insincerity, and blindness of public officials made it possible for the strong to exploit the weak. Morals seemed all but forgotten. Into such a society walked the prophet of Tekoa and denounced it with such vigor, clarity of thought, and authority, that his message is still eagerly read and applied to modern situations.

The Call of Amos to Prophesy. In the seventh chapter of Amos we glean the information that the prophet was called from his flock to prophesy against Israel.

> Then answered Amos, and said to Amaziah: 'I was no prophet, neither was I a prophet's son; but I was a herdman, and a dresser of sycomore-trees; and the Lord took me from following the flock, and the Lord said unto me: Go, prophesy unto My people Israel.'[2]

The prophet went without question from his native Judean home to Bethel, the sanctuary of the court of Israel, the Northern Kingdom, to deliver the message the Lord confided to him. Fearlessly he delivered it in forceful, classical Hebrew—the best in the Old Testament. The prophecy falls naturally into three great divisions:

1. The coming judgment—Chapters 1 and 2.
2. The grounds for God's judgment—Chapters 3 to 6.
3. Visions of judgment and the dawn of a brighter day—Chapters 7 to 9.

The Lord Roars From Zion. The first division, judgment, is masterly in its conception and execution. The Lord is portrayed as "roaring" from Zion. In the words of Professor McFadyen:

> The clear eyes of Amos saw the symptoms of rottenness and inevitable decay; and the words of his first recorded message are that Jehovah, the God of this easy-going people, would roar from His temple in Jerusalem, like a lion just before he makes his spring. The implication is that Jehovah will soon spring upon his people, to tear

---

[2]Amos 7:14, 15.

them in pieces; and Amos's message we might describe as the Gospel of the Lion's Roar.[3]

The prophet spins a web about his listeners and, at the same time, holds their interest by first pronouncing God's judgments upon successive nations outside of Israel. The nations in order are Damascus, Philistia, Phoenicia, Edom, Ammon, Moab and Judah.[4] Amos begins each of his denunciations with the words: "Thus saith the Lord, for three transgressions, yea, for four, I will not reverse it." By "three transgressions" is meant much sin. One sin is then named out of many to justify the coming judgment upon each nation. Amos's words thrill and delight his audience, particularly his pronouncements upon Judah, its hated rival kingdom. But suddenly, as a bolt from the blue, Amos turns upon his audience and the nation it represents. He stalks Israel as a lion does its prey. Israel, too, is as guilty of misconduct as the nations before-mentioned. The wealthy mistreat the poor and humble, prostitution is rampant, the people are wine-bibbers, prophets are disregarded, and young men are made to break their covenants.[5] But retribution is to come upon the guilty nation. God will strike and the strong shall not be delivered.[6]

Law Reigns in the Realm of the Spirit. In this day of scientific method and observation, we are far too prone to assume that while law and order reign in the realm of material things, it is questionable that they do so in the realm of spiritual values. It is to the eternal honor of Amos that he perceived law reigning as inexorably in the realm of the spirit as it does in the physical world. Amos applied his observation with characteristic vigor and clarity to the position of Israel before the Lord.

---

[3]John E. McFadyen, *A Cry for Justice* p. 2.
[4]The student is advised to locate these countries in succession upon a map. Note the web Amos spins around Israel.
[5]Amos 2:6-12.
[6]Amos 2:13-16.

Hear this word that the Lord hath spoken against you, O children of Israel, against the whole family which I brought up out of the land of Egypt, saying:

> You only have I known of all the families of the earth;
> Therefore I will visit upon you all your iniquities.[7]

The two poetic lines above form one of the grandest passages in all scripture. In the Hebrew scriptures, "to know" often signifies "to care for", both with the understanding and the heart. Thus Amos pointed out the unique place God had assigned to Israel in the world. Amos understood that Israel was the "chosen" people of God in the sense that it was a covenant people. But we can easily imagine Amos saying:

Special privilege implies corresponding responsibility, O Israel, and you have not measured up to it. "There is a law, irrevocably decreed in heaven before the foundations of this world, upon which all blessings are predicated—and when we obtain any blessing from God, it is by obedience to that law upon which it is predicated."[8]

As Professor McFadyen said it: "They [Israel] believed in their election without understanding the reasons for it; they failed to realize that election to privilege is always election to duty and responsibility."[9]

Amos then proceeded to clinch, by a series of homely illustrations from the physical world, his point that law reigns also in the realm of spirit.

> Will two walk together,
> Except they have agreed?
> Will a lion roar in the forest,
> When he hath no prey?
> Will a young lion give forth his voice out of his den,
> If he have taken nothing?[10]

Women Determine the Temper and Quality of a Civilization. Amos must have been a man of superb

---

[7]Amos 3:1-2.
[8]See D&C 130:20-21; also 78:6.
[9]McFadyen, *op. cit.*, p. 23.
[10]Amos 3:3-4, etc.

courage and daring. He boldly continued that part of his address dealing with the reasons for God's coming judgments by giving a scathing rebuke to women in high places. Many of our English translations are too elegant to reveal effectually Amos's contempt for the women of Israel. These women were helping to make its social life cruel and rotten and its religion a gorgeous sham. What he actually said was:

> Hear this word, you cows of Bashan,
> Who are on the Mount of Samaria,
> Who oppress the poor, who crush the needy,
> Who say to their lords: 'Bring, and let us drink.'
> The Lord Jehovah has sworn by His holiness:
> Behold, days come upon you,
> That He will carry you away with hooks,
> And the remnant of you with fish-hooks.[11]

Amos compares the women of Samaria with the fat and well-fed cows roaming on pastures to the east of the Sea of Galilee. These rich, voluptuous, and violent women are qualified partners for their lords whom Amos has already denounced, who "store up violence and robbery in their palaces."[12] The sin of these sleek women consisted in their tyrannical oppression of poor people in that they requested their husbands to procure them wine bought with money squeezed from their victims.

A country is largely what its women make it; if they are cruel or careless or unwomanly, the country is on the road to ruin. But these cattle on the hills of Samaria at whom Amos flings his words of scorn are worse than the cattle on the hills of Bashan; for they have done what no animal could do—they have made coarse pleasure the deliberate end of life. . . . Intemperance and cruelty went together then, as they go so often still. When women, who should be pitiful, sink to such depths of shame and heartlessness, it must be made plain that God will soon appear to mete out to them what they had meted to the poor.[13]

[11]Amos 4:1, 2.
[12]Amos 3:10.
[13]McFadyen, *op. cit.*, pp. 36 f.

Like so many fish pulled out of their element with fish-hooks, these women with all their luxury would be taken in hand by Israel's enemies. They would be insulted, abused, and cast around like old rags. In sorrow and shame they would realize that repentance came too late.

Every Disaster a New Call to Repentance. Amos's heart was bleeding over the sinful state of Israel. It was no pleasure for him to pronounce judgment upon his brethren. So he took up a lamentation over them:

> The virgin of Israel is fallen,
> She shall no more rise;
> She is cast down upon her land,
> There is none to raise her up.

For thus saith the Lord God: 'The city that went forth a thousand shall have a hundred left, and that which went forth a hundred shall have ten left, of the house of Israel.'[14]

After this lament Amos paradoxically proceeds to exhort his listeners to change their ways:

> For thus saith the Lord unto the house of Israel:
> Seek ye Me, and live;
> But seek not Beth-el,
>
> . . .
> Seek the Lord, and live—
> Lest He break out like fire in the house of Joseph,
> And it devour, and there be none to quench it in Beth-el—
> Ye who turn justice to wormwood,
> And cast righteousness to the ground.[15]

A nation in the process of moral decay can still repent and find God if it will. And here is the paradox of prophecy: When God makes threats against His people, His threatenings are conditional.

When God threatens he is promising . . . when he comes near in any way it is for our salvation . . . God is not obliged to fulfill his threats, but he is obliged to fulfill his promises.[16]

---

[14]Amos 5:2, 3. Note the *tithe* of Israel left. A rather grim figure!

[15]Amos 5:4-7. Note the satirical word play on Bethel. Beth-el was the Israelite court and means "house of God".

[16]G. L. Robinson, *The Twelve Minor Prophets*, pp. 91 f.

Israel's disaster in the realm of morals and spiritual perspective, so Amos thinks, should constitute a new call to repentance.

> Seek good, and not evil, that ye may live;
> And so the Lord, the God of hosts, will be with you, as ye say.
> Hate the evil, and love the good,
> And establish justice in the gate;
> It may be that the Lord, the God of hosts,
> Will be gracious unto the remnant of Joseph.[17]

Note Amos's emphasis on the word *live*. He uses the word here in much the same sense as the Syriac version of the New Testament uses the word *life*. *Life* stands equally for *salvation*, and *to be saved is to live*. Note also his insistence on justice. Amos had a passion for social justice. Goodness to Amos had a strong social color— he wanted justice in society and fair play between man and man. Few lines better portray his love of justice than the following:

> But let justice well up as waters,
> And righteousness as a perennial stream.[18]

This clarion call to repentance is one of the finest of all time.

Jehovah's Love for All Nations. There are three passages in Amos that clearly portray the prophet's conception that God loves and cares for all nations. We have already considered two of them in other connections. The first is found in Amos 1:3-2:3 which, it will be remembered, was a pronouncement of doom upon a number of peoples living near Israel. Jehovah's very pronouncement upon them, however, shows how interested He was in their doings. Failure to live up to better ideals of living caused Jehovah regret and disappointment. The second is found in Amos 3:2.

> You only have I known of all the families of the earth;
> Therefore I will visit upon you all your iniquities.

---

[17]Amos 5:14, 15.
[18]Amos 5:24.

This passage, as pointed out above, implies that Israel is "chosen" only in the sense that she accepts greater responsibility. The greater the privileges given, the greater the responsibilities. Therefore, God's dealings with all peoples are essentially equal. "God is no respecter of persons," or we may add, of races.[19]

In still another passage, Amos makes even clearer the point in question:

> Are ye not as the children of the Ethiopians unto Me,
> O children of Israel? saith the Lord.
> Have not I brought up Israel out of the land of Egypt,
> And the Philistines from Caphtor,
> And Aram from Kir?[20]

Because of her sins, Amos considers Israel on the same level as other nations.

The Dawn of a Better Day. Amos has painted to his audience a sorrowful picture of sin and doom. Here and there to be sure are flashes of hope.[21] But mostly it is doom. Suddenly Amos ceases his message of doom and portrays a future of hope and promise.[22] Someday—presumably far in the future—the remnant of Israel that has escaped destruction shall be restored to its inheritance, the captivity of its people is to be turned, it shall build cities and plant vineyards and never be dispossessed.

> And I will turn the captivity of My people Israel,
> And they shall build the waste cities, and inhabit them;
> And they shall plant vineyards, and drink the wine thereof;
> They shall also make gardens, and eat the fruit of them.
> And I will plant them upon their land,
> And they shall no more be plucked up
> Out of their land which I have given them,
> Saith the Lord thy God.[23]

---

[19]Acts 10:34.

[20]Amos 9:7.

[21]Consider Amos 3:12; 5:3. A remnant to escape. These passages are in essential harmony with 9:8b.

[22]Amos 9:8b-15.

[23]Amos 9:14, 15.

This section, a rosy picture of Israel's future blessed state, has been denied to Amos by many scholars. But the writer can see no reason to doubt its authenticity. What would be the point in warning a people if it were completely doomed and without a ray of hope? Furthermore, Amos is in harmony with other prophets who looked forward to Israel's future blessings.

So far as Israel, as a kingdom and people, is sinful, it is to be destroyed from off the face of the earth. But there is always a divine kernel in the nation, by virtue of its divine election, a holy seed out of which the Lord will form a new and holy people and kingdom of God.[24]

---

[24]C. F. Keil and F. Delitzsch, *Biblical Commentary on the Old Testament* (The Twelve Minor Prophets), I, 328. For negative views see J. E. McFadyen, *Introduction to the Old Testament*, pp. 219 f.; Sir G. A. Smith, *The Book of the Twelve Prophets* (New and Revised Edition), I, 204 f.

Chapter XVII

JONAH–DIVINE GRACE
IS UNIVERSAL

The Man and His Time. The Book of Jonah gives little information about the prophet and his times. The inscription at the head of the book merely states that Jonah was "the son of Amittai". We know, however, from II Kings 14:25 that he was born in Gath-Hepher, which according to Joshua 19:10-13 was in the tribe of Zebulun. St. Jerome[1] (circa 400 A.D.) states that Gath-Hepher was "two miles from Sepphorim which is now called Diocaesarea, in the way to Tiberias, where his tomb also is pointed out."[2] To modern Arabs the reputed site of Gath-Hepher is known as El-Meshed. Jonah's supposed tomb is still pointed out there. According to the reference in II Kings, Jonah lived in the reign of Jeroboam II (circa 786 B.C.), and prophesied to him about the success of his war with Syria for the restoration of the ancient borders of the kingdom. That Jonah was an historical person is a fact accepted by most scholars.

Jonah Turns Down God's Call to a Mission. A call on a mission! Jonah thinks it over, but rebels in his heart because the call is to Nineveh, the capital of the hated Assyrians who, after all, were nothing but heathens. Hadn't Father Abraham and his family fled that country in order to avoid contact with their wicked practices?

But Jonah rose up to flee unto Tarshish from the presence of the Lord; and he went down to Joppa, and found a ship going to Tarshish; so he paid the fare thereof, and went down into it, to go with them unto Tarshish, from the presence of the Lord.[3]

---

[1]Eusebius Hieronymus, one of the great Biblical scholars of his day.

[2]As quoted by E. B. Pusey, *The Minor Prophets*, I, 372.

[3]Jonah 1:3. Tarshish or Tartessus is supposed to have been a city in southwestern Spain. Some scholars doubt this. The word may mean "foundry" or "refinery." Tarshish ships may have made up refinery fleets engaged in the metals trade, especially in the Red Sea.

Some scholars interpret the above passage as meaning that Jonah was attempting to flee from Jehovah's jurisdiction, i.e., Jehovah was the national God of Palestine, and all one had to do to get away from God was to get out of His territory. Others think it means that he simply sought to abandon his office as a prophet and get away from a distasteful job.[4] In any event, Jonah learned what so many of us learn sooner or later—God is not mocked, neither can we get away from His power and influence. God "hurled" a great wind into the sea and soon both ship and passengers were in trouble. Note that the mariners, despised heathens also, did something about it. First they prayed to their gods, then set about throwing the ship's wares into the sea to lighten her. But Jonah slept through it all. The ship's master called upon him to wake up and pray.

What meanest thou that thou sleepest? arise, call upon thy God, if so be that God will think upon us, that we perish not.[5]

In this, and succeeding passages, there is most delicious irony. Instead of Jonah preaching to the heathen, God is preaching to Jonah by means of a heathen. Imagine one of these despised people calling upon a Hebrew prophet to pray! The watchman on the tower of Zion has fallen asleep at his post. Lots are cast and it is determined that Jonah is the cause of the trouble to the ship. Jonah's conscience smites him and he asks to be thrown in the sea —all will be quiet then. He "came to himself"[6] at last. "The awakening of the conscience," says Victor Hugo, "is the grandeur of the soul." But the seamen, out of fear, reverence, pity and respect, refused to sacrifice one of

---

[4]See Pusey, *op. cit.*, p. 371. C. F. Keil and F. Delitzsch, *Biblical Commentary on the Old Testament* (The Twelve Minor Prophets), I, 384, says: "Jonah tries to escape from the command to proclaim the word of God in Nineveh by flight to Tarshish, because he is displeased with the display of divine mercy to the great heathen world, and because, according to ch. 4:2, he is afraid lest the preaching of repentance should avert from Nineveh the destruction with which it is threatened."

[5]Jonah 1:6.

[6]Jonah 1:12.

their fellow men. They rowed[7] hard to bring the ship to land, but all to no avail.

Only when all measures to save Jonah and the ship had failed did they finally consent to throw the Hebrew prophet overboard.[8] The miraculous cessation of the storm seems to have further convinced the sailors that Jonah's God was the true "God of heaven who hath made the sea and the dry land."[9] They seemingly were converted to Him for the record says:

> Then the men feared the Lord exceedingly; and they offered a sacrifice unto the Lord, and made vows.[10]

Jonah Turns to God. Jonah had to be saved physically and receive a spiritual resuscitation—otherwise we should have had no Book of Jonah. So the Lord appointed a large fish (a fish large enough to swallow a minor prophet like Jonah) to engulf him three days and nights. From the bowels of the fish Jonah cried mightily to God. Most men in their desperate need pray to God, when in less trying circumstances they completely forget Him.[11] The book ironically points out that God hearkens to Jonah's prayer and has the fish "vomit" Jonah upon the dry land.[12]

Jonah Accepts God's Second Call to a Mission. Through bitter experience Jonah learned that life is much sweeter and better if one runs *with* God rather than *from* Him. Repentance gives a man another opportunity to serve and that is why it is so important. God repeated the call to Jonah and this time he accepted by going to Nineveh.[13] He began to preach and apparently relished the message he delivered:

---

[7]The word in Hebrew literally means "to dig".

[8]Jonah 1:14-15.

[9]Jonah 1:9.

[10]Jonah 1:16.

[11]Read Jonah's prayer in Ch. 2; cf. Ps. 42:8; 31:23; 18:5; 69:2; 142:4; 31:7; 42:5; 50:14, 23.

[12]Jonah 2:10.

[13]Jonah 3:3 states that Nineveh "was an exceeding great city, of three days journey." The phrase "three days journey" is an oriental expression referring to superior size. See G. L. Robinson, *The Twelve Minor Prophets*, p. 80.

Yet forty days, and Nineveh shall be overthrown.[14]

The Book of Jonah records that the people of Nineveh received the prophet's message—greatest miracle of all—and repented of their evil deeds with the result that God turned away the punishment He had decreed.[15]

But it displeased Jonah exceedingly and he was angry.[16]

Therefore God had to teach His representative another lesson.

God Teaches Jonah a Profound Lesson. Jonah went out of Nineveh and sat in a safe place on the east side of the city, still hoping that God's judgments would descend on the repentant heathen. So God appointed a gourd to shade Jonah from the sun. It pleased him very much. Soon, however, a worm cut down the plant and Jonah fainted by reason of both a hot east wind and the sun. He requested that he might die.

And God said to Jonah: 'Art thou greatly angry for the gourd?' And he said: 'I am greatly angry, even unto death.' And the Lord said: 'Thou hast had pity on the gourd, for which thou hast not labored, neither madest it grow, which came up in a night, and perished in a night; and should not I have pity on Nineveh, that great city, wherein are more than sixscore thousand persons that cannot discern between their right hand and their left hand,[17] and also much cattle?'[18]

It is apparent throughout the story that Jonah could not stand to see God's love, so much promised to Israel, and cherished by her, bestowed on others, particularly her heathen oppressors.

God has vindicated His love to the jealousy of those who thought that it was theirs alone. And we are left with this vague vision of the immeasurable city, with its multitude of innocent children and cattle, and God's compassion brooding over all.[19]

---

[14]Jonah 3:4.
[15]Jonah 3:5-10.
[16]Jonah 4:1. Note his prayer in next verse.
[17]Presumably, therefore, children.
[18]Jonah 4:9-11.

[19]G. A. Smith, *The Book of the Twelve Prophets*, II, 528.

Abiding Lessons of Jonah.[20] Many think that Jonah "stands pre-eminent as the noblest, broadest, and most Christian of all Old Testament literature."

The greatest lesson of the book is that God's divine grace is universal.[21] Another and very obvious lesson is that of obedience.[22] Another important lesson is that prophecy is conditional. "Judgment, indeed, through repentance may be exchanged for salvation." Still another lesson lies in the spirit of higher patriotism which is in the book. We can agree with Professor Robinson that:

> Over against the narrow patriotism of the mean and contemptible little spirit of Jonah, who was a mirror for the nation, the author gives us, as we have already seen, a picture of the loving, fatherly, catholic God. The comparison was meant to sting Israel to the quick for their bigotry and hardness of heart.[23]

We must conclude, however, that if Jonah was the author of the book by his name he finally learned his lesson and thought it of enough value to pass it on to future generations.[24] That is evidence of a big man.

Some Important Considerations. We are more concerned with the teachings of the Book of Jonah than with mere technicalities or problems of criticism. It is necessary, however, in the case of this important book to point out certain facts that should be taken into consideration by those who wish to interpret it more technically than we have above. 1. First of all, let us ask ourselves whether Jonah wrote the book. If he didn't, readers may perhaps be justified in giving it a very free and "liberal" interpretation. If he did write it,—that is something else again. Most modern writers assume that the book was not written by Jonah. They take this position for the following reasons: 2. The book does not claim to be by Jonah, nor does it give any proof of having come from an eye-witness of

[20]See Robinson, *op. cit.*, p. 89-93.
[21]Cf. John 3:16.
[22]Cf. I Sam. 15:22; Acts 5:29.
[23]Robinson, *op. cit.*, pp. 90 f.
[24]Study carefully the following section of the chapter.

the events it describes.[3] The book is written in the third person. 3. One verse (3:3) seems to imply that at the time the book was written Nineveh had ceased to be a great city. "Now Ninevah *was* an exceeding great city," etc. 4. Certain words and grammatical elements in the book point to a late date—perhaps 300 B.C. 5. If the book had been written by Jonah himself (circa 786 B.C.) it would have been put first in the collection of the Minor Prophets instead of fourth.[25]

Against the above views the following are urged: 1. No books were admitted among the prophets except those which the arrangers of the canon *believed* or knew were written by men called to be prophets. Such is the uniform tradition of the Jews. 2. That Jonah is written in the third person is no argument that the prophet did not write the book, for it is the *exception* rather than the rule when sacred writers speak of themselves in the first person. Ezra and Nehemiah write in the first person, but they give accounts, not of God's dealings with His people, but of their own discharge of a definite office allotted to them by man. The prophets, on the contrary, unless they speak of God's revelations to them, speak of themselves in the third person. As a good example of this note that Amos related in the first person, what God shows him in vision, but passes at once to the third person when relating his persecution by Amaziah.[26] "Also Amaziah said unto Amos . . . Then answered Amos, and said to Amaziah."[27] 3. The verse (3:3) quoted above neither proves that Nineveh had already been destroyed when the Book of Jonah was written, nor that Nineveh's greatness was unknown to Jonah's contemporaries. *Was* is the synchronistic imper-

---

[25]For more detailed treatment of the above points consult Smith, *op cit.*, II, 482-488; W. O. E. Oesterley and T. H. Robinson, *An Introduction to the Books of the Old Testament*, pp. 372-374.

[26]See the challenging discussion on the above two points by Pusey, *op. cit.*, pp. 373ff. In reference to (1) H. E. Ryle, *The Canon of the Old Testament* (First Edition), p. 194, says: "There is no evidence to show that the recognition of Jonah as a book of Canonical Scriptures was ever seriously imperilled."

[27]Amos 7:12, 14.

fect, just as in Gen. 1:2. Nineveh was a great city when Jonah reached it, i. e., he found it so.[28] 4. Words pointed to in Jonah as late can not be *proved* late, they are only *allegedly* so, (a) It can not be maintained that because a word occurs only in a late document the word is therefore late. (b) It can not be maintained that a document is late merely because it contains words which do not occur in earlier ones, that are well known to us. (c) A word cannot be used as evidence of the lateness of a document in which it occurs simply because it occurs again in documents known to be late, such as the Hebrew parts of the Talmud.[29] 5. The position of the Book of Jonah among the Minor Prophets would, in the light of modern critical views, be no criterion as to the time it was written. Thus Obadiah which just precedes Jonah has been dated anywhere from 900 B. C. to 300 B. C.[30] Where ought its place in the canon to be? Joel is often dated about 400 B. C. to 350 B. C. or even later. Why does it occupy second place in the canon?

II. The second important consideration relates to the character of the Book of Jonah. Three views have held the field, the historical, the mythical, and the allegorical or parabolic. We may dismiss the mythical because it has not proved very convincing to most scholars. The historical view is that the Book of Jonah is historically correct, since it is based upon the prophet's actual experiences. In favor of this are the following facts: (a) The form of the book is simple historical narrative and was so regarded by most Jews and Christians until a little over a century ago. (b) The Book of Tobit, [31] the Book of III Maccabees,[32] and the *Antiquities*[33] of Josephus all treat of Jonah's call

---

[28]Keil and Delitzsch, *op. cit.*, I, 382.

[29]For (a), (b), (c), consult R. D. Wilson, *A Scientific Investigation of the Old Testament*, pp. 131-136, where statistical proof is given. For a note on grammar see p. 108 in the same work. The older commentators, Keil and Delitzsch, *op. cit.*, p. 381 and Pusey, *op. cit.*, pp. 375-378, also argue against the late date.

[30]See Smith, *op. cit.*, II, 164.

[31]Tobit 14:4, 8.

[32]III Maccabees 6:8.

[33]*Antiquities*, ix, 10, 2.

and preaching to Nineveh as an actual fact. (c) There were other prophets than Jonah who preached to foreign nations. Elijah and Elisha did so.[34] (d) Many modern critics have agreed that there is a kernel of history in the Book of Jonah and that Jonah actually preached to Nineveh.[35]

The allegorical or parabolic view holds the following: (a) The stay of Jonah in the belly of the fish for three days and nights is sufficiently extraordinary to warrant the suspicion of allegory. (b) The account of Nineveh's conversion is very general and no attempt is made to describe precise events. The absence of precise data is very conspicuous throughout the Book of Jonah. (c) The abrupt close of the story when its moral becomes obvious very strongly points to symptoms of the parable.[36]

III. The third and last consideration has to do with the Savior's reference to the Book of Jonah.[37] When the Scribes and Pharisees requested a sign of Him the Christ replied in terms that seem strongly compatible with the historical view of the Book of Jonah given above. Those who believe the book is a parable reply:

> We do not believe that our Lord had any thought of confirming or not confirming the historic character of the story. His purpose was one of exhortation and we feel the grounds of that exhortation to be just as strong when we have proven the Book of Jonah to be a parable. Christ is using an illustration: it matters not whether that be drawn from the realms of fact or of poetry.[38]

To which those of the historical persuasion might reply:

> In the same connection he (Christ) goes on to speak of the Queen of the South, how she came "from the ends of the earth, to hear the wisdom of Solomon, and behold a greater than Solomon is here"; and it certainly seems unlikely that he would mingle real and fictitious names in the same context. If the account of the Queen

---

[34]I Kings 17:8 ff.; II Kings 8:7 ff.

[35]We are indebted to G. L. Robinson, *op. cit.*, p. 84 f. for the facts in the above summation of the historical view.

[36]For a fuller account see Smith, *op. cit.*, pp. 488 f.

[37]See Matt. 12:38-42; 16:4; Luke 11:29-32.

[38]Smith, *op. cit.*, II, 496 f.

of the South were history, and the story of Jonah were fiction, Jesus surely might have discriminated between them in the interests of intellectual honesty.[39]

Before coming to definite conclusions respecting the interpretation of the Book of Jonah the careful student will, of course, give due weight to all of the considerations pointed out above.

---

[39]Robinson, *op. cit.*, p. 88.

Chapter XVIII

ISAIAH—POET, PROPHET, STATESMAN

The Greatness of the Man. Isaiah was one of the greatest men of all time. Certainly none of the prophets of the Old Testament, so far as we can tell from their writings, was greater than he. In the first place, Isaiah had great natural gifts, which were disciplined and sharpened by the best education that his time afforded. He was blessed with fine judgment and insight together with the courage to defend to the uttermost a cause he knew to be right. Secondly, he possessed great spiritual intuition and insight which made him a marvelous and ready instrument in the hands of Jehovah, whom he loved and served with all his heart. Isaiah thus combined earthly and heavenly wisdom to a most unusual degree. All this he, of course, used for the benefit of his fellow men. Valeton gives the following tribute to him:

> Never perhaps has there been another prophet like Isaiah, who stood with his head in the clouds and his feet on the solid earth, with his heart in the things of eternity and with mouth and hand in the things of time, with his spirit in the eternal counsel of God and his body in a very definite moment of history.[1]

Some Facts About Isaiah's Personal History. As the superscription[2] of the book makes plain, Isaiah was the son of Amoz (not to be confused with Amos) and his ministry took place during the last half of the eighth century B.C. His name means "Jehovah saves" or, perhaps, "Jehovah brings salvation". Isaiah seemed to be keenly aware of the meaning of his name for he continually used the words that comprise it. (The name is composite.) As far as can be ascertained, Isaiah was a native of Jerusalem and there-

---

[1] As quoted by G. L. Robinson, *The Book of Isaiah* (First Edition), p. 22.
[2] Isa. 1:1.

fore a city prophet. Throughout the book he mentions
Jerusalem and, since he was a close confidant of the king,
he is sometimes spoken of as a court prophet. According
to tradition, Isaiah was a cousin of King Uzziah; from
the prophet's own statements it may be deduced that he
apparently came from a family of high rank.[3] Isaiah was
married, though we do not know the name of his wife. She
is simply spoken of as the "prophetess".[4] Two sons are
mentioned, Shear-jashub[5] and Maher-shalal-hash-baz.[6]
The meanings of these names are respectively, "a remnant
shall return" and "the spoil speedeth, the prey hasteth" and
symbolize, at least in part, Isaiah's message to his people.[7]

Isaiah as Poet and Statesman. Isaiah has no rival
in the Old Testament for his versatility of expression and
brilliancy of imagery. Dr. G. L. Robinson pays the following tribute to his literary ability:

> His style marks the climax of Hebrew literary art. Both his
> periods and descriptions are most finished and sublime. "Every word
> from him stirs and strikes its mark," says Dillman. Beauty and strength
> are characteristic of his entire book. He is a perfect artist in words.
> No other Old Testament writer uses so many beautifully picturesque
> illustrations (5:1-7; 12:3; 28:23-29; 32:2).
>
> Epigrams and metaphors, particularly of flood, storm and
> sound (1:13; 5:18, 22; 8:8; 10:22; 28:17, 20; 30:28, 30), interrogation
> and dialogue (10:8; 6:8), anthithesis and alliteration (1:18; 3:24; 17:10,
> 12), hyperbole and parable (2:7; 5:1-7; 28:23-29), even paranomasia,
> or play on words (5:7; 7:9), characterize Isaiah's book as the master-
> piece of Hebrew literature. He is also famous for his vocabulary and
> richness of synonyms. Ezekiel uses 1535 words; Jeremiah, 1653; the
> Psalmist, 2170; Isaiah, 2186.
>
> Isaiah was also an orator. Jerome likened him to Demosthenes.
> He was likewise a poet. He frequently elaborates his messages in
> rhythmic or poetic style (12:1-6; 25:1-5; 26:1-12; 38:10-20; 42:1-4;
> 49:1-9; 50:4-9; 52:13-53:12; 60-62; 66:5-24); and in several instances

---

[3]See Isa. 7:3. Note Isaiah's ready access to the king. Note also 8:2 where he
seems to have easy access to the religious leaders.
[4]Isa. 8:3.
[5]Isa. 7:3.
[6]Isa. 8:3.
[7]Isa. 8:18.

slips into elegiac rhythm: for example, in 37:22-29 there is a fine taunting poem on Sennacherib, and in 14:4-21 another on the king of Babylon. As Driver remarks, "Isaiah's poetical genius is superb."[8]

Isaiah not only had great literary gifts, his fine mind, education, and broad acquaintance with men in all walks of life qualified him to be a statesman of the first rank. Judging from his book, the political horizon of the prophet, both foreign and domestic, was very extended and included Assyria, Babylonia, Syria, Egypt, Moab, Edom, Ethiopia, Arabia, Ammon, the isles of the sea, and all parts of Palestine. Isaiah's counsel to his people was to trust in God and not to make entangling alliances with other powers who would only lead them into trouble. When his counsel was kept, the kingdom profited, otherwise not. It was due to the prophet's wise counsel and advice that Jerusalem was saved from Sennacherib in 701 B.C.

The Period of Isaiah's Ministry. Isaiah lived and prophesied during the reigns of four kings of Judah— Uzziah, Jotham, Ahaz, and Hezekiah.[9] The chronology of the regal period of Israel and Judah is somewhat uncertain,[10] but it is reasonable to believe that Isaiah's ministry occupied at least forty years. It began in the year that king Uzziah died (circa 742 B. C.) and lasted until near the end of Hezekiah's reign (circa 687 B. C.). There is a tradition that Isaiah suffered martyrdom by being sawed asunder with a wooden saw during the reign of king Manasseh. The main political and social facts of Isaiah's time may be summarized as follows:

1. During the reigns of Uzziah and Jotham the kingdom of Judah was wealthy and relatively powerful.

2. During the reign of Ahaz there occurred the Syro-Ephraimite war, one of the great events in Isaiah's career, during which Judah was brought low because of the king's decidedly baneful religious and political policies.[11]

---

[8]Robinson, op. cit., p. 23.
[9]Isa. 1:1.
[10]See W. O. E. Oesterley and T. H. Robinson, A History of Israel, I, 454-464.
[11]II Chron. 28:19; II Kings 16:10-16.

3. During Hezekiah's reign Isaiah saw the end of the kingdom of Israel with the capture of Samaria by the Assyrians in 721 B.C., the religious reform of Hezekiah,[12] and the constantly increasing pressure and power of Assyria which finally culminated in Judah being over-run by Sennacherib (701 B.C.). Jerusalem was saved, due, as we have already pointed out, to Isaiah's good judgment. The Assyrian crisis was the greatest event in the long ministry of Isaiah.

4. During Isaiah's time great wealth and extremes of poverty existed together. The poor were oppressed by the wealthy classes, religion was a hollow sham,[13] idolatry increased in the land due to the influence of Assyrian colonists in Northern Israel, drunkenness and carousing prevailed, women were guiltyof low standards of conduct, great moral laxity prevailed and judges and civic leaders failed to keep faith with the people. The terrible effects of war upon Judah were especially apparent toward the end of Isaiah's ministry.

Isaiah's Vision and Call to the Ministry. God had said to Amos, years before this time:

> For the Lord God will do nothing,
> But He revealeth His counsel unto His servants the prophets.[14]

Near the end of king Uzziah's reign the sin and pride of the people of Israel was such that they needed stern warning. Isaiah was the man chosen by God to receive "His counsel" and to deliver the message desired. One day—presumably in the temple—Isaiah was suddenly vouchsafed a vision:

> In the year that king Uzziah died I saw the Lord sitting upon a throne high and lifted up, and His train filled the temple.[15]

Round about, seraphim cried one to another:

---

[12]II Kings 18:4, 22.
[13]II Kings 16:10-16; II Chron. 28. Note how Ahaz introduced foreign worship and even burned his children in the fire. All of this was reminiscent of the terrible Canaanite religious practices.
[14]Amos 3:7.
[15]Isa. 6:1.

> Holy, holy, holy, is the Lord of hosts;
> The whole earth is full of His glory.[16]

Isaiah in his humility thought of the unworthy state of himself and his people. He exclaimed:

> Woe is me! for I am undone;
> Because I am a man of unclean lips,
> And I dwell in the midst of a people of unclean lips;
> For mine eyes have seen the King,
> The Lord of hosts.[17]

His sin was forgiven in symbol of which one of the seraphim touched his lips with a hot stone from off the altar. Then he heard Jehovah say:

> Whom shall I send,
> And who will go for us?
> Then I said: 'Here am I send me.'
> And he said: 'Go, and tell this people:
> Hear ye indeed, but understand not;
> And see ye indeed, but perceive not.
> Make the heart of this people fat,
> And make their ears heavy,
> And shut their eyes;
> Lest they, seeing with their eyes,
> And hearing with their ears,
> And understanding with their heart,
> Return, and he healed.'[18]

Isaiah was commissioned and sent forth, but as the above words imply, his message was to fall on deaf ears and unrepentant hearts. As the rest of the chapter points out, only disaster and exile could be the end of such a people though, to be sure, there would remain a little stock from which life would spring.

An Overview of Isaiah's Prophecies. Since it is obviously impossible in two short chapters to give a detailed exposition of Isaiah, we shall at least give an overview of

---

[16]Isa. 6:3.
[17]Isa. 6:5.
[18]Isa. 6:8-10.

the whole book. It divides readily into six general divisions as follows:

1. Chapters 1-12, prophecies concerning Judah and Jerusalem, closing with promises of restoration and a psalm of thanksgiving.

2. Chapters 13-23, prophecies of judgment and salvation, for the most part concerning those foreign nations whose fortunes affected Judah and Jerusalem.

3. Chapters 24-27, Jehovah's world-judgment, issuing in the redemption of Israel.

4. Chapters 28-35, a cycle of prophetic warnings against alliance with Egypt, closing with a prophecy concerning Edom and a promise of Israel's ransom.

5. Chapters 36-39, history, prophecy and song intermingled; serving both as an appendix to chapters 1-35, and as an introduction to chapters 40-66.

6. Chapters 40-66, prophecies of comfort, salvation, and of the future glory awaiting Israel.[19]

The student who wishes to better appreciate Isaiah will do well to study carefully the above analysis of the book before making extensive readings in it.

The Great Arraignment. Such is the title suggested by the famous German scholar Ewald for the first chapter of Isaiah. This chapter forms an excellent preface to the book because it contains a summary of certain characteristic and essential teachings of Isaiah. It is one of the finest specimens of prophetic oratory in the Old Testament.[20] The student is strongly urged to read it through with care.

The preface takes the form of a court scene in which Jehovah appears to be plaintiff and judge, Israel the defendant, and Isaiah a bystander and interlocutor. The prophecy naturally falls into four sections.

1. Verses 1-9, the first section, contains the charge

---

[19]According to Robinson, *op. cit.*, p. 27, with slight changes. A fuller overview of Isaiah's prophecies will be found in Sperry, *The Voice of Israel's Prophets*, p. 19.

[20]T. K. Cheyne, *The Prophecies of Isaiah*, I, 1.

and appeal to the witnesses. Note the vigor of the opening
lines in which Israel is accused of rebellion:

> Hear, O heavens, and give ear, O earth,
> For the Lord hath spoken:
> Children I have reared, and brought up,
> And they have rebelled against Me.[21]

Israel's rebellion is evidence of the highest degree of
sin. The Lord then accuses the people of a lack of knowledge and understanding. They do not even know how
to do right.

> The ox knoweth his owner,
> And the ass his master's crib;
> But Israel doth not know,
> My people doth not consider.[22]

Lack of knowledge under some circumstances might
be forgiven, but Israel had no excuse. She had had teachers aplenty, but had rejected them, therefore her sin was
the greater. Here we have a fine teaching of Isaiah's:
Good religion demands knowledge in its scheme of things
and men will be held accountable if they do not obtain it,
insofar as they are able.

The Lord continues His accusation:

> Ah sinful nation,
> A people laden with iniquity,
> A seed of evil-doers,
> Children that deal corruptly;
> They have forsaken the Lord.[23]

The section ends by Isaiah saying:

> Except the Lord of hosts
> Had left unto us a very small remnant,
> We should have been as Sodom,
> We should have been like unto Gomorrah.[24]

---

[21]Isa. 1:2.
[22]Isa. 1:3; cf. Amos 3:10.
[23]Isa. 1:4.
[24]Isa. 1:9.

The doctrine that a remnant of Israel should be saved
is similar to what we met with in Amos 3:12; 5:3; 9:8b-15.

2. The next section, verses 10-17, anticipates Israel's
preliminary objection to a charge. Note the allusion to
Canaanite practices in the opening lines. This must have
been bitterly received by Isaiah's audience.

> Hear the word of the Lord,
> Ye rulers of Sodom;
> Give ear unto the law of our God,
> Ye people of Gomorrah.[25]

Isaiah was a brave man to confront his people with such a
statement. Then in anticipation of Israel's defense of
herself, based on precise observance of ritualistic practices,
the Lord says:

> To what purpose is the multitude of your sacrifices unto Me?
> Saith the Lord:
> I am full of the burnt-offerings of rams,
> And the fat of fed beasts:
> And I delight not in the blood
> Of bullocks, or of lambs, or of he-goats.
> . . .
> Bring no more vain oblations;
> It is an offering of abomination unto Me:
> New moon and sabbath, the holding of convocations—
> I cannot endure iniquity along with the solemn assembly.
> Your new moons and your appointed seasons
> My soul hateth;
> They are a burden unto Me;
> I am weary to bear them.[26]

Many writers have supposed these verses to mean
that Jehovah had no use for sacrifices and that the ritual
of Israel was distasteful to Him. Far more probable is
the view that He was not denouncing sacrifices and worship as such, but only rejecting their efficacy and value
when performed by a wicked and hypocritical people.[27]

---

[25]Isa. 1:10.

[26]Isa. 1:11, 13, 14.

[27]In support of this view note Isa. 1:15. It might be argued from this verse that
God is opposed to prayer. But no one would believe that. The point is that those
offering prayer are unworthy. "I will not hear; your hands are full of blood."

If the nation, as Isaiah says, has revolted from God, and become like Sodom, then . . . the basis of the sacrificial system ordained by God has fallen away; the means of grace have lost their force, and the conduct of the multitude in matters of worship is a self-willed course of no value before God, and bringing no blessing to the people. Outward worship without the accompaniment of true fear of God, and a corresponding walk, the Lord rejects as utterly foreign and repugnant to Him.[28]

3. The third section, verses 18-23, offers reconciliation to Israel on condition of repentance. Three verses follow:

> Come now, and let us reason together,
> Saith the Lord;
> Though your sins be as scarlet,
> They shall be as white as snow;
> Though they be red like crimson,
> They shall be as wool.
> If ye be willing and obedient,
> Ye shall eat the good of the land;
> But if ye refuse and rebel,
> Ye shall be devoured with the sword;
> For the mouth of the Lord hath spoken.[29]

In this passage the Lord points out to Israel that it is not too late to repent. Bad as conditions are, she can stave off destruction and ruin by undergoing a change of heart if such be coupled with righteous actions. The Lord again (as if his mind could not be kept off the subject) speaks of the sinners of his people as harlots, murderers, companions of thieves, lovers of bribes and forsakers of the cause of the orphan and widow.[30]

4. In the fourth and concluding section, verses 24-31, it is assumed that Jehovah's judgment will take place because His people will inevitably reject the gracious offer made to them.

> Therefore saith the Lord, the Lord of hosts,
> The Mighty One of Israel:
> Ah, I will ease Me of Mine adversaries,
> And avenge Me of Mine enemies.[31]

[28]C. von Orelli, *The Prophecies of Isaiah*, p. 16.
[29]Isa. 1:18-20.
[30]Isa. 1:21-23.
[31]Isa. 1:24.

This seems to be directed to the people as a whole. But Jehovah also seems to stress His remarks to a special class of sinners, probably among the higher classes,[32] and speaks of their destruction. However, He makes clear that Israel shall be purged of her baser elements and will some-day—presumably far in the future—be redeemed and re-stored.

> And I will turn My hand upon thee,
> And purge away thy dross as with lye,
> And will take away all thine alloy;
> And I will restore thy judges as at the first,
> And thy counsellors as at the beginning;
> Afterward thou shalt be called the city of righteousness,
> The faithful city.
> Zion shall be redeemed with justice,
> And they that return of her with righteousness.[33]

The doctrine of Israel's redemption is emphasized throughout Isaiah and is one of the keys to the under-standing of the book.

Professor G. L. Robinson has summed up the practical lessons of the chapter in the following words:

> The paramount lessons of the discourse are the too oft-forgotten facts that true religion is the prime condition of a healthy social order; that irreligion or formal ritual is a social vice; that no man liveth to himself; and that what a peasant or a prince believes is of public concern to all. All social evils are traceable ultimately to rebellion against God.[34]

---

[32]Isa. 1:28-31. (Notice the allusion to practices reminiscent of Canaanite religion in verse 29). "The whole people is indicted, but it is the judges, princes, and coun-sellors who are denounced. Judah's disasters, which she seeks to meet by worship, are due to civic faults: bribery, corruption of justice, indifference to the rights of the poor and the friendless." G. A. Smith, *The Book of Isaiah* (New and Revised Edition), 1, 14.

[33]Isa. 1:25-27.

[34]Robinson, *op. cit.*, pp. 69 f.

Chapter XIX

ISAIAH—POET, PROPHET, STATESMAN (Cont'd)

The Mountain of the Lord's House. Isaiah saw clearly the wickedness and moral degeneration of his people, but as a seer he looked into the future and saw that in the latter days his people, the house of Jacob, would still be existent (probably a righteous remnant) and playing a glorious role in the world.

And it shall come to pass in the latter days,
That the mountain of the Lord's house shall be established in the top of the mountains,
And shall be exalted above the hills;
And all nations shall flow unto it.
And many peoples shall go and say:
'Come ye, and let us go up to the mountain of the Lord,
To the house of the God of Jacob;
And He will teach us of His ways,
And we will walk in His paths.'
For out of Zion shall go forth the law,
And the word of the Lord from Jerusalem.[1]

These verses give an exalted and idealized vision of Zion's future. Isaiah sees a great commonwealth to which all nations gather to be governed by the God of Jacob. This great religious commonwealth is composed of the people of Israel who have returned to their God and who have forsaken the evil ways of their fathers. Through them God will teach the peoples of all nations who flock to hear His word. The word "mountain" in the phrase, "the mountain of the Lord's house," would seem to be nearly equivalent to "dwelling place" or "abode".[2] But the picture is not

---

[1]Isa. 2:2, 3: These verses and the one following are, with slight variations, like Micah 4:1-4. Many scholars are not certain which of the two prophets is the author of them or whether both quote from a still earlier prophet. Some regard the verses as a post-exilic insertion. The writer rejects the latter hypothesis.

[2]See Ps. 68:16, 17; Isa. 8:18; 11:9; D&C 84:2-4; 133:12-13.

complete. Isaiah sees in this glorious vision that there shall be no more war.

Isaiah and the Crime of War. In the war-shattered world in which we live it seems strange to read Isaiah's intensely idealistic and beautiful word picture of a world in which there is no war. And yet, it has been about 2700 years since the Hebrew prophet wrote the vision. We sometimes wonder how far human beings have progressed in that time. Let us examine Isaiah's words as he continues the vision of which we have already read two verses.

> And He shall judge among the nations,
> And shall rebuke many peoples;
> And they shall beat their swords into plowshares,
> And their spears into pruning-hooks;
> Nation shall not lift up sword against nation,
> Neither shall they learn war any more.[3]

Wars are bred because men and nations seem never to learn how to get along with each other. Selfishness and greed for power are still rampant in the world. In the midst of it all, we are apt to conclude that Isaiah was an impractical dreamer. But was he? In the physical world we do not progress without much planning and toil. But in that field we *are* making progress. In the realm of the moral and spiritual, can we likewise expect to progress without effort and without setting up goals and ideals? Isaiah knew, as all men should know, that war is a crime against humanity. He knew, as few men have known before or since, the weaknesses and failings of mankind. But in spite of that knowledge he boldly writes that someday war shall cease. He doesn't argue the point. He writes as if it were certain of accomplishment. His faith is magnificent.

Speaking of the vision, Alexander R. Gordon has said:

The insight of this prophecy is as deep as its outlook is broad. War may have its place in the Divine drama of history; but the end

---
[3]Isa. 2:4.

towards which all move is peace. God is a God of peace, who desires that His children should live and work together in peace. And the way of peace is no base surrender of justice, but the carrying of its claims to the highest court of appeal—the mind and purpose of God— which is identical with the arbitrament of sound reason, trust and goodwill. "Peace on earth to men of goodwill." Won by this motive, peace transforms the very instruments of war.[4]

In still another beautiful passage, Isaiah refers to the conditions that shall ensue in the earth when war has ceased and peace and happiness reign.

> And the wolf shall dwell with the lamb,
> And the leopard shall lie down with the kid;
> And the calf and the young lion and fatling together;
> And a little child shall lead them.
> And the cow and the bear shall feed;
> Their young ones shall lie down together;
> And the lion shall eat straw like the ox.
> And the sucking child shall play on the hole of the asp,
> And the weaned child shall put his hand on the basilisk's[5] den.
> They shall not hurt nor destroy
> In all My holy mountain;
> For the earth shall be full of the knowledge of the Lord,
> As the waters cover the sea.[6]

In Chapter 2:2-4 we read the description of peace among men and nations; here we have a description of peace as it will then exist among the brute creation,— *And a little child shall lead them.*

Note Isaiah's reference to knowledge. The narrow and particularistic has no place in it. He looked forward to the day when the knowledge of God should be over the earth as a sea covers the land. His statement is one of the glories of the Old Testament.

The Recovery of the Remnant of Israel. We have already seen how Isaiah's vision encompassed a glorious future of man and nature in which the arts of peace should be practiced. In the picture which Isaiah draws for us he

---

[4]Alexander R. Godon, *The Faith of Isaiah,* p. 248.
[5]A small, very poisonous species of viper.
[6]Isa. 11:6-9; cf. Rom. 8:18-22.

sees the house of Jacob in a glorious position. But Isaiah
has also foreseen Israel's dispersion among the nations.
In order for Israel to be effective in teaching these nations
she must be gathered, instructed, and prepared for her
mission. The glorious age of peace cannot be ushered in
until the chosen remnant has been gathered, prepared, and
sent forth with the message of the God of Israel. Isaiah
would not forget God's promise to Abraham, that all the
nations of the earth should be blessed in him.

And it shall come to pass in that day,
That the Lord will set His hand again the second time
To recover the remnant of His people,
That shall remain from Assyria, and from Egypt,
And from Pathros, and from Cush, and from Elam,
And from Shinar, and from Hamath, and from the islands of the sea.
And He will set up an ensign for the nations,
And will assemble the dispersed of Israel,
And gather together the scattered of Judah
From the four corners of the earth.
The envy also of Ephraim shall depart,
And they that harass Judah shall be cut off:
Ephraim shall not envy Judah,
And Judah shall not vex Ephraim.[7]

In the rest of the passage (verses 14-161, Isaiah shows
that Israel's enemies shall be overcome and that by a miracle,
a great highway shall be made for the remnant of his
people like as there was when they came up out of Egypt.

The whole of this passage (verses 10-16) is usually
denied to Isaiah and considered to be on a lower level than
what precedes.

In passing from the second to the third part of this prophecy, we
cannot but feel that we descend to a lower point of view and a less
pure atmosphere of spiritual ambition. Isaiah has just declared peace
between man and beast, but now we read that Judah must clear off
certain scores against her neighbors before there can be peace between
man and man. Were these verses also Isaiah's they would form an interesting psychological study. . . . He admits, indeed, the reconciliation
of Ephraim and Judah; but the first act of the reconciled brethren, he

---

[7]Isa. 11:11-13.

prophesies with exultation will be to *swoop down upon* their cousins Edom, Moab, and Ammon, and their neighbors the Philistines.[8]

In the opinion of the writer, those who adopt this view or others like it fail to do Isaiah justice. In the first place, they are loathe to accept the passage as the prophet's because it assumes a knowledge of the Exile and the Jewish Dispersion, hence, they assume it could only have been written *after* those events. As Professor G. B. Gray says:

> Most of it is clearly post-exilic since it presupposes the Exile and the Dispersion of the Jews as existing facts.[9]

In other words, the fact of prediction on the part of Isaiah is clearly denied. It is not convenient for us here to uphold the Isaianic authorship of the verses in view of the limitations of space. We merely point out that those who reject it do so without attempting to name the author or to explain satisfactorily how it got into the canon of scripture.[10] We point out all these facts to the reader in order to show how differences in what the Germans call *weltanschauung* (conception of the world or world-philosophy) will cause variant interpretations of a given passage of scripture on the part of different individuals. We may also assume that differing parties are sincere and intellectually honest in coming to their various conclusions.

Then secondly, they think that the passage descends "to a lower point of view and a less pure atmosphere of spiritual ambition" than what goes before, hence Isaiah probably did not write it. But such a conclusion may be reached because the interpreter has failed to enter into the spirit of the prophet and misinterprets him. That is what the writer thinks has happened here. We believe that Isaiah was looking far down the stream of time to a day

---

[8]George A. Smith, *The Book of Isaiah*, I, 198.

[9]Quoted by Smith, *ibid.*, p. 184, note.

[10]Furthermore, it is no exaggeration to say that the very essence of Isaiah's message is *prediction*. That is true regardless of what we think of it. This all brings up the literary problem of Isaiah which will be briefly treated a little later in the chapter.

long after Edom, Moab, and Ammon (verse 14) had ceased
to exist as nations and that consequently "to *swoop down
upon* their cousins" is to misinterpret Isaiah's prophecy
with respect to Israel's remnant. What did he mean, then,
when he mentions the countries by name? Edom, Moab
and Ammon were sworn enemies of Israel, often doing her
great wrongs. Consequently, in Isaiah's time the Hebrews
regarded them as synonymous with all that was evil.[11]
In his prophecy, therefore, they are symbols of wicked
nations or forces working against God and His people
in the "latter" days. These nations or forces, whatever
they are, shall face a day of reckoning. Isaiah had nothing
narrow or particularistic in mind when he uttered the
prophecy. We accept it unreservedly as coming from his
hand.

Isaiah and Predictions of the Coming of the Messiah.
The Christian Church has held through the ages that Isaiah
foresaw the coming of the Christ. The New Testament
writers themselves saw in Christ's birth and life the fulfilment of certain of Isaiah's prophecies. We shall, therefore, examine a number of the latter.

In Isa. 7:14 there is the famous "Immanuel" passage.

Therefore the Lord Himself shall give you a sign: behold, the
young woman shall conceive, and bear a son, and shall call his name
Immanuel.

Matthew in speaking of Mary the mother of the Christ
says:

And she will bring forth a son, and thou shalt call his name Jesus;
for he is the One who will save his people from their sins. Now this
has come to pass, that it might be fulfilled which was spoken by the
Lord through the prophet, saying,
    Behold, the virgin will be with child,
    And will bring forth a son,
    And they will call his name Immanuel;
    Which is being interpreted, God with us.[12]

---

[11]See Amos 1:9-13; 2:1-3; Obad. 1:10-14.
[12]Matt. 1:21-23.

There is, therefore, no doubt that the early Christians viewed this prophecy of Isaiah's as being fulfilled in Christ and His mother. This may be correct, but a careful examination of the context of the verse will reveal many difficulties, and scholars have been at their wits' end to explain them. Our readers ought to examine carefully the relevant passages for themselves.

Isa. 9:1, 2 has been claimed to have been fulfilled by Christ.

But there shall not always be gloom to her who is in anguish.
In the former time he brought into contempt the land of Zebulun and
    the land of Naphtali,
But in the latter time he makes glorious the way to the sea,
Beyond Jordan, the district of the nations.
The people who walked in darkness behold a great light:
They who dwelt in the land of deep darkness, upon them the light
    shines.

The Gospel of Matthew refers to these verses as follows:

And leaving Nazareth, He [Christ] came and dwelt in Capernaum, which is by the sea, in the borders of Zebulun and Naphtali; that it might be fulfilled which was spoken through Isaiah the prophet. . . .[13]

Strange as it may seem, the famous passage in Isa. 9:6-7 is apparently not referred to in the New Testament.

For unto us a child is born, unto us a son is given;
And the government shall be upon his shoulder:
And his name shall be called Wonderful, Counselor,[14]
The Mighty God, The Everlasting Father, The Prince of Peace.
Of the increase of government and peace there is no end.
Upon the throne of David, and upon his kingdom,
To order it, and to establish it with judgment and with justice.
From henceforth even forever. The zeal of the Lord of Hosts will
    perform this.

This scripture will be remembered by music-lovers for the use made of it in Handel's *Messiah*. Many scholars

---

[13]Matt. 4:13, 14. See also verses 15 and 16.
[14]Many scholars combine these as Wonderful-Counselor.

have either denied this passage to Isaiah or have denied its application to the Christ; nevertheless, it is not likely that the masses of Christian peoples will do so.

We should be remiss if we made no reference to Isa. 53. In it most Christian people through the ages have seen prophetically portrayed the sufferings and sorrows of the Christ. We reproduce herewith some of the most important verses, but advise our readers to study carefully the whole chapter.

> He is despised, and rejected of men,
> A man of sorrows, and acquainted with grief,
> And we hid as it were our faces from him:
> He was despised, and we esteemed him not.
> Surely he hath borne our griefs, and carried our sorrows;
> Yet we did esteem him stricken,
> Smitten of God, and afflicted.
> But he was wounded for our transgressions,
> He was bruised for our iniquities;
> The chastisement of our peace was upon him,
> And with his stripes we are healed.
> All we like sheep have gone astray,
> We have turned every one to his own way;
> And the Lord hath laid on him
> The iniquity of us all.
> He was oppressed, and he was afflicted
> Yet he opened not his mouth;
> He is brought as a lamb to the slaughter,
> And as a sheep before her shearers is dumb;
> So he openeth not his mouth.
> He was taken from prison and from judgment,
> And who shall declare his generation?
> For he was cut off out of the land of the living,
> For the transgression of my people was he stricken.
> And he made his grave with the wicked,
> And with the rich in his death;
> Because he had done no violence,
> Neither was any deceit in his mouth.[15]

The text above reproduces the Authorized Version rendering. Its beauty and musical quality in part make up for the few places where the translation could have been improved.

---

[15]Isa. 53:3-9.

Practically the whole of Isa. 53 has been reproduced in the New Testament and applied to the Christ. This is a remarkable tribute to Isaiah's prophecy.

Part of the chapter is also used in Handel's *Messiah.* It will be remembered that the second part of his oratorio opens with Isa. 53:3. The story is told that at this point in the writing of the composition he was found with his head upon a table, weeping.

The Literary Problem of Isaiah. Before dealing with the prophecies of Israel's redemption in Chapters 40-66, a little should be said about the literary problem that centers around the Book of Isaiah. Most modern scholars deny that Isaiah wrote the bulk of the book that goes under his name and especially do they deny to him Chapters 40-66. Many deny the unity even of these and the names "Deutero-Isaiah" and "Trito-Isaiah" are applied to Chapters 40-55 and 56-66 respectively. Nor is Trito-Isaiah looked upon as the work of one writer. In fact, the Book of Isaiah has been chopped into what Professor Charles C. Torrey called "hopeless chunks".[16] Much of Isaiah has been assigned to a later age than the prophet, to the days of the Exile and later.

Isaiah's authorship of many parts of the book is denied because of certain technical reasons such as differences in style, vocabulary, and theological outlook in its different parts, as well as presuppositions respecting the predictive element in prophecy with which the study of the book is approached.

However, some very able scholars through the years have maintained the Isaianic authorship of the book and by no means has such authorship been disproved. The writer believes that the evidence for Isaiah's authorship is very strong. He has presented this in some detail in another publication and the reader is referred to it. A selected bibliography will be found therein.[17]

---

[16]Charles C. Torrey, *The Second Isaiah,* p. 13.

[17]See Sidney B. Sperry, "The Isaiah Problem in The Book of Mormon"; in the *Improvement Era,* XLII, No. 9, pp. 525, 526, 564-569 (September, 1939). See also Sperry, *The Voice of Israel's Prophets,* pp. 75-94.

Prophecies of Israel's Redemption. The general theme of Isa. 40-66 is Israel's redemption. These chapters are to be accounted the most brilliant jewels of Old Testament prophetic literature. In masterful and beautiful language, Isaiah comforts his people and points to the time when they shall be redeemed and God's kingdom shall triumph over the earth. His first words form the beginning of Handel's *Messiah*, so much loved by cultured people.

> Comfort ye, comfort ye My people,
> Saith your God.
> Speak ye comfortably to Jerusalem,
> And cry unto her,
> That her warfare is accomplished,
> That her iniquity is pardoned;
> That she hath received of the Lord's hand
> Double for all her sins.[18]

This passage has no reference at all to Israel's deliverance from the Babylonian Captivity as many have supposed, but applies to a day far more distant than that, to the latter days, to the time spoken of previously in Isa. 2:2-4. Isaiah has in mind the period at and just preceding the time when peace shall come to man and the brute creation (see Isa. 11:6-9). He sees that after Israel has paid the penalty for her sins, God will again choose her and remember His promise to Abraham.

> But thou, Israel, My servant,
> Jacob whom I have chosen,
> The seed of Abraham My friend;
> Thou whom I have taken hold of from the ends of the earth,
> And called thee from the uttermost parts thereof,
> And said unto thee: 'Thou art My servant,
> I have chosen thee and not cast thee away;
> Fear thou not, for I am with thee,
> Be not dismayed, for I am thy God;
> I strengthen thee, yea, I help thee;
> Yea, I uphold thee with My victorious right hand.[19]

---

[18]Isa. 40:1, 2.
[19]Isa. 41:8-10; note also Isa. 42:1-9.

He then goes on to show that Israel's enemies shall come to nought[20] and that God's sons and daughters shall return from the end of the earth.[21]

Every one that is called by My name.[22]

Then, taking a look a little nearer his own time, he sees the Babylonian Empire fall,[23] describes the makers of idols and scorns them,[24] then reverts back to the scenes of redemption again.

I have blotted out, as a thick cloud, thy transgressions,
And, as a cloud, thy sins;
Return unto Me, for I have redeemed thee.
Sing, O ye heavens, for the Lord hath done it;
Shout, ye lowest parts of the earth;
Break forth into singing, ye mountains,
O forest, and every tree therein;
For the Lord hath redeemed Jacob,
And doth glorify Himself in Israel.[25]

Isaiah then proceeds to take note of Israel's release from the Babylonian Captivity, even so far as to mention the Persian king, Cyrus, who is to be her deliverer.[26] Chapter 47 is a wonderful poem depicting Babylon's fall and abject humiliation.

The reader's attention is especially called to the four famous "Servant Songs" in which Isaiah seems, according to many authorities, to personify righteous Israel or else refers to some unique person in Israel. These songs are as follows:

1. Chapter 42:1-9. The Servant's world-wide mission and gentle manner.
2. Chapter 49:1-13. The Servant's mission and spiritual success; followed by promises of comfort to Zion (49:14-50:3).
3. Chapter 50:4-11. The Servant's soliloquy concerning his perfection through suffering; followed again by messages of comfort and encouragement to the believers in Zion (51:1-52:12).[27]

---

[20]Isa. 41:12.
[21]Isa. 43:6.
[22]Isa. 43:7.
[23]Isa. 43:14.
[24]Isa. 44:9-20.
[25]Isa. 44:22, 23.
[26]Isa. 44:28-45:13.
[27]See D&C 113:7-10.

4. Chapters 52:13-53:12. The Servant's vicarious suffering and
ultimate exaltion;[28] followed by a vivid description of Zion's future
prosperity and glory (chapter 54), and an urgent invitation to men
immersed in business to accept of God's proffered salvation (chapter
55): even proselytes and eunuchs being allowed to share in the blessings of redemption (56:1-8); the section closing with a scathing
rebuke to faithless shepherds and sensual idolaters (56:9-57:21).[29]

The reader must decide, of course, for himself who
the suffering Servant is in these poems. Latter-day Saints
know that he is the Savior. (See Mos. 13:35-14:12.)

In Chapter 60 Isaiah draws a graphic and beautiful
picture of the future Zion. Note verses 1-3.

Arise, shine, for thy light is come,
And the glory of the Lord is risen upon thee.
For, behold, darkness shall cover the earth,
And gross darkness the peoples;
But upon thee the Lord will arise,
And His glory shall be seen upon thee.
And nations shall walk at thy light,
And kings at the brightness of thy rising.

Finally, Isaiah sees the climax of God's work and His
triumph over wickedness in the earth.

For, behold, I create new heavens
And a new earth;
And the former things shall not be remembered,
Nor come into mind.
But be ye glad and rejoice for ever
In that which I create;
For, behold, I create Jerusalem a rejoicing,
And her people a joy.
And I will rejoice in Jerusalem,
And joy in My people;
And the voice of weeping shall be no more heard in her,
Nor the voice of crying.[30]

---

[28]As we have already seen, the New Testament considers Isaiah 53 as applying to
the Christ.
[29]Adapted from George L. Robinson, *The Book of Isaiah* (First Edition), p. 141 f.
[30]Isa. 65:17-19.

Truly "great are the words of Isaiah".[31] He was a spiritual giant whose vision and intellect transcend that of ordinary men as the mountain peak overshadows the hills. His voice will continue to ring down through the centuries, bringing joy and happiness to those whose hearts and spirits are attuned to the same spiritual rock as his.

---

[31]3 Nephi 23:1.

Chapter XX

MICAH—PROPHET OF JUDGMENT, COMFORT, AND SALVATION

Some Facts About Micah. From the superscription of the Book of Micah it is apparent that the prophet preached during the reigns of Jotham, Ahaz, and Hezekiah, kings of Judah. We can therefore set a date for Micah of about 765 B.C. This means that he was a contemporary of Isaiah the Prophet.

Micah's name means "who is like unto Jehovah?" and that would seem to indicate that he was the offspring of parents who were zealous worshippers of the true God. The fact that the prophet is called the Morashtite would point strongly toward his being a native of Moresheth-Gath, which is mentioned in the text.[1] The name of the town means *Territory* or *Property of Gath,* and seems to have been located in the Shephelah or low hill region some twenty miles southwest of Jerusalem. If our location of Moresheth is correct, the writer may claim to have walked all over the place which is located upon a relatively high (1000 feet) terrace. It commands a marvelous view of the surrounding country and anciently must have been of considerable importance. Micah was, therefore, a product of the open hills and valleys and would seem to have had no special love for the cities.[2]

Since Micah was a contemporary of Isaiah, the problems he faced were much the same. In fact, he does portray the political, moral, and religious condition of Palestine in essentially the same colors as does Isaiah: he speaks of the corruption of the people's leaders, priests, law-givers, and prophets, and of the greediness and avaricious nature of the rich. But Micah was not a statesman

---

[1]Micah 1:14.
[2]Micah 1:5; 5:11; 6:9.

like Isaiah, consequently, he was not so much concerned about his nation's political sins. Neither was he so much concerned about ritual as his Jerusalem contemporary.[3] Micah was more like Amos in that his grievances were more social in character. Like others of the prophets, he envisioned the day when Israel would be redeemed and restored to her rightful inheritance.

Characteristics of the Book of Micah. The Book of Micah divides quite naturally into three sections. 1. Chapters 1 to 3 deal with the coming judgments because of Israel's sins, the destruction of Samaria, the devastation of Judah and deportation of her inhabitants, a threat to Jerusalem, and a brief promise of eventual restoration of the remnant of Israel. 2. Chapters 4 to 5 have to do with the glorification and blessing of Zion in the latter days, of the restoration to Israel of her former dominion, of the Babylonian captivity and subsequent rescue, of the birth of the Savior in Bethlehem and, finally, of the beneficent and terrible power of the remnant of Jacob among the nations. 3. Chapters 6 to 7. By the expedient of a very dramatic controversy, or law-suit, the Lord shows Israel the way to salvation, that she had repaid His loving care and benefits with ingratitude, that her worship is mistaken if not insincere, and that her social sins point to her doom. The Lord will again have compassion on His people and show forth His marvelous works to the nations, if Israel will but confess her sins and turn to Him. A beautiful prayer concludes the book.

The Pronouncement of Judgment Upon Israel. In vivid language reminding one of Isaiah's prophecies, Micah opens his discourse:

> Hear, ye peoples, all of you;
> Hearken, O earth, and all that therein is;
> And let the Lord God be witness against you,
> The Lord from His holy temple.
> For, behold, the Lord cometh forth out of His place,
> And will come down, and tread upon the high places of the earth.[4]

---

[3]These statements are necessarily based on the short text at our disposal.
[4]Micah 1:2, 3.

He then proceeds to show the reason for the Lord's actions:

> For the rebellion[5] of Jacob is all this,
> And for the sins of the house of Israel.[6]
> What is the rebellion of Jacob? is it not Samaria?
> And what are the high places of Judah? are they not Jerusalem?[7]

Micah identifies the source of apostasy or rebellion of Israel as the capital cities of the Northern and Southern kingdoms respectively. Samaria and Jerusalem are the centers of corruption from whence Israel's evil examples come. The reference to the "high places" in line six is an allusion to the sinister Canaanite religious practices adopted by Israel. The prophets can never forget them. And what will be God's judgment upon Samaria? The answer comes without equivocation:

> Therefore I will make Samaria a heap in the field,
> A place for the planting of vineyards;
> And I will pour down the stones thereof unto the valley,
> And I will uncover the foundations thereof.[8]

In the process of Samaria's destruction, the prophet is very careful to note the end of certain religious paraphernalia and practices taken over from the Canaanites.

> And all her graven images shall be beaten to pieces,
> And all her harlot-gifts shall be burned with fire,
> And all her idols will I lay desolate;
> For of the hire of a harlot hath she gathered them,
> And unto the hire of a harlot shall they return.[9]

How far Canaanite religion had penetrated Israel the reader can judge for himself. The lesson to modern Israel is apparent.

Nor does Micah spare Judah and Jerusalem. In an ominous series of puns or word plays on Judean towns,

---

[5]Meaning apostasy.
[6]Note synonymous parallelism. The whole of Israel is meant as the following lines indicate.
[7]Micah 1:5.
[8]Micah 1:6.
[9]Micah 1:7.

Micah warns them of their coming fate. Following is Moffatt's attempt to bring out the thought in English:

Weep *tears* at *Tear*town (Bochim),
Grovel in the *dust* at *Dust*town (Beth-ophrah)
Fare forth stripped, O *Fair*town (Saphir)!
*Stir*town (Zaanan) dare not *stir*,
Beth-esel . . .
and Moroth hopes in vain;
for doom descends from the Eternal
to the very gates of Jerusalem.

Harness your steeds and away, O Horsetown (Lakhish)
O source of Sion's sin,
where the crimes of Israel centre!
O maiden Sion, you must part with
Moresheth of Gath;
and Israel's kings are ever *balked*
at *Balk*ton (Achzib).
I will march the conqueror on you yet,
O men of Moreshah;
and Israel's pomp shall perish utterly.
Israel, shave your head and *hair*,
in mourning for your children dear,
shave it like a vulture's *bare*,
for they are lost to you.[10]

Micah Denounces Social Wrongs. We are today in the midst of a world revolution. It is due in part to social wrongs that have constantly beset the poor and innocent in every country. Micah keenly felt the social injustices that plagued Israel in his own day. Coming from the country as he did, he no doubt felt these wrongs more acutely than if he had come from the city.[11] Micah could not help but cast his invective at the wealthy, greedy, land grabbers who descended upon the rural districts and made the poor their debtors. And even today, the agricultural communities in our own nation could well take a leaf from

---

[10]Micah 1:10-16.

[11]"Social wrongs are felt most acutely, not in the town, but in the country. So in the days of Rome, whose earliest social revolts were agrarian. So in the Middle Ages . . ." G. A. Smith, *The Book of the Twelve Prophets* (New and Revised Edition, I, 413 f.

Micah's note book and beware letting their properties go into the hands of money lenders.

> Woe to them that devise iniquity
> And work evil upon their beds!
> When the morning is light, they execute it,
> Because it is in the power of their hand.
> And they covet fields, and seize them;
> And houses, and take them away;
> Thus they oppress a man and his house,
> Even a man and his heritage.[12]

Micah was not so much concerned about the taking of mere chattels. What ground his soul and made him righteously indignant was that unscrupulous men were allowed to commit wrongs so easily and put human beings in their power. Personal independence was lost, and the security of home and family was put in the hands of a few capricious men.

> Micah feels that by themselves the economic wrongs explain and justify the doom impending on the nation. When this doom falls, by the Divine irony of God it shall take the form of a conquest of the land by the heathen, and the disposal of those great estates to the foreigner.[13]

In the same indignant vein, Micah continues;

> And I said:
> Hear, I pray you, ye heads of Jacob,
> And rulers of the house of Israel:
> Is it not for you to know justice?
> Who hate the good, and love the evil;
> Who rob their skin from off them,
> And their flesh from off their bones;
> Who also eat the flesh of my people,
> And flay their skin from off them,
> And break their bones;
> Yea, they chop them in pieces, as that which is in the pot,
> And as flesh within the caldron.[14]

What Micah said in his day applies with equal force today. As Professor George A. Smith writes:

---

[12]Micah 2:1, 2.
[13]Smith, *op. cit.*, I, 416. Micah is, after all, very modern.
[14]Micah 3:1-3.

Is there nothing of the same with ourselves? While Micah spoke he had wasted lives and bent backs before him. Pinched peasant-faces peer between his words and fill the ellipses. Among the poor today are there not starved and bitten faces—bodies with the blood sucked from them with the Divine image crushed out? We cannot explain all of these by vice. Drunkenness and unthrift account for much; but how much more only the following facts! Men among us live in fashionable streets and keep their families comfortable by paying their employees a wage on which it is impossible for men to be strong or women to be virtuous. Are those not using these as their food? They say that if they gave higher wages they must close their business, and cease paying wages at all; and they are right if they continue to live on the scale they do. As long as any families are maintained in comfort by the profits of business in which some or all of the employees work for less than they can nourish their bodies upon, the fact is that the one set are feeding upon the others.[15]

Micah Versus the Hireling Prophets. We have already noted that Amos the prophet was not a "prophet nor a son of a prophet".[18] That is, he was not a professional or a hireling. Micah also makes reference to hireling prophets. It seems that in the generation of Amos and Micah the leaders—better tyrants—of Israel used professional prophets and seers to cloak their misdeeds. Religion, unfortunately, lends itself, or rather its cloak, very easily to the uses of the hypocrite. So the rich and unscrupulous leaders of Israel found it easy—for a price—to hire professional religionists to cover their actions by flattery and falsehood. The hireling prophet depended upon his rich clients for a living. He could not, therefore, be independent in his thinking and in his judgment. He was high-pressured into siding with the rich, and consequently shut his eyes to the real condition among the people. Naturally he could not attack the sins of the day that made it possible for his clients to exploit Israel's common people. Micah exposed the pseudo-prophet as follows:

Thus saith the Lord concerning the prophets that make my people to err; That cry: 'Peace,' when their teeth have anything to bite;[17]

---

[15]Smith, *op. cit.*, I, 422 f. At the present writing (1969), it might be noted that many employees don't earn their pay. That is also wrong.

[16]Amos 7:14.

[17]That is, they preach if they receive something to bite (eat).

And whoso putteth not into their mouths,
They even prepare war against him:
Therefore it shall be night unto you, that ye shall have no vision;
And it shall be dark unto you, that ye shall not divine;
And the sun shall go down upon the prophets,
And the day shall be black over them.
And the seers shall be put to shame, and the diviners confounded;
Yea, they shall all cover their upper lips;
For there shall be no answer of God.[18]

On the other hand, Micah shows that the true prophet has the spirit of God and the necessary insight, vision, and courage to tell what was wrong among the people.

> But I truly am full of power by the spirit of the Lord,
> And of justice, and of might,
> To declare unto Jacob his transgression,
> And to Israel his sin.[19]

Because of the lack of justice on the part of Israel's leaders and the "prophets that divine for money," Micah goes on to emphasize Israel's doom:

> Therefore shall Zion for your sake be plowed as a field,
> And Jerusalem shall become heaps,
> And the mountain of the house as the high places of a forest.[20]

Micah's Vision of the Latter Days. In spite of Micah's pronouncement of doom upon the two kingdoms of Israel, he cannot help but give a ray of hope and comfort to that little remnant of Israel that has proved faithful to their prophetic leaders. Micah, like all of the prophets, remembered the promises God made to Abraham. Through Abraham's descendants should all nations be blessed. How could that promise be fulfilled if all Israel were destroyed? Micah knows that it will not be. Even in the midst of his predictions of woe he had quoted the Lord as saying:

---

[18]Micah 3:5-7.
[19]Micah 3:8.
[20]Micah 3:12. A very famous passage of scripture and one that was later to be instrumental in saving Jeremiah's life. See Jer. 26:18.

> I will surely assemble, O Jacob, all of thee;
> I will surely gather the remnant of Israel;
> I will render them all as sheep in a fold;
> As a flock in the midst of their pasture.[21]

Not only was the remnant of Israel to be assembled (he means in the latter days), but it would be glorified in the eyes of all nations. Micah had the same view as did Isaiah of its future.[22] The mountain of the Lord's house was to be established on the tops of the mountains, and many nations and people should go up there to be taught in the ways of Jacob's God. As a result of Divine judgments, nations shall not learn war any more, and every man shall sit in the security of his own vine and fig-tree with none to make afraid. Finally, Micah sees God reigning over His people, Israel.

> In that day, saith the Lord, will I assemble her that halteth,
> And I will gather her that is driven away,
> And her that I have afflicted;
> And I will make her that halted a remnant,
> And her that was cast far off a mighty nation;
> And the Lord shall reign over them in mount Zion
>   from thenceforth even for ever.[23]

The Prediction of the Coming of a Messiah. Micah now turns for a moment from his predictions concerning Israel in the latter days and turns back the wheel of time to the little village of Bethlehem. Out of this village, one of Judah's smallest, he sees coming one who is to be ruler over all Israel. This is to be the Messiah, or Savior of His people. His goings forth, Micah sees, reach back into eternity.

---

[21]Micah 2:12.

[22]Micah 4:1-3 and Isa. 2:2-4 are very nearly the same. Scholars differ in their opinions as to whether Isaiah copied from Micah and vice versa or whether both quote from a common earlier source.

[23]Micah 4:6, 7. For certain powers granted Israel read Micah 4:11-14; 5:6-14. Read the Savior's interpretation in 3 Nephi 20:15-22; 21:12-25.

And thou, Bethlehem Ephratha,
Too small to be among the thousands of Judah,
Out of thee will He come forth to Me who will be
     Ruler over Israel;
And His goings forth are from the olden time, from
     the days of eternity.[24]

Many writers deny that this prophecy has reference to Christ or that it was written by Micah, but we think upon insufficient grounds. Even the Old Jewish synagogue unanimously regarded this passage as containing a prophecy of the birth of the Messiah in Bethlehem.[25] But whatever the view now taken, certainly the writers of the Gospels of Matthew and John regarded the birth of the Christ in Bethlehem as the fulfilment of Micah's prophecy.[26]

Micah Points the Way to Salvation. Having pointed out the judgment that shall burst upon Israel and the future glory awaiting the righteous remnant, Micah now proceeds to point out the true way of salvation, by showing that Israel only brings distress and punishment upon herself through ingratitude and resistance to God, and that only by true repentance can she participate in His promised blessings. In a mood reminiscent of court procedure, Micah asks.

For the Lord hath a controversy with His people,
And He will plead with Israel.
O My people, what have I done unto thee?
And wherein have I wearied thee?
Testify against Me.[27]

The Lord then points out briefly how He brought up Israel from Egypt and performed other great deeds in her behalf, in order that she might know the righteous acts of God.[28]

---

[24]Micah 5:2.
[25]C. F. Keil and F. Delitzsch, *Biblical Commentary on the Old Testament* (The Twelve Minor Prophets), I, 481.
[26]See Matt. 2:5, 6: John 7:42.
[27]Micah 6:2, 3.
[28]Micah 6:4, 5.

Because of these loving acts of God which cannot be questioned, the audience is made to reply (in the first person singular) in its sincere but mistaken way:

> Wherewith shall I come before the Lord,
> And bow myself before God on high?
> Shall I come before Him with burnt-offerings,
> With calves of a year old?
> Will the Lord be pleased with thousands of rams,
> With ten thousands of rivers of oil?
> Shall I give my first-born for my transgression,
> The fruit of my body for the sin of my soul.[29]

The answer to this is of course obvious, God desires something more of His people than formalized worship. The above answer to God betrayed the darkened minds of His people.

Micah conveyed to the people the requirements of true salvation in an answer that is one of the noblest of all time.

> It hath been told thee, O man, what is good,
> And what the Lord doth require of thee:
> Only to do justly, and to love mercy, and to walk
>   humbly with thy God.[30]

In these few lines, Micah has summed up the teachings of the prophets. They were, in our opinion, coined in the same Eternal Mint as the lines of Christ when he said:

> Thou shalt love the Lord thy God with all thy heart, and with all thy soul, and with all thy mind. This is the great and first commandment. A second is like it, Thou shalt love thy neighbor as thyself.[31]

---

[29]Micah 6:6, 7.
[30]Micah 6:8. The student will do well to memorize this passage.
[31]Matt. 22:37-39.

Chapter XXI

JEREMIAH—PROPHET OF REBUKE AND JUDGMENT

Jeremiah and His Times. The name of Jeremiah is of doubtful meaning. Some writers have thought it signifies "Jehovah hurls," others suggest "Jehovah founds, sets, appoints." According to the superscription of his book, Jeremiah was a son of Hilkiah, "of the priests that were in Anathoth in the land of Benjamin." When Joshua had entered Canaan he gave to the children of Aaron, the priest, a number of cities as an inheritance and Anathoth was one of them.[1] It is quite probable, therefore, that Hilkiah's priestly ancestors had lived in the city for generations.[2] Anathoth was probably located very near the present little Arab village of Anata. It took the writer and some friends over an hour to walk the distance separating it on the northeast from Jerusalem. We should judge that it is about four miles from the capital city. The village of Anata is not a very prepossessing place and we were greeted by barking dogs and a few dirty, ragged children. Anathoth was located within the confines of the territory of Benjamin. For that reason Jeremiah's forebears must have been identified with the kingdom of Israel and not with Judah as was the prophet. It will be remembered that many years before Jeremiah's time Israel had been taken captive by the Assyrians. After 721 B.C., therefore, Jeremiah's family must have concerned itself more and more with the fortunes of the kingdom of Judah.

The superscription of the Book of Jeremiah further tells us that the prophet began his ministry in the thirteenth year of Josiah's reign which would be about 627

---

[1]See Josh. 21:13-19.

[2]Hilkiah was possibly a descendant of Abiathar the priest who was banished by Solomon and sent to Anathoth. Abiathar was a descendant of Eli. Jeremiah may therefore have descended from a distinguished family of priests. See I Kings 2:26, 27.

B.C. Since Jeremiah was very young when called to the ministry[3] we can assume that he was born about the year 645 B.C. or perhaps even a little later. We know that the prophet preached during the reigns of the last five kings of Judah, namely, Josiah, Jehoahaz (Shallum), Jehoiakim, Jehoiachin and Zedekiah and for a considerable time into the Captivity, perhaps until about 575 B.C. His ministry probably extended, therefore, over a period of fifty years and the prophet must have died at about seventy years of age.

How stirring the times in which Jeremiah lived (and sad) is shown by the fact that Jehovah commanded him not to marry.

> Thou shalt not take thee a wife,
> Neither shalt thou have sons or daughters in this place.[4]

The reason given for this command is as follows:

> For thus saith the Lord concerning the sons and concerning the daughters that are born in this place, and concerning their mothers that bore them, and concerning their fathers that begot them in this land:
> They shall die of grievous deaths;
> They shall not be lamented, neither shall they be buried.[5]

Jeremiah's life was, therefore, to be filled with grief and sorrow. His suffering was to be even more poignant because his own brethren and kinsmen in Anathoth opposed him.

> For even thy brethren, and the house of thy father,
> Even they have dealt treacherously with thee,
> Even they have cried aloud after thee;
> Believe them not, though they speak fair words unto thee.[6]

All of this, in addition to the rejection of his message by his countrymen, was to fill the cup of bitterness full to overflowing. Few men outside of the Savior Himself have experienced so many years of abject sorrow or have

---

[3]See Jer. 1:6, 7.
[4]Jer. 16:2.
[5]Jer. 16:3, 4.
[6]Jer. 12:6.

felt the weight of their nation's sin as did he. It is not to
be wondered at that occasionally his soul rebelled at it.
One is reminded of Job when he exclaims:

> I am become a laughing-stock all the day
> Everyone mocketh me.
>
> . . .
>
> Cursed be the day
> Wherein I was born;
> The day wherein my mother bore me.[7]

With the exception of Josiah, all the kings of Judah
during Jeremiah's ministry were unworthy men under
whom the country suffered severely. Idolatry and hill-
worship and heathen religious practices generally were
rampant among the people. There was a carry over of
many of the old Canaanite religious practices of which
we have already said so much. Heathen idols stood in
the temple,[8] children were sacrificed to Baal-Moloch,[9]
and Baal is especially mentioned as the usual heathen
deity. The worship of the "Queen of Heaven" ought also
to be mentioned.[10] The corruption of the nation's religious worship was, of course, accompanied by all manner of immorality and unrighteousness, against which the
prophet had to continually testify.[11] The poor were forgotten.[12] Jeremiah was surrounded on all sides by almost
total apostasy. Professional prophets there were aplenty.

He was surrounded by plenty of prophets, but they were the
smooth, easy-going, popular, professional preachers whose words
awakened no conscience, and who assured the people that the nation
was safe in the protecting care of God. This was a true message in
Isaiah's day, but that time was long since past, and Jerusalem was
destined for captivity. Thus Jeremiah was doomed to preach an
unwelcome message, while the false prophets persuaded the people
that he was unpatriotic, uninspired and pessimistic (14:13, 14).[13]

---

[7]Jer. 20:7, 14.
[8]Jer. 32:34.
[9]Jer. 7:31; 19:5; 32:35.
[10]Jer. 7:18; 44:19.
[11]See Jer. 5:1-5, 7, 8, 26, 27; 6:7, 13; 7:5-9.
[12]Jer. 5:28.
[13]Herbert L. Willett, *The Prophets of Israel*, p. 96.

Jeremiah was a very sensitive and lovable individual. He was a sincere and ardent patriot who loved his nation so much that it wrung his soul to see its destruction on the way. So great was his love that at times he seemed blind to the higher claims of justice and righteousness and the Lord found it necessary to rebuke him.

> Though Moses and Samuel stood before Me, yet My mind could not be toward this people; cast them out of My sight, and let them go forth.[14]

The very human qualities displayed by Jeremiah make us love him, though at times we wonder how he dared speak as he did. Gentle and patient as he was, occasionally the machinations of his enemies caused him to break out in a very storm of fury.

Therefore deliver up their children to the famine,
And hurl them to the power of the sword;
And let their wives be bereaved of their children, and widows;
And let their men be slain of death,
And their young men smitten of the sword in battle.[15]

And as if that were not enough, his wrath at times came up against the Lord because of the persecution he received.

> Wilt Thou indeed be unto me as a deceitful brook,
> As waters that fail?[16]

Jeremiah was a great poet. He knew the human heart to its depths, and possessed a power of remarkably terse and vivid expression.[17]

Characteristics of the Book of Jeremiah. The Book of Jeremiah is rather complex and involved in structure, as is witnessed to by the fact that it is much differently divided by commentators. Perhaps the reasons for this may be seen in the following:

---

[14]Jer. 15:1.
[15]Jer. 18:21.
[16]Jer. 15:18.
[17]John E. McFadyen, *Introduction to the Old Testament* (New Edition, Revised), p. 168. See Jer. 4:23-25; 9:21, 22 as samples of his poetry.

In the fourth year of the reign of Jehoiakim (circa 605), the Lord commanded Jeremiah to write down all of the words previously given him in the hope that Judah would repent of her evil. Jeremiah called his scribe Baruch and dictated all of the words of the Lord. These were written upon one roll. We need not suppose that some of Jeremiah's utterances had not been written down before, the chances are that they were. But there is no assurance that the order of the prophecies as written down by Baruch was the same as before. Furthermore, when Baruch, at Jeremiah's solicitation, read the prophecies to the people of Jerusalem the king heard of them and insisted on a reading. After three or four columns had been read to him he callously took a penknife, cut the manuscript in pieces and committed it to the flames. Jeremiah then re-dictated the words of the Lord and "added besides unto them many like words."[18] How did these prophecies reach the form in which we now have them?[19] The book seems to indicate that if the prophecies were originally written in chronological order that order has been disturbed. There are many knotty problems concerning the text of Jeremiah that we should like to see cleared up. Apparently Jeremiah's prophecies were considerably worked over by later scribes. In the Greek translation (Septuagint) of Jeremiah there are approximately 2700 words less than in our Hebrew text, a clear indication of editorial revision.

At the risk of over-simplification we offer to the student who is reading Jeremiah for the first time the following analysis of the book:

1. Chapter 1. Jeremiah's call.
2. Chapters 2-6. Judah's sins.
3. Chapters 7-10. Judah called to repentance.

---

[18]See Jer. 36.

[19]See I Nephi 5:13. Who was responsible for recording Jeremiah's prophecies upon the Brass Plates? Were they written down before or after Baruch recorded them upon the rolls mentioned in Jer. 36? Answers to these questions would be of great interest to us.

4. Chapters 11-13. An appeal to the covenant between God and His people.

5. Chapters 14-22. The people do not heed Jeremiah; Judah's disaster and captivity foretold.

6. Chapters 23-29. Israel's eventual redemption; Jeremiah sees little present hope for his people; the seventy years of captivity and return; Jeremiah and the false prophets.

7. Chapters 30-33. Israel and Judah to be restored in latter days; Jeremiah buys a field.

8. Chapters 34-45. Incidents during and after the siege and destruction of Jerusalem. (Chapters 35, 36 out of place, belonging to Jehoiachim's reign. Chapter 45 a supplement to Chapter 36:1-8.)

9. Chapters 46-51. Jeremiah's prophecies concerning foreign nations.

10. Chapter 52. An excerpt, mainly from II Kings 24:18-25:30. An account of the capture of Jerusalem.

Jeremiah's Call to the Ministry. The account of Jeremiah's call is especially interesting because it involves a doctrinal principle not mentioned in the call of any other prophet we have studied. The Lord said to the youth:

> Before I formed you in the belly I knew you,
> And before you came forth from the womb, I set you apart;
> I have appointed you a prophet to the nations.[20]

This passage points to the fact that Jeremiah was foreordained before his birth to perform the work of a prophet. God does not leave His work to chance; He sees the qualifications of His servants in advance and calls them to the labors they can best perform.

Jeremiah, a young man, perhaps even a child,[21] was astounded at the Lord's words and replied:

> Ah, Lord Jehovah!
> Behold, I do not know how to speak,
> For I am a boy.[22]

The Lord was not impressed by his answer, and in that fact young people may extract a profound lesson.

---

[20]Jer. 1:5.
[21]The Hebrew word *na'ar* may mean *child, infant, boy or young man.*
[22]Jer. 1:6.

Say not: I am a child;
For to whomsoever I shall send thee thou shalt go,
And whatsoever I shall command thee thou shalt speak.
Be not afraid of them;
For I am with thee to deliver thee,
Saith the Lord.[23]

Jehovah told Jeremiah that He had put him over nations and kingdoms

To root out and to pull down
And to destroy and to overthrow;
To build, and to plant.[24]

Jeremiah was then shown an almond tree and a boiling pot that faced northward. These symbols meant respectively that God would "watch"[25] His word to perform it and that an evil from the north should come to bring judgments upon Judah for its wickedness.[26] And "judgment" is the watchword of Jeremiah's ministry.

Jeremiah's Indictment of Judah. Jeremiah's whole ministry was an indictment of Judah for her sins; not that, indeed, there were no bright spots in his conception of her future. He shows the influence of the prophet Hosea in comparing Judah to a harlotrous wife.

But thou hast played the harlot with many lovers;
And wouldst thou yet return to Me?
Saith the Lord.
Lift up thine eyes unto the high hills, and see:
Where hast thou not been lain with?
By the ways hast thou sat for them,
As an Arabian in the wilderness;
And thou hast polluted the land
With thy harlotries and with thy wickedness.[27]

---

[23]Jer. 1:7, 8; cf. I Nephi 3:7.

[24]Jer. 1:10.

[25]There is a play upon words here. The word for *almond-tree* in Hebrew is *shaked* and that for *watch* is *shoked*. Jer. 1:11, 12.

[26]Jer. 1:13-16. Many scholars have thought the evil was a threatened invasion by the Scythians. This view is now practically abandoned. The writer thinks it more likely that Jeremiah had in mind the Babylonians.

[27]Jer. 3:1, 2.

The spirit of harlotry seems to have permeated Judah as it had her sister kingdom, Israel, over a hundred years before. Consequently, Jeremiah uses the symbols of harlotry in his discussion of Judah's waywardness.

And I saw, when, forasmuch as backsliding Israel had committed adultery, I had put her away and given her a bill of divorcement, that yet treacherous Judah her sister feared not; but she also went and played the harlot; and it came to pass through the lightness of her harlotry, that the land was polluted, and she committed adultery with stones and stocks.[28]

Like the Canaanites before them, the Jews make idols and worship them:

> Hath a nation changed its gods,
> Which yet are no gods?
> But My people hath changed its glory
> For that which doth not profit.
> . . .
> But where are thy gods that thou hast made thee?
> Let them arise, if they can save thee in the time
>   of thy trouble;
> For according to the number of thy cities
> Are thy gods, O Judah.[29]

The priests and rulers who should have known and kept God's law would not:

> The priests said not: 'Where is the Lord?'
> And they that handle the law knew Me not,
> And the rulers transgressed against Me.[30]

Baal worship in all its Canaanite glory went on apace:

> The prophets also prophesied by Baal,
> And walked after things that do not profit.
> . . .
> How canst thou say: 'I am not defiled,
> I have not gone after the Baalim'?[31]

---

[28]Jer. 3:8, 9.
[29]Jer. 2:11, 28.
[30]Jer. 2:8.
[31]Jer. 2:8, 23.

Children are burned in sacrifices contrary to God's word:

And they have built the high places of Topheth, which is in the valley of the son of Hinnom, to burn their sons and their daughters in the fire; which I commanded not, neither came it into My mind.

. . .

And have built the high places of Baal, to burn their sons in the fire for burnt offerings unto Baal.

. . .

And they build the high places of Baal . . . to set apart their sons and their daughters unto Molech.[32]

There is no need to further harrow up our souls with the sins of Judah pointed out by Jeremiah. Apparently human beings couldn't commit much worse sins than those indicated by him. In as forceful terms as he could, the prophet indicted Judah throughout his ministry. Judah had the greatest of vices and the most trivial religious practices. But the central requirements of God, love, mercy, and kindness seemed not to have touched the lives of the most of her people.

Run ye to and fro through the streets of Jerusalem,
And see now, and know,
And seek in the broad places thereof,
If ye can find a man,
If there be any that doeth justly, that seeketh truth;
And I will pardon her.[33]

The Threatened Penalty. Jeremiah, of course, preached in the hopes that his people would repent.[34] But when they didn't, it became necessary to pronounce a penalty. So Jeremiah spoke of a nation that the Lord would bring from far. It would eat up Judah's harvest, her sons and daughters, flocks and herds, vines and fig-trees, and would batter her fortified cities. Taken captive, her people should serve strangers in a land not hers.[35] They should run the

---

[32]Jer. 7:31; 19:5; 32:35.
[33]Jer. 5:1.
[34]Jer. 7:3-7.
[35]Jer. 5:15-19.

gamut of nearly every form of human suffering for their sins.[36] Many should be consumed by the sword, by famine and pestilence.[37] Finally, Jeremiah became specific and predicted that Nebuchadrezzar, the king of Babylon, would come against Judah and make her a desolation and a waste. The people of Judah were to be taken into captivity for seventy years.[38]

Jeremiah Gives a Charge Concerning the Sabbath. It is strange, but true, that the Book of Jeremiah is the first of the prophetic books to give a specific charge to observe the Sabbath day.

> Thus saith the Lord: Take heed for the sake of your souls, and bear no burden on the sabbath day, nor bring it in by the gates of Jerusalem; neither carry forth a burden out of your houses on the sabbath day, neither do ye any work; but hallow ye the sabbath day, as I commanded your fathers.[39]

In connection with this charge, the prophet also looks with favor upon burnt offerings, frankincense, and sacrifice.[40] Jeremiah promised that if the Jews would properly observe the Sabbath, the city of Jerusalem should be inhabited forever. This is a remarkable promise but the Lord seems always to make much of proper Sabbath observance.[41] Probably Jeremiah thought that a people who had ideals high enough to observe properly the Sabbath were not far from the kingdom of God.

The Doctrine of the Potter and the Clay. Many times while in Jerusalem the writer visited a certain potter and watched him make vessels of clay. The workman was very skillful and adroit in turning out vessels of many shapes and sizes. All usually went well until the potter got hold of a batch of clay that wouldn't work as it should. The only recourse, then, was to take the clay off the wheel

---

[36]Jer. 7:33-8:1-3, 9, 10, 15; 9:1.
[37]Jer. 14:12; 16:3-7; 24:8-10.
[38]Jer. 25:1-14.
[39]Jer. 17:21, 22.
[40]Jer. 17:25, 26. This bears out what we said about the prophetic view of sacrifice in Chapter XVIII.
[41]See D&C 59:9-24.

and rework it until it assumed the proper consistency. Then it could be used again in fashioning the desired product.

The Lord had Jeremiah view a potter at work and turned the incident into a remarkable lesson:

> O house of Israel, cannot I do with you as this potter? saith the Lord. Behold, as the clay in the potter's hand, so are ye in My hand, O house of Israel. At one instant I may speak concerning a nation, and concerning a kingdom, to pluck up and to break down and to destroy it; but if that nation turn from their evil, because of which I have spoken against it, I repent of the evil that I thought to do unto it. And at one instant I may speak concerning a nation, and concerning a kingdom, to build and to plant it; but if it do evil in My sight, that it hearkeneth not to My voice, then I repent of the good, wherewith I said I would benefit it.[42]

In addition to the more obvious lessons of this scripture, the reader should note the emphasis laid on man's freedom. The failure of clay to work properly at times as applied in the parable implies, of course, the fact that man has his free agency.

Jeremiah's Teachings Concerning the Restoration of Israel. Like most of the other prophets we have studied, Jeremiah looked into the future and saw the restoration of Israel. He knew that most of his contemporaries were corrupt, nevertheless, God would someday restore to her rightful position the righteous remnant of Israel. This fact must have comforted the agonized prophet through his ministry not a little. Consequently, his message to Judah held out hope for those who would repent:

> Return, O backsliding children, saith the Lord; for I am a Lord unto you, and I will take you one of a city, and two of a family, and I will bring you to Zion; and I will give you shepherds according to My heart, who shall feed you with knowledge and understanding.[43]

Jeremiah also sees a time when all nations shall gather to Jerusalem, and Israel and Judah together shall

---

[42]See Jer. 18:6-10.

[43]Jer. 3:14, 15.

come from the land of the north to inherit Palestine. Jerusalem shall be called the Throne of the Lord.[44]

So wonderful would the gathering of Israel be that the bringing of Israel out* of Egypt should be no more spoken of:

> Therefore, behold, the days come, saith the Lord, that it shall no more be said: 'As the Lord liveth, that brought up the children of Israel out of the land of Egypt,' but: 'As the Lord liveth, that brought up the children of Israel from the land of the north, and from all the countries whither He had driven them;' and I will bring them back into their land that I gave unto their fathers.[45]

In that day a descendant of David should be raised up to be a ruler:

> Behold, the days come, saith the Lord,
> That I will raise unto David a righteous shoot,
> And he shall reign as king and prosper,
> And shall execute justice and righteousness in the land.
> In his days Judah shall be saved,
> And Israel shall dwell safely;
> And this is his name whereby he shall be called;
> The Lord is our righteousness.[46]

In Chapters 30 and 31 Jeremiah gives a beautiful picture of Israel's restoration and goes on to point out that the Lord will make a higher covenant with them at that time. That is, a covenant higher than the Mosaic requirement.

> But this is the covenant that I will make with the house of Israel after those days, saith the Lord, I will put My law in their inward parts, and in their heart will I write it; and I will be their God, and they shall be My people; and they shall teach no more every man his neighbor, and every man his brother, saying: 'Know the Lord'; for they shall all know Me, from the least of them unto the greatest of them, saith the Lord; for I will forgive their iniquity, and their sin will I remember no more.[47]

---

[44]Jer. 3:16-18.
[45]Jer. 16:14, 15.
[46]Jer. 23:5, 6. See Joseph Fielding Smith, *Teachings of the Prophet Joseph Smith*, p. 339. Consult also Jer. 30:9; Ezek. 34:23-24.
[47]Jer. 31:33, 34.

This declaration of Jeremiah is one of the high water marks of his teaching. He knew that the law of Moses was not sufficient to save a man notwithstanding all of its ritual and technical requirements. The prophet did not oppose sacrifice and the ritual requirement of the Mosaic law since it was binding upon the people for the time being. In this respect he was like the other prophets. But he did foresee a day when Israel's remnant should be redeemed and live under the higher law of the gospel. The gospel law is the new covenant Jeremiah speaks of.

The Lord Executes the Penalty on Judah. True to Jeremiah's predictions[48] the king of Babylonia came against Judah and Jerusalem. Jeremiah's constant advice to the cowardly and vacillating king Zedekiah had been to subject himself to Babylon's overlordship until the Lord saw fit to change the situation. Despite every warning of the prophet, Judah rebelled. The nobles relied especially on Egypt, but that did no good. Zedekiah was told by Jeremiah what should happen to him when the Babylonians began the siege of Jerusalem. Even during the long siege he repeatedly gave good advice to him.[49] The king was much impressed by Jeremiah's words and could plainly see they were coming to pass, but his vain and flippant nature, and his concern with the views of his counselors, prevented him from acting upon his convictions. He allowed the prophet to be almost slain by his foes and Jeremiah's sufferings reached a climax during the siege of Jerusalem.[50] Even during a lull in the siege when Jeremiah went home, Judah's military leaders had him arrested as a deserter and put in close confinement for a long period.[51] He finally prevailed upon the king to give him milder imprisonment.[52] But again the prophet's enemies got control of him, and he would have perished quickly if

---

[48]See above.
[49]See Jer. 21:1-10; 34:1-22; 37:1-10, 17-21; 38:14-23.
[50]Jer. 37, 38.
[51]Jer. 37:11-16.
[52]Jer. 37:18-21.

help had not come at once.[53] He was brought back to his former place where he remained until Jerusalem was captured.[54]

When Nebuchadrezzar captured Jerusalem, he broke down its walls, and the houses of the people and the temple he burned. With the exception of the poor, he took the people captive to Babylon. As for king Zedekiah, he took him to Riblah on the Orontes river, slew his sons and nobles before his eyes, and finally blinded the unfortunate ruler. He was then led captive to Babylon in shackles.[55] Thus were literally fulfilled the judgments of God upon His people as declared by Jeremiah.

Jeremiah After the Capture of Jerusalem. Because of Jeremiah's advice to Zedekiah, namely, to be in subjection to Babylon, Nebuchadrezzar spared him when Jerusalem was captured. He was left free to go to Babylon or stay in Judah.[56] He chose the latter because the trustworthy Gedaliah, who had been appointed governor over Judah, was a good man for the Jewish people left in the land to rally around. Unfortunately, however, Gedaliah was assassinated.[57]

Jeremiah was then forced by frightened remnants of the people to accompany them to Egypt. There they went against the advice of the Lord given to Jeremiah.[58] Thus, even toward the end of his life, the prophet met constant and unremitting persecution and trial. But through all of these difficulties Jeremiah still remained God's mouthpiece.[59] There is a tradition to the effect that he died in Egypt, being stoned to death at Daphne.

Thus passed one of the great men of the earth, whose records and prophecies are among the imperishable legacies of our generation.

---

[53]Jer. 38:1-13.
[54]Jer. 38:28.
[55]Jer. 39:5-10. See also II Kings 25:1-21.
[56]Jer. 39:11-14; 40:1-6.
[57]Jer. 41:2.
[58]Jer. 42:1-43:7.
[59]Jer. 43:8-13; 44.

Chapter XXII

SOME LASTING CONTRIBUTIONS OF THE OLD TESTAMENT TO MANKIND

The Contribution of Hebrew Culture to the Western World. Before dealing with some specific contributions of the Old Testament to mankind, let us consider for a moment the general contribution of Hebrew culture to the West. Historically, our civilization rests back upon three great ancient civilizations, the Hebrew, the Greek and the Roman. From the Greeks we inherited science, philosophy, art, literature and many other things that we should be infinitely the poorer without. From the Romans we inherited much of law and the science of government, literature, and a language whose roots underly many of our Western tongues. But it is to the Hebrews that we owe so much in the realm of religion, and it is thought by many that their contribution is the greatest of the three. Not only did they contribute the magnificent volume of religious literature known to us as the Old Testament—incidentally one of the greatest single contributions from the ancient world—but they contributed Christianity and the New Testament, not to mention Judaism. The earliest Christians were Jews, and they came into the Church with a good knowledge of the Hebrew scriptures. The latter had a profound influence upon the writings that later formed the New Testament. It goes without saying that Christianity, Judaism, and the Old and New Testaments have had an enormous and far-reaching effect upon civilization.

The Old Testament Contribution to the Idea of God. One of the outstanding contributions of the Old Testament to mankind is the conception of the one true God to whom should go man's undivided allegiance. The pagan nations round about Israel had many gods and these they played off, one against another. Not so in Israel. The God of Abraham, Isaac and Jacob alone could answer prayers and grant men their needs. There was no conflict between the will of God and the will of other supernatural beings. One supreme law and one standard of righteousness determined for the man of Israel his course of action.

Not only that, but the Hebrew God taught men to strive for higher ideals of righteousness, even holiness.

> You must be holy; for I, the Lord
> Your God, am holy.[1]

The Hebrew people, instead of attributing vices and human weaknesses to many gods as did their pagan neighbors, had the training and advantage of ascribing all great qualities to the one true God. This developed within them great spiritual insight. They, as few other people, realized that God with all His marvelous attributes demanded similar personal qualities in those who worshiped Him.

It will be well to call attention to the fact that the Fatherhood and love of God is distinctly taught in the Old Testament; it belongs not alone to the New Testament. Hosea,[2] Jonah, Isaiah,[3] the Psalmist[4] and many others make us distinctly aware of that fact. Along with this teaching, the Hebrews never lost sight of God's majesty and glory. This produced in them a sense of awe and reverence. Furthermore, to them He was a God of redemption. This was constantly borne home to them from the day He redeemed them from slavery and bondage in Egypt.

Israel's idea of God developed a great conception of man and the seriousness of sin. When men sinned, they

---

[1]Lev. 19:2.
[2]Hos. 11:1.
[3]Isa. 64:8.
[4]Ps. 103:13.

were not only offending God, but were warping and breaking down the elements of godliness in themselves.

Finally, we may point out that to Israel God was not just a shadow or a figment of the imagination, but a sure and everlasting reality whose power and influence were abundantly manifested in the crucible of living experience.

The Contribution of the Old Testament to the New Testament. Some people have advocated the elimination of the Old Testament from religious teaching. We fear, however, that they know not what they do. In the first place, purely as literature, the Old Testament is highly superior to the New Testament, and secondly, the great essentials of true religion are to be found in it beautifully expressed. Furthermore, much of the New Testament is unintelligible without an understanding of the Old Testament. The very nerve-threads of Christian life in the first century of our Era lead back into the Old Testament. There is much in the idiom of the New Testament that strongly reflects the Aramaic and Hebrew idiom of the Jewish authors. The great use of the Old Testament by New Testament writers is a fact well known to Bible scholars. The scriptures (the Old Testament) were carefully searched by early Christians for proof texts illustrative of their claims. The Gospel of Matthew, for instance, quotes liberally from the Old Testament, and its aim is to show that the Christ is the true Messiah foreshadowed by the prophets of the Hebrew scriptures. In the two first chapters of the Gospel of Luke we are undeniably in an Old Testament atmosphere. Many other places in the Gospels give the same impression. In the Book of Revelation the Old Testament literary forms and religious conceptions are apparent throughout. The influence of the Old Testament upon Paul's epistles is of course widely acknowledged. Dr. Thackeray has truly said:

> There is perhaps no aspect of the Pauline theology in which the influence of the Apostle's Rabbinic training is so clearly marked as the

use which is made of the Old Testament. It appears at first sight paradoxical that whereas the Law is constantly spoken of as done away in Christ and as powerless to produce man's salvation, yet the Apostle as constantly bases his arguments for the truth of Christianity on the Law in the wider sense of the term. The Epistle which may be regarded as summing up the main ideas of St. Paul begins and ends with a reference to the "holy" and "prophetical" writings which foretold the coming of Christ (cf. Rom. 1:2; 16:26). The proof for his arguments is sought again and again in the Old Testament. He never for a moment thought of disparaging the Scriptures to which the Jew appealed, on the contrary he recognized that the chief privilege of his nation was the possession of the oracles of God; but he maintained that these oracles had been misinterpreted. . . . He met the Jew on his own ground and bade him search the Scriptures in the light of the coming of Christ.[5]

This should emphasize the fact that the Old Testament is a book of supreme importance to us and instead of being read less should be read more.

The New Testament makes two hundred and eighty-three quotations from the Old Testament. These statistics reinforce the view that the connection between "the Old Testament and the New is of a vital and organic character. They stand in a single line of development."[6]

The Old Testament Contribution to Worship. It is not generally realized how deeply indebted our civilization is to Hebrew methods of worship. The history of the Jewish synagogue would be intensely interesting if we knew the details of its centuries of pre-Christian development. At any rate, early Christianity fell heir to the methods of Jewish worship and with perhaps slight modifications adopted and used them. We use them in great measure today, though usually unconscious of our debt.

When the apostles of Christ and other early Christian missionaries went into the Mediterranean world to preach, they found Jewish synagogues in most of the principal cities and in many of the lesser ones. Into these they

---

[5]St. John Thackeray, *The Relation of St. Paul to Contemporary Jewish Thought*, pp. 180 f. Quoted in *The People and The Book* (Edited by A. S. Peake), pp. 462 f.
[6]*Ibid.* (Peake), p. 465.

entered and often found opportunities to preach. The privilege of preaching or expounding a message can be appreciated better if we understand the worship of other peoples. Note the following by a British scholar, Professor H. H. Rowley:

> I shall never forget the impression made upon me when I first stood in a pagan shrine in China. Within a large courtyard I found some tiny shrines, no larger than the rooms of an ordinary house, and each of these was more than half-filled with the table on which stood the idols. I realized, as I had never realized from anything I had read, that anything like worship in our sense of the word was impossible, and that worshippers must come singly to place their incense before the gods, do their obeisance, and leave their coin. On feast days, when numbers attended the shrine, there might be fellowship in the courtyard, but there could be none in the act of worship. I had been before into Mohammedan mosques, where the differences from our churches are less striking. But Islam is in some measure the heir of Judaism, and for her form of worship she, no less than Christianity, owes a debt to the Jews. For it was Judaism that created the form of worship which, in differing ways, has been adopted and adapted in Christianity and in Islam.[7]

Nor should we forget that Hebrew worship developed as it did mainly because it provided the people with an opportunity to gather together where they could be instructed in their scriptures and the holy faith that it represented. Psalms were sung and a place was provided where a preacher could instruct and edify the people. Professor Rowley also writes: "And if Judaism had given us nothing but the Psalter, our debt would still have been inexpressibly great. But she contributed much more than that to our worship."[8]

The Old Testament Contribution to Law. Hebrew law as reflected in the Old Testament has had tremendous influence upon our civilization. In the past seventy years, thanks to archaeological discoveries and linguistic studies, we have obtained a fairly clear picture of the laws of Israel's neighbors, the Assyrians, Babylonians, and Hittites.

---

[7]H. H. Rowley, *Israel's Mission to the World*, p. 122.
[8]*Ibid.*

And it must be admitted in the light of these studies that Old Testament laws were generally much superior in spiritual and moral content.[9] In the Mosaic era there was, to be sure, much of the spirit of an eye for an eye and a tooth for a tooth, but that is as far as retaliation could go. There could not be two eyes for an eye or two teeth for a tooth. Among the prophets the law relative to social justice, honesty, regard for the poor, and other important matters was on an exceedingly high plane and leaves little to be asked. But even if we consider only the contribution of the Decalogue to mankind what a magnificent thing it is! And what an incomparably better world we would be living in today if only it were reasonably lived up to. But the voice from Sinai has steadily thundered down the centuries and holds true today as then:

> Thou shalt have no other gods before me.
> Thou shalt not make unto thee any graven image.
> Thou shalt not take the name of the Lord thy God in vain.
> Remember the sabbath day, to keep it holy.
> Honor thy father and thy mother.
> Thou shalt not kill.
> Thou shalt not commit adultery.
> Thou shalt not steal.
> Thou shalt not bear false witness against thy neighbor.
> Thou shalt not covet.

These laws would seem to be the very minimum necessary in a civilized society and the Old Testament supplied them in clear-cut language.

Then in the matter of sexual morality the Old Testament has made and still makes a great contribution to society. In making this statement we refer to the idealistic side of the Old Testament, Israel at its best. Neither should we forget the high standards of the prophets in the matter of divorce.

> Take heed to your spirit, and let none deal treacherously against the wife of his youth. For I hate putting away saith the Lord.[10]

---

[9]See J. M. P. Smith, *The Origin and History of Hebrew Law*, p. 279.
[10]Mal. 2:15, 16.

In these two matters the world has yet a long way to go before it reaches the Old Testament ideal.

The Contribution of the Old Testament to Education. With the contribution of the Old Testament to education there must of course be reckoned that of the New Testament. The two go together. The influence of these books is well nigh incalculable and it is possible only to tell of it here in general terms.

The history of England is replete with examples of the influence of the Bible on education. Think of the Venerable Bede with his knowledge of Latin, Hebrew and Greek, all so useful in his Bible studies. The Bible was the main inspiration of his scholarship. And think also of Alcuin (circa 600 A.D.) who was saturated with Bible knowledge.

> The name Alcuin might well be inscribed over the doorway of every free school, every private school, every college and every university, yes, and every Sunday-school, too, of the entire English-speaking race, for he it was that started the movement that eventually led to their existence.[11]

Alcuin's influence extended even into France.

We may also mention Caedmon and King Alfred who did so much for early English education by spreading abroad their knowledge of the Bible.

The great universities, Oxford and Cambridge, started as Bible schools.[12] From these universities there came many other universities whose inspiration was the same book.

In America eight great and well-known universities were founded very early as a result of prayer over the Bible and for Bible continuance. They are Harvard, William and Mary, Yale, Princeton, Washington and Lee, Pennsylvania, Rutgers, and Dartmouth.[13]

---

[11]James G. K. McClure, *The Supreme Book of Mankind*, p. 90.

[12]*Ibid.*, p. 95.

[13]*Ibid.*, p. 102.

The famous old New England Primer for one hundred and fifty years or more had a tremendous effect on early American education. It had a sale of 3,000,000 copies, notwithstanding the sparse population. And it was essentially a Bible primer.[14]

It is a fact that Bible-trained men planted colleges in the developing West and that the Bible school paved the way for public education in America.

Nor is it necessary to point out in detail the enormous effect the Old and New Testaments had on European education before and after the Reformation. Education centered in Bible studies and the student of art, music and literature is usually well aware of that fact. Such studies led to the freedom of speech and action that many of us still enjoy and the right to worship God according to the dictates of our own conscience. Let it never be forgotten that modern democracy owes a vast debt of gratitude to Bible studies and translations made by such men as Wyclif, Luther, Tyndale, Calvin, and many others. The common man as never before seized on and made use of the truth he was able to read in a Bible printed in his own language.

The greatest music, the greatest literature, and the greatest art that we enjoy today rests back on the marvelous religious influence exerted by the Old and New Testaments upon the hearts and minds of great geniuses.

Let us hope that the great heritage left us by the Old Testament and its companion volume will never be forgotten and that they will continue to inspire us in our attempts to make a better world in which to live.

---

[14]See P. Marion Simms, *The Bible in America*, pp. 43 f.

Chapter XXIII

SOME LATTER-DAY SAINT VIEWS
CONCERNING THE BIBLE

The Latter-day Saints are great believers in the Bible
but they have never viewed it as the inerrant word of God,
completely true (in its present form) from cover to cover.
Indeed, in the early history of the Church, the Mormon
Prophet, Joseph Smith, wrote as follows: "We believe the
Bible to be the word of God as far as it is translated correctly."[1] These words seem to be a clear enough statement
of belief, but in reality they need some explanation. There
are a number of passages in the Bible that are correctly
translated from the texts that have been handed down to us
that Latter-day Saints do not believe. It is a well-known fact
that certain passages of the Bible contradict each other in a
number of places. None of us denies that these passages are
correctly translated. Yet who would presume to assert that
all of them are correct *in fact?* Our point can be made clear
by reference to a revelation given by the Lord through
Joseph Smith in the year 1833. The revelation refers to the
Apocrypha in the following language: "Verily, thus saith
the Lord unto you concerning the Apocrypha—There are
many things contained therein that are true, and it is mostly
translated correctly; there are many things contained
therein that are not true, which are interpolations by the
hands of men."[2] It will be noticed that in spite of the fact
that the Apocrypha is "mostly translated correctly," it contains many things "that are not true." What is true of the
Apocrypha is in a measure true of the Bible. Nor need we
suppose that Joseph Smith was not aware of this fact. Between the years 1830 and 1833 the Prophet, at the Lord's

---

[1]See *The Articles of Faith of the Church of Jesus Christ of Latter-day Saints,*
Article 8.
[2]D&C 91:1, 2.

command, made a revision of the Bible (Authorized Version) by the spirit of revelation. In many parts of it he made profound changes. The reader is invited to examine such passages as Gen. 1 (first portion); 50; Isa. 29; Matt. 4, etc.[3] Many of the changes made go far beyond anything we understand at this day by a "correct" translation. What, then, did Joseph Smith mean when he said, "We believe the Bible to be the word of God as far as it is translated correctly"? Let him give his own answer. "I believe the Bible as it read when it came from the pen of the original writers. Ignorant translators, careless transcribers, or designing and corrupt priests have committed many errors. As it read, Gen. VI. 6, 'It repented the Lord that he had made man on the earth;' also, Num. XXII. 19, 'God is not a man, that he should lie; neither the Son of man, that he should repent;' which I do not believe. But it ought to read, 'It repented *Noah* that God made man.' This I believe, and then the other quotation stands fair."[4] It is plain that the Prophet's use of "translation" in the 8th Article of Faith is much broader than one may at first suppose.

Oliver Cowdery who was closely associated with Joseph Smith at the time the Church was first organized, pointed out that the scriptures were given through men and subject to men's limitations. "When looking over the sacred scriptures we seem to forget they were given through men of imperfections and subject to passion."[5]

President Brigham Young during his long ministry said much about the Bible that reflects the views of the Church in his day about it. The great colonizer had come under the influence and tutelage of Joseph Smith in the so-called School of the Prophets in Kirtland, Ohio. In this school, the great Mormon Prophet impressed upon the body of men who were to become future leaders of the Church the necessity and importance of a knowledge of ancient

---

[3]See *Holy Scriptures* as published by the Reorganized Church of Jesus Christ of Latter-day Saints.

[4]DHC, 6:57.

[5]*Times and Seasons*, 2:212.

Biblical languages. In his journal history for December 22, 1835, Joseph Smith wrote as follows: "At home. Continued my studies. O may God give me learning, even language; and endue me with qualifications to magnify His name while I live." The next day he wrote, "In the forenoon, at home, studying the Greek language." It is well known that the Prophet, along with his brethren, studied Hebrew under the direction of Prof. Joshua Seixas who was engaged from the Hudson seminary for that purpose.[6] So enthused did the Prophet become over his studies that he wrote in his journal for Feb. 17, 1836, the following: "Attended the school and read and translated with my class as usual. My soul delights in reading the word of the Lord in the original, and I am determined to pursue the study of the languages, until I shall become master of them, if I am permitted to live long enough. At any rate, so long as I do live, I am determined to make this my object; and with the blessing of God, I shall succeed to my satisfaction."[7]

It is not surprising, therefore, to find Brigham Young, years later, when he was president of the Church, saying, "Take the Bible just as it reads; and if it be translated incorrectly and there is a scholar on the earth who professes to be a Christian, and he can translate it any better than King James' translators did it, he is under obligation to do so. If I understood Greek and Hebrew as some may profess to do, and I knew the Bible was not correctly translated, I should feel myself bound by the law of justice to the inhabitants of the earth to translate that which is incorrect and give it just as it was spoken anciently. Is that proper? Yes, I would be under obligation to do it. But I think it is translated just as correctly as the scholars could get it, although it is not correct in a great many instances. But it is no matter about that. Read it and observe it and it will not hurt any person in the world."[8]

---

[6]See DHC, 2:356-368, 376.

[7]*Ibid.*, 396.

[8]*Jour. Dis.*, 14:226.

On still another occasion President Young said, "I have heard ministers of the Gospel declare that they believed every word in the Bible was the word of God. I have said to them, 'You believe more than I do.' I believe the words of God are there; I believe the words of the Devil are there; I believe that the words of men and the words of angels are there; and that is not all, —I believe that the words of a dumb brute are there. I recollect one of the prophets riding, and prophesying against Israel, and the animal he rode rebuked his madness."[9]

Apparently following in part the lead of Brigham Young, Elder George Reynolds, a prominent writer and leader in the Church, wrote his views of the Bible in the following words, "There are in the Bible the words of God, the words of Angels, of men and of the devil. Some parts of the Bible are simply history written from the writer's standpoint and according to his knowledge. Then again all servants of the Lord were not equally inspired at all times and on all occasions, consequently we have in the sacred scriptures revelations which the Lord dictated word by word, revelations, equally binding, in which the will of the Lord is directly expressed, but clothed in the language of the prophet, who was for the occasion, His mouthpiece; and again, we have the divine word given under some general law of Heaven in which not only the words but the argument was that of the speaker, but the word of the Lord nevertheless."[10]

President George Q. Cannon, speaking on the same subject, said, "A certain amount of reverence for it is good. It is good to read here of the holy and good. It is good to have confidence in goodness, in holiness, in good and pure men. But if we were to place all our confidence in this book, we should put something between us and that God, the light of whose wisdom illuminates its pages and gives it all its worth. To do this is to worship the book. I call it

---

[9]*Ibid.*, 12:280.
[10]*Mill. Star*, 64:181.

idolatry. . . . I would as soon worship Peter, or the Virgin
Mary, or any other mortal, as to worship a book. . . . It is
through the substitution of the book for God that confusion
prevails through the religious world."[11]

President Charles W. Penrose gave an interesting view
of the translators of the King James Version. Incidentally,
he gave us an insight into his views concerning how free
the Bible is from error. "It is not claimed that the men who
translated the Old and New Testaments, in the time of King
James, were inspired of God. They were learned men, experienced men, educated men, and no doubt they did the
best they could, and gave to the work committed to them
the benefit of their erudition, their experience, and their
research. . . . When you say that *all* scripture is given by
inspiration of God, you say something that is not true."[12]

The citations given above clearly reveal the fact that
the Mormon Church leaders have never viewed the Bible
as being completely correct, word for word. But it must
not be supposed that because they did not believe everything written in it that they handled it loosely and care-
lessly. To the contrary. They knew that the gospel could
not be well understood without a knowledge of the Bible.
They clearly understood the extreme value of the Old Testament as well as the New Testament in the study of the
plan of salvation. In accordance with this statement we
find President Brigham Young saying, "By reading the Bible
we find that the Gospel is contained not only in the New
Testament, but also in the Old. Moses and the Prophets
saw and predicted the apostasy of the Church. They saw
that the Lord would strive with the children of men from
time to time, that he would deliver to them the truth and
the Priesthood; they also saw that through the wickedness
of the people they would change his ordinances, break the
covenants, and transgress his laws, until the Priesthood
would be taken from the earth, and its inhabitants be left

---

[11]*Ibid.,* 23:513.
[12]*Ibid.,* 55:544.

in apostasy and darkness."[13] On another occasion, in speaking of the Bible, Brigham Young said, "I say we take this book for our guide, for our rule of action; we take it as the foundation of our faith. It points the way to salvation like a fingerboard pointing to a city, or a map which designates the locality of mountains, rivers, or the latitude and longitude of any place on the surface of the earth that we desire to find, and we have no better sense than to believe it; hence, I say that the Latter-day Saints have the most natural faith and belief of any people on the face of the Earth."[14] Again, "I ask you, brother B, how I must believe the Bible, and how shall you and every other follower of the Lord Jesus Christ believe it? 'Brother Mormon, how do you believe it?' I believe it just as it is. I do not believe in putting any man's interpretation upon it, whatever, unless it should be directed by the Lord himself in some way. I do not believe we need interpreters and expounders of the Scriptures, to wrest them from their literal, plain, simple meaning."[15]

It may be of some interest to notice the views of certain Church authorities on problems in the Bible that have engaged the attention of many laymen and scholars alike. President Charles W. Penrose handled the famous problem of the Pentateuch as follows: "There is a great dispute as to whether Moses wrote the Pentateuch—the "five books of Moses," as they are called. What is the reason of so much contention? We say, in the first place, that Moses wrote the books. How do we know? Because the Lord has said so. He has said that He inspired Moses to write these books. But years after the time of Moses—in the time of Ezra—these books were revised; and there may have been other revisions; and the books as they have been handed down to us are not just as they were originally written. For instance . . . [Deut. 34:5-6 is quoted] Do you think

---

[13]*Jour. Dis.*, 16:74.
[14]*Ibid.*, 13:236.
[15]*Ibid.*, 1:237.

God revealed that? I am satisfied He did not. The person who revised these books added that by way of explanation."[16] It is seen that President Penrose accounted for the difficulties involved in the problem on the hypothesis that revisions and changes in the process of transmission altered the original text.

President Brigham Young dealt with the Creation and the Antediluvian world in the following words: "There are a great many people in the world who are so wise in their own eyes that they are not disposed to believe the account contained in the Bible of the Creation of Adam and Eve in the Garden of Eden, the antediluvian world and other things; but we profess to believe, and we do or should believe these things."[17] Many scholars have viewed the early accounts in Genesis as mere folklore of the Hebrew people.

Orson Pratt commented on systems of chronology as follows: "In this Alexandrian era, the time from the creation to the birth of Christ is set down as 5,500. Father Pezron makes it 5,873 years . . . Then you take the one who has given the chronology to the Bible, Archbishop Usher, and he makes it 4,004 years from the creation to Christ . . . We are no more sure that Archbishop Usher's chronology is correct, than we are to suppose that many of those others are correct."[18]

Modern scholarship often attributes the authorship of few, if any, of the Psalms to David. Orson Pratt taught otherwise. He said, "These Psalms were written by the Inspiration of the Holy Ghost, and most of them were prophetic in their nature. David was a man especially inspired of the Lord . . . to utter forth many predictions in the form of Psalms to be sung in the congregations of Israel."[19]

The Mormon Church leaders have consistently preached and written about the predictive elements in the

[16]*Mill. Star*, 55:558 f.
[17]*Jour. Dis.*, 13:313 f.
[18]*Ibid.*, 16:324.
[19]*Ibid.*, 14:138.

Bible. The two following citations may be regarded as typical. President Anthon H. Lund said, "The book [Bible] itself proves to us that it is genuine. Its own prophecies, fulfilled since it was written, prove to us that it is a book containing the word of God. Look at Daniel's prophecy. In what a nutshell is the history of the future portrayed there? We could not any better describe it to-day, after we have followed history down for more than two thousand years. Daniel's prophecies are like history written beforehand, showing that they were inspired."[20]

President Wilford Woodruff said, "I testify . . . that God has set His hand to fulfil the word of the Lord as given in the Bible . . . the revelations of St. John, the predictions of Isaiah, Ezekiel, Jeremiah, Joel, Micah, and others . . . who spoke of the great work of the last days; and I testify that the day has come which Daniel saw, the day referred to by him in his interpretation of Nebuchadnezzar's dream, when the God of heaven would set up a kingdom which should never be destroyed."[21] Those who are well acquainted with current scholarly views of the Bible will recognize at once how far the above sentiments differ from them.

The following quotation from the pen of the late Brigham H. Roberts probably voices as well as any the general sentiments of the Church leaders concerning the "Higher" criticism of the Bible: "You recognize, do you not, that the methods of higher criticism are legitimate, that is to say, it is right to consider the various books of the scriptures, the Old Testament and the New, as a body of literature, and to examine them internally, and go into the circumstances under which they were written, and the time at which they were written, and the purpose for which they were written? All that we recognize as legitimate, though I must say, in passing, that when one enters into the details of these methods, it is rather astonishing, at

---

[20]Mill. Star, 62:50.
[21]Ibid., 51:788.

least it is to me, to see what heavy weights are hung upon very slender threads. The method, then, of higher criticism we recognize as proper; but we must disagree as to the correctness of many of the conclusions arrived at by that method."[22]

The general views on the Bible as quoted above probably represent quite fairly those held in the Church today. If they do not altogether comport with the generally accepted ones in the field of biblical scholarship, it must be remembered that The Church of Jesus Christ of Latter-day Saints has an exceptional message to proclaim to the world. The revelations of the Lord to the Church demand a somewhat distinctive approach to the Bible. It was part of our purpose in this book to portray that approach so far as it affects the Old Testament.

---

[22]*Improvement Era*, 14:667.

BIBLIOGRAPHY

Albright, W. F., *Archaeology and the Religion of Israel* (2nd ed., John Hopkins Press, 1946).

Albright, W. F., *From the Stone Age to Christianity* (New York: Doubleday Anchor Book, 1957).

Albright, W. F., *The Biblical Period from Abraham to Ezra* (Harper Torchbook, 1963).

Albright, W. F., *Yahweh and the Gods of Canaan* (Athlone Press. London, 1968).

Anderson, B. W., *Understanding the Old Testament* (Prentice-Hall, 1957).

Anderson, G. W., *A Critical Introduction to the Old Testament* (Duckworth, 1959).

Andrus, H. L., *Doctrinal Commentary on the Pearl of Great Price* (Deseret Book, 1967).

Baly, Denis, *The Geography of the Bible* (Lutterworth, 1957).

Bentzen, Aage, *Introduction to the Old Testament*, I and II (2nd ed., Gad Copenhagen, 1952).

Bentwich, Norman, *Josephus* (Phila. Jewish Publication Society of America, 1914).

Berrett, W. E., *Teachings of the Book of Mormon* (Deseret Book Co., 1962).

Burrows, Millar, *The Dead Sea Scrolls* (Viking Press, 1955).

Burrows, Millar, *More Light on the Dead Sea Scrolls* (Viking Press, 1958).

Bright, John, *Early Israel in Recent History Writing* (SCM Press, 1956).

Bright, John, *A History of Israel* (Westminster, 1959).

Brockington, L. H. *A Critical Introduction to the Apocrypha* (Duckworth and Co., London, 1961).

Bruce, F. F., *Second Thoughts on the Dead Sea Scrolls* (2nd ed., Eerdmans, 1961. 1st ed., 1956).

Bruce, F. F., *The English Bible:* A history of translations. (Oxford Univ. Press, 1961).

Cameron, Duncan, *Songs of Sorrow and Praise.* Studies in the Hebrew Psalter. (T. and T. Clark, 1924).

Cansdale, G. S., *Animals of Bible Lands.* To be published in Spring, 1970. Should be good. (Obtain through James Thin Co., Edinburgh).

Charles, R. H., *The Apocrypha and Pseudepigrapha of the Old Testament* (2 vols. Oxford: Clarendon Press, 1913).

Cheyne, T. K., *The Prophecies of Isaiah* (2 vols. C. Kegan Paul and Co., 1880).

Clark, Pres. J. Reuben, Jr., *Why The King James Version* (Deseret Book, 1956).

Clark, James R., *The Story of the Pearl of Great Price* (Bookcraft, 1955).

Contenau, Georges, *Everyday Life in Babylon and Assyria* (Edward Arnold Publishers, 1954).

Cross, F. M., Jr., *The Ancient Library of Qumran and Modern Biblical Studies* (Rev. ed., Doubleday, 1961).

Dalman, Gustaf, *Jesus-Jeshua* (tr. Levertoff. Macmillan, 1929).

Dana, H. E., *New Testament Criticism* (2nd ed., Fort Worth: The World Co., 1924).

Dana, H. E., *The New Testament World* (2nd ed., rev., Forth Worth: Pioneer Pub. Co., 1928).

Daniel - Rops, *Israel and the Ancient World* (tr. K. Madge. Eyre and Spottiswoode, 1949. Reprints in 1957 and 1960).

Danker, F. W., *Multipurpose Tools for Bible Study* (St. Louis: Concordia Pub. House, 1960. Very useful to teachers).

Davidson, A. B., *An Introductory Hebrew Grammar* (Rev. by J. E. McFayden, 22nd ed., Edinburgh: T. and T. Clark, 1923).

Davidson, A. B., *The Theology of the Old Testament* (Scribners, 1904).

De Vaux, Roland, *Ancient Israel: Its Life and Institutions* (McGraw-Hill, 1962).

Dobschutz, Ernst von, *The Influence of the Bible on Civilization* (New York, 1914).

Doxey, Roy W., *The Latter-day Prophets and the Doctrine and Covenants* (4 vols. Deseret Book, 1963-64).

Driver, G. R., *The Judaean Scrolls* (New York: Schocken Books, 1966).

Driver, S. R., *An Introduction to the Literature of the Old Testament* (New ed., rev. 1913. Scribners, 1923).

Duncan, J. G., *The Accuracy of the Old Testament* (London: S.P.C.K., 1930).

Eichrodt, Walther, *Theology of the Old Testament*, Vol. I (Westminster, 1961).

Elliott, M. E., *The Language of the King James Bible*. A glossary explaining its words and expressions (Doubleday, 1967).

Ellis, E. E., *Paul's Use of the Old Testament* (Oliver and Boyd, Edinburgh, 1957).

Encyclopedia Britannica (14th ed., London, 1929).

Finegan, Jack, *Light from the Ancient Past*, 2nd ed., (Princeton Univ. Press, 1960).

Foakes - Jackson, *Josephus and the Jews* (New York: Harper, 1930).

Frankfort, Henri, *Ancient Egyptian Religion* (Harper Torchbook, 1961).

Gaster, T. H., *The Dead Sea Scriptures in English Translation* (Doubleday, 1957, 1964).

Goodspeed, E. J., *The Story of the Apocrypha* (Univ. of Chicago Press, 1939).

Gordon, A. R., *The Faith of Isaiah* (London: James Clark and Co., No date).

Grant, F. C., *Translating the Bible* (Seabury Press, 1961).

Green, W. H., *General Introduction to the Old Testament. The Canon.* (New York: Charles Scribner's Sons, 1899).

Grollenberg, L. H., *Atlas of the Bible* (Nelson, 1957). Available in abridged edition.

Guillaume, Alfred, *Prophecy and Divination* (Harper, 1938).

Hahn, H. F., *The Old Testament in Modern Research* (Fortress Press, 1966).

Harrison, R. K., *A History of Old Testament Times* (Zondervan, 1957).

Harrison, R. K., *Introduction to the Old Testament.* To be published in Jan., 1970. Should be very useful. (Obtain through James Thin Co., Edinburgh).

Heaton, E. W., *Everyday Life in Old Testament Times* (B. T. Batsford, 1956).

History of the Church of Jesus Christ of Latter-day Saints (6 vols. Deseret Book, B. H. Roberts, editor. Editions and vols. of various dates).

Holy Bible. The King James Version and many modern translations available.

Hunter, Milton R., *Pearl of Great Price Commentary* (Bookcraft, 1951).

Jacob, Edmund, *Theology of the Old Testament* (Harper, 1958).

Kaufmann, Yehezkel, *The Religion of Israel,* Trs. and abridged by Moshe Greenberg (Allen and Unwin, Ltd., 1961).

Keil, C. F. and Delitzsch, F., *Biblical Commentary on the Old Testament* (2 vols. The Twelve Minor Prophets. Tr. Martin. T. and T. Clark, 1889).

Kent, C. F., *The Origin and Permanent Value of the Old Testament* (New York: Charles Scribner's Sons, 1912).

Kenyon, Kathleen M., *Archaeology in the Holy Land* (Praeger Paperback, 1960).

Kirkham, F. W., *A New Witness for Christ in America* (3rd ed., enlarged. Independence: Zion's Printing Co., 1951).

Kittel, R., *Great Men and Movements in Israel* (KTAV, 1968).

Köhler, Ludwig, *Old Testament Theology* (Lutterworth, 1957).

Lods, A., *Israel* (tr. S. H. Hooke, New York: Alfred A. Knopf, 1932).

Macdonald, D. B., *The Hebrew Literary Genius* (Princeton Univ. Press, 1935).

Macdonald, D. B., *The Hebrew Philosophical Genius* (Princeton Univ. Press, 1936. Reissued, 1965, by Russell and Russell, Inc., New York).

Malden, R. H., *The Apocrypha* (Oxford Press, 1936).

Maly, E. H., *The World of David and Solomon* (Prentice-Hall, 1966).

Mansoor, M., *The Dead Sea Scrolls*. Textbook and Study Guide (Eerdmans, 1964).

Matthews, R. J., *Joseph Smith's Revision of the Bible* (Provo: BYU Press, 1969).

May, Herbert J., ed., *Oxford Bible Atlas* (Oxford Univ. Press, 1962).

McClure, J. G. K., *The Supreme Book of Mankind* (Scribners, 1930).

McFayden, J. E., *A Cry for Justice* (Scribners, 1912).

McFayden, J. E., *Introduction to the Old Testament* (New Edition, revised. London: Hodder and Stoughton Ltd., 1932).

McKenzie, J. L., *The Two-Edged Sword* (Bruce, 1956).

McKenzie, J. L., *The World of the Judges* (Prentice-Hall, 1966).

Meek, T. J., *Hebrew Origins* (New York, 1936. Revised ed., Harper, 1950).

Mercer, S. A. B., *Extra-Biblical Sources for Hebrew and Jewish History* (Longman's, Green, and Co., 1913).

Metzger, B., *An Introduction to the Apocrypha* (Oxford Univ. Press, 1957).

Milik, J. T., *Ten Years of Discovery in the Wilderness of Judaea* (Naperville: A. R. Allenson, 1959).

Miller, M. S. and J. L., *Encyclopedia of Bible Life* (Harper, 1944).

Miller, M. S. and J. L., *Harpers Bible Dictionary* (7th ed., 1961).

Moore, G. F., *Judaism* (3 vols. Cambridge: Harvard Univ. Press, 1927-30).

Moriarty, F. L., *Foreword to the Old Testament Books* (Weston College Press, 1954).

Moriarty, F. L., *Introducing the Old Testament* (Bruce Pub. Co., 1960).

Moulton, R. G., *The Literary Study of the Bible.* (Rev. and partly rewritten. Boston: D. C. Heath and Co., 1899).

Murphy, R. E., *Seven Books of Wisdom* (Bruce Pub. Co., 1960).

National Geographic Society, *Everyday Life in Bible Times* (By many specialists. A sumptuous volume, magnificently illustrated. Washington, D. C., 1967).

Nibley, Hugh, *An Approach to the Book of Mormon* (Deseret News Press, 1957).

Nibley, Hugh, *Since Cumorah* (Deseret Book, 1967).

Noth, Martin, *The History of Israel* (A. & E. Black, 1958).

Oesterley, W. O. E., *An Introduction to the Books of the Apocrypha* (Macmillan, 1935).

Oesterley, W. O. E., *The Psalms* (2 vols. S. P. C. K., 1939).

Oesterley, W. O. E., and Robinson, T. H., *A History of Israel* (2 vols. Oxford: Clarendon Press, 1932).

Oesterley, W. O. E., and Robinson, T. H., *An Introduction to the Books of the Old Testament* (S. P. C. K., 1934).

Olmstead, A. T., *History of Palestine and Syria* (Scribners, 1931).

Orelli, C. von, *Old Testament Prophecy* (tr. Banks. T. and T. Clark, 1889).

Orelli, C. von, *The Prophecies of Isaiah* (tr Banks. T. and T. Clark, 1889).

Orlinsky, H. M., *Ancient Israel* (Cornell Univ., 1954).

Orr, James, *The Problem of the Old Testament* (Scribners, 1906).

Paterson, John, *The Goodly Fellowship of the Prophets* (Scribners, 1950).

Peake, A. S., Ed., *The People and the Book* (Oxford: Clarendon Press, 1925).

Pedersen, Johannes, *Israel: Its Life and Culture* (Branner Og Korch, 1940).

Perowne, J. J. S., *The Book of Psalms* (2 vols. Third London ed., rev. Andover: W. F. Draper, 1889).

Peters, J. P., *The Psalms as Liturgies* (Macmillan, 1922).

Pfeiffer, R. H., *Introduction to the Old Testament* (Rev. ed., Harper, 1948).

Pfeiffer, R. H., *History of New Testament Times with an Introduction to the Apocrypha* (Harper, 1949).

Pope, Marvin, *Job* (Anchor Bible, Doubleday, 1965).

Pritchard, J. B., *Ancient Near Eastern Texts* (Princeton Univ. Press, 1955).

Pritchard, J. B., *Archaeology and the Old Testament* (Princeton University Press, 1958).

Pritchard, J. B., *The Ancient Near East in Pictures Relating to the Old Testament* (Princeton Univ. Press, 1954).

Pusey, E. B., *The Twelve Prophets* (2 vols. Funk and Wagnalls, 1885, 1888).

Rankin, O. S., *Israel's Wisdom Literature* (Edinburgh: T. and T. Clark, 1936).

Ranston, Harry, *Old Testament Wisdom Books and Their Teaching* (Epworth Press, 1930).

Ricciotti, G., *The History of Israel* (2 vols. Tr. Penta and Murphy. Bruce Pub. Co., 1955).

Ricks, Eldin, *The Case of the Book of Mormon Witnesses* (Olympus Pub. Co., 1961).

Roberts, B. J., *The Old Testament Text and Versions: The Hebrew Text in Transmission and the History of the Ancient Versions* (Cardiff, 1951).

Robertson, A. T., *A Grammar of the Greek New Testament in the Light of Historical Research* (Fifth ed. Harper. No date).

Robinson, G. L., *The Book of Isaiah* (1st ed. YMCA Press, 1910).

Robinson, G. L., *The Twelve Minor Prophets* (Richard R. Smith, 1930).

Robinson, T. H., *The Genius of Hebrew Grammar* (London: Oxford Univ. Press, 1928).

Rowley, H. H., ed., *The Old Testament and Modern Study* (Oxford, 1951).

Rowley, H. H., *Israel's Mission to the World* (SCM Press, 1939).

Rowley, H. H., *Men of God* (Thos. Nelson and Sons Ltd., 1963).

Rowley, H. H., *The Biblical Doctrine of Election* (Lutterworth, 1950).

Rowley, H. H., *The Faith of Israel* (S. C. M. Press, 1956).

Rowley, H. H., *The Re-Discovery of the Old Testament* (Westminster Press, 1946).

Ryle, H. E., *The Canon of the Old Testament* (1st ed., Macmillan, 1892).

Scott, R. B. Y., *Proverbs* (Anchor Bible, 1965).

Scott, R. B. Y., *The Relevance of the Prophets* (Rev. ed., Macmillan, 1969).

Sellin - Fohrer, *Introduction to the Old Testament* (tr. D. Green. Abingdon Press, 1968).

Simms, P. M., *The Bible in America* (Wilson-Erickson, Inc. 1936).

Smith, G. A., *Jeremiah* (4th ed., rev. and enlarged, Harper, 1929).

Smith, G. A., *The Book of the Twelve Prophets* (2 vols. Rev. ed. Doubleday, Doran, 1929).

Smith, G. A. *The Book of Isaiah* (2 vols. New and rev. ed., Doubleday, Doran, No date).

Smith, Joseph Fielding, *Teachings of the Prophet Joseph Smith* (Deseret News Press; many printings).

Smith, J. M. P., *The Origin and History of Hebrew Law* (Univ. of Chicago Press, 1931).

Smith, J. M. P., *The Prophet and His Problems* (Scribners, 1914).

Smith, J. M. P., *The Prophets and Their Times* (Univ. of Chicago Press, 1925).

Snaith, Norman, *The Distinctive Ideas of the Old Testament* (4th ed., Epworth, 1950).

Sperry, S. B., *Ancient Records Testify* (Salt Lake City: M.I.A. Manual, 1938).

Sperry, S. B., *Answers to Book of Mormon Problems* (Bookcraft, 1967).

Sperry, S. B., *Book of Mormon Compendium* (Bookcraft, 1968).

Sperry, S. B., *Doctrine and Covenants Compendium* (Bookcraft, 1960).

Sperry, S. B., *Our Book of Mormon* (Bookcraft, 1963).

Sperry, S. B., *The Voice of Israel's Prophets* (Deseret Book, 1952).

Thackeray, H. St., J., *Josephus, The Man and the Historian* (New York: Jewish Inst. Press, 1929).

The Holy Scriptures. Inspired Version. (Corrected Edition. Independence, Missouri. Herald Publishing House).

The Holy Scriptures (Jewish Publication Society of America. Philadelphia, 1917).

The Interpreter's Dictionary of the Bible (4 vols. George A. Buttrick, Editor-in-chief. Abingdon Press, 1962).

The Inter-Varsity Fellowship, *A Guide to Christian Reading* (London, 1952).

Thomas, D. W., *Archaeology and Old Testament Study* (Oxford: Clarendon Press, 1967).

Thomas, D. W., (ed.,) *Documents from Old Testament Times* (Thos. Nelson and Sons, 1958).

Torrey, C. C., *The Apocryphal Literature* (Yale Univ. Press, 1945).

Torrey, C. C. *The Second Isaiah* (Scribners, 1928).

Unger, M. F., *Introductory Guide to the Old Testament* (Zondervan, 1951).

Vriezen, T., *An Outline of Old Testament Theology* (Blackwell's, 1958).

Waxman, Meyer, *A History of Jewish Literature* (3 vols. Bloch Pub. Co., 1930).

Wight, F. H., *Manners and Customs of Bible Lands* (Moody Press, 1965).

Willett, H. L., *The Prophets of Israel* (Christian Board of Publication, 1899).

Wilson, Robert D., *A Scientific Investigation of the Old Testament* (The Sunday School Times Co., 1926).

Wright, G. E., *Biblical Archaeology* (Westminster Press, 1957, Very valuable for teachers).

Wright, G. E., *The Pottery of Palestine from the Earliest Times to the End of the Early Bronze Age* (New Haven: American Schools of Oriental Research, 1937).

Wright, G. E. and Filson, F. V., *The Westminster Historical Atlas to the Bible* (Rev. ed., Westminster, 1956).

Wright, G. E. and Freedman, D. N., eds., *The Biblical Archaeologist Reader* (Doubleday, 1961).

Young, E. J., *An Introduction to the Old Testament* (Eerdmans, 1963).

Young, E. J., *Who Wrote Isaiah?* (Eerdmans, 1958), An able defense of the traditional view that Isaiah was the author of the whole book).

Periodicals

Biblical Archaeologist. (American Schools of Oriental Research).
Bulletin of the American Schools of Oriental Research.
Catholic Biblical Quarterly.
Interpretation.
Journal of Biblical Literature.
Vetus Testamentum.

Standard Works of
The Church of Jesus Christ of Latter-day Saints

Holy Bible. (King James Version)
Book of Mormon.
Doctrine and Covenants.
Pearl of Great Price.

INDEX